PLANET OF
THE UMPS

PLANET OF THE UMPS

A Baseball Life from Behind the Plate

KEN KAISER

AND

DAVID FISHER

THOMAS DUNNE BOOKS

ST. MARTIN'S PRESS NEW YORK

THOMAS DUNNE BOOKS.
An imprint of St. Martin's Press.

Design by Phil Mazzone

ISBN 0-312-30416-1

First Edition: March 2003

10 9 8 7 6 5 4 3 2 1

I'm thrilled to dedicate this book to my mom and dad,
who always had time for my fantasies.

I would also like to dedicate this book to two
extraordinary people, Mo Vaughn and Rafael Palmeiro,
for their friendship and support. Both of them are
All-Stars in life as well as on the field.

INTRODUCTION

Don't make me throw you out of this book before it's even started. . . .

To be a successful major league umpire you need to have a knowledge of the rules of the game, strength of character, good size, great judgment, perfect vision, selective hearing, the ability to make and defend a quick decision, and the fortitude to remain calm and collected even when surrounded by a bunch of infantile people yelling and screaming right in your face and kicking dirt on you and threatening you and cursing you and calling your entire family including every single one of your ancestors—particularly those who first came to this great country of ours—the kinds of names that would embarrass a gangsta rapper.

That's what it takes, and if you don't understand that, *then just what kind of reader are you!? Just who do you think you are to be putting your %$&%@ hands all over this page! You couldn't read a stop sign on a sunny day if I spotted you the 's' and the 'p'! You're the kind of reader who doesn't even know the difference between a gerund and a gerbil! A comma and a quotation thing! I can't believe it. I mean, I can't believe it. I've never been read by such an incompetent. . . .*

There is no other job in the world like being an umpire. If you like having every close decision you make criticized, if you like doing your job surrounded by thousands of people ready to blame you for mistakes other people make, every one of them believing they can do your job better than you can, if you like spending at least six months every year traveling thousands of miles and living in hotels and eating ballpark food, and if you don't mind the only response you get for a job done absolutely perfectly being silence, then maybe you would like being an umpire.

I loved it. I really loved it. Maybe not the constant complaining and the arguing and the traveling and the occasional death threats, and I definitely didn't love that short manager in Baltimore, but I was a professional umpire for thirty-six years. I spent twenty-three seasons in the major leagues. I was on the field for at least 3,000 big league games—for 153,000 outs. I worked under five commissioners, and I still love the game of baseball. Admittedly, I'm not real crazy about some of the people currently running that game—maybe it would even be better to describe them as the people crippling it—but I still love the game. I still like most of the thousands of players I've known, and I probably will miss being part of it for the rest of my life.

PLANET OF
THE UMPS

Two things nobody grows up dreaming about being are broke and an umpire. Thanks to baseball, I got to be both. I didn't grow up wanting to be an umpire. I grew up in Rochester, New York. I was a pretty tough kid—in my senior year in high school my classmates voted me Most Likely to Hold Up a Grocery Store. Some of the people I grew up with are in prison. Throughout my whole life I was always the biggest kid and I was always strong. I didn't work out with weights, I didn't exercise, I was just naturally strong. In high school I probably weighed 260 pounds. I guess I inherited my size and strength from my father and my uncles, who were all big men. I was born in 1945 while my father was serving in the Army. He was a military policeman stationed in North Africa guarding German prisoners. The prisoners loved him—because his name was Kaiser, they figured he was one of them. My father wasn't much of a drinker, but he celebrated my birth by going into a bar and getting drunk and ending up in a fight with three sailors. For years he didn't finish that story, so one day I asked him about that fight. Naturally I expected him to tell me in detail what he did to those sailors. I liked to imagine him celebrating my birth by beating up three sailors.

Instead he said, "They beat the daylights out of me. What'd you expect? There were three of them."

My father and mother were hardworking people, good people. After the war my father worked as a security guard at Eastman Kodak. For a long time my mom had her own television repair shop, The Tube Center. My parents taught me the difference between right and wrong and to respect and tolerate other people. I got my temper all by myself. I never looked for trouble, but when it showed up I didn't walk away. For a big kid, I was a reasonably good athlete. In baseball I played first base. I could hit the ball a long way, but I didn't hit it that often. Even though I was such a big kid, I didn't play football until my freshman year at Thomas Aquinas High School.

I didn't really want to play football. I didn't particularly like it. But one day in science class the teacher, Father Klein, was demonstrating the strength of a vacuum. He sucked all the air out of a sphere which caused its two halves to lock together. Even a team of horses couldn't pull them apart, he explained. He had each kid in the class come up to the front of the room and try to pull them apart. When my turn came I went up to the front of the room and pulled them apart. I don't know who was more surprised, Father Klein or me. He couldn't believe it. Truthfully, neither could I. "Maybe they're broken," I suggested.

I don't know how I was able to do it. I was lefthanded, so I figured that might have made a difference. But, as a reward they made me play football. *Mr. Kaiser, you're so good in science you should go out and smash into other people.* I didn't know very much about playing the game of football. On my first day of practice they put me on the defensive line. On the very first play of my football career the ball carrier came running right towards me. This game isn't so tough, I thought. But as I went to tackle him he stiff-armed me in the face. He stuck his finger through my face mask and got me right in the eye. That kid knocked me down with his finger. Oh, I get it, I thought, now I understand how to play football. The next time that guy came running at me I grabbed his face mask, ripped his helmet off his head, and slugged him right in the mouth.

That's not how you play the game, they said. I lasted maybe a week before my football career ended.

I wasn't a great student. I have no doubt I would have been a much better student if only I had gone to class. My parents had sent me to Thomas Aquinas, a strict Catholic high school, hoping I would learn discipline. I didn't last there very long. One day in class a teacher named Rosey smacked me on the knuckles with his ruler. I glared at him, "Don't you ever do that again," I warned.

He did it again. That probably was a mistake. I stood up and rammed him backwards into the chalkboard, knocking him down. He sent me to the principal's office. Father Hart, the principal, was a stern man and told me, "You're going to get ten whacks."

"I don't think so," I said. "I'm going to West High School." I turned around and walked out of the building. I respected authority, but I didn't allow authority figures to abuse me.

The only person I ever heard of who grew up intending to become an umpire was Bill Haller, my first crew chief and one of the finest people I've ever known. He claimed he knew he wanted to be an umpire when he was twelve years old. Bill must have had an interesting childhood. I think if people really knew how tough a job it is, even if you make it to the big leagues, they wouldn't even try it. I'll tell you how tough it is. An old-time American League umpire named Bill Kinnamon said that if he had known how tough it was to become an umpire he never would have given up his job with the Internal Revenue Service!

This was a guy who thought working for the IRS was better than being an umpire.

People decide to become an umpire for all kinds of reasons. Don Denkinger became an ump because his girlfriend who worked for the airlines ran away with a pilot. In that situation some people get drunk; he decided to become an umpire. Terry Cooney quit his job as a prison guard when he got a zero on the oral part of the sergeant's exam. Actually, it wasn't his idea; one of the inmates saw an ad for the umpire school on baseball's *Game of the Week* and suggested it to Cooney. While in college Teddy Barrett started umpiring high school games because it paid $45 a game. But Teddy really intended to become a professional boxer. He ended up sparring with heavyweights like George Foreman and Greg

Page. Eventually he figured out that getting yelled at by some manager or player was a lot better than getting punched in the mouth by George Foreman.

And it amazes me sometimes that people think umpires aren't that intelligent.

When I graduated high school in 1964 I had no precise plans for my future. I would basically describe my life as sort of a day-to-day proposition. When I got up in the morning my long-range plan was lunch. But, in those days, winters in Rochester were brutal. It was always cold and we got a lot of snow. A friend of mine, an ex-boxer named Eddie O'Hara, told me he had enrolled in umpire school in Daytona, Florida. He asked me to drive down there with him and split the expenses. I didn't really focus on the part about umpire school. The only thing I heard him say was Florida. Everybody in Rochester knew all about Florida: It was where the sun went for winter vacation. I closed my eyes and saw beautiful beaches and pretty girls in bikinis, I felt the warmth of the sun on my face and heard the surf rolling in. . . .

Umpire school definitely was not part of my fantasy. I had never umpired a game of baseball in my life. In fact, I had never been to a major league game. The only thing I knew about umpire school was that they didn't look at your SAT scores. Hey, if you could afford the tuition they didn't even care if you could pass a blood test. But it was the only school I'd ever heard of that didn't have detention. I had no desire to be an umpire, but I really didn't want to stay in Rochester for the winter—so I went to Florida and enrolled in Al Sommers' Umpire School.

Umpire school is sort of like military basic training, but

without any of the fun. The first umpire school was started in 1935 by a National League umpire named George Barr. Four years later, American League umpire Bill McGowan opened the second school. That was pretty much it for expansion. Two schools, that's the way it's been ever since then. This was not exactly a growing business. Before the schools were established people would learn how to umpire by working in the minor leagues. In those days, long before the existence of television, just about every small town had its own minor league team. There were more than fifty different minor leagues, so they needed a lot of umpires. Those umpires were paid terribly and treated worse; about the only thing they ever got for free was tar and feathers. People were always quitting, so it wasn't too hard to get a minor league job.

The first graduate of umpire school to get to the major leagues was Bill McKinley, in 1946—and he had attended both of them. For a long time nobody took the schools too seriously. Managers used to yell at McKinley, "You're telling me you had to go to a school to learn how to be so stupid?" But by the time I enrolled it was pretty much impossible to progress as an umpire without attending one of the two schools.

There were about a hundred people in my class. For me, umpire school was a winter vacation, but most of the other people really wanted to be there. I couldn't figure out what they had been doing with their lives, so that being cursed at, having things thrown at you, having your car vandalized, sharing a room with another young umpire in five-buck-a-night motels, driving unbelievably long hours and not seeing your family for six months—for a salary of $100 a week—

was an improvement. I was eighteen years old, the youngest person in the school, so I didn't know any better. Clearly, what motivated most of the other students was the dream of eventually making it to the major leagues.

Almost definitely that wasn't going to happen. Chances of even one person in any class getting to the majors were very slim, and, realistically, chances of that one person being Ken Kaiser were probably a little less than me winning the swimsuit competition in The Miss America Pageant.

There were all types in my class. People with money and people who were struggling. We had some really bright guys and some people whose ladders didn't have all their rungs. People from the inner city and people from small towns. We had guys who had been driving trucks, teaching school, working in plants, and even some former major league players. Dale Long, who hit home runs in eight consecutive games while playing for the Pittsburgh Pirates, was in my class. Danny McDevitt, a Dodgers pitcher who looked like he was going to be a big star before he hurt his arm, was in my class. Long and McDevitt had been in the major leagues, so everybody sort of assumed they couldn't miss making it back as umpires. But, neither one of them ever got out of the minors.

We had good athletes and not such good athletes. I'll never forget one kid from Boston was so uncoordinated that every time he tried to do a jumping jack he'd smack himself in the side of the head. This is absolutely true, he just couldn't do a jumping jack. He'd throw his hands up into the air but his feet wouldn't move, and then, when he focused on moving his feet, he'd hit himself in the head. It was more like a jumping jackass.

I think he eventually became the commissioner of baseball.

Okay, maybe not.

Every class had its share of characters. For example, a classmate of mine claimed he had been beamed up to a Martian spaceship. One of the most memorable students to attend Al Sommers' school was a kid from Chicago who looked like he had some talent. The staff had decided to recommend him for a minor league job, until the day he surprised everyone by running into the office shaking and crying. He wasn't exactly the person he claimed to be, he explained. Apparently, back in Chicago he and a partner had beaten some people out of some money. As a result his partner had been murdered, but he'd gotten away. He was hiding out in umpire school. Talk about finding the last place in the world people would look. He had decided he was going to change his life, he was going to become an umpire. Things had gone really well until he'd gone into town that day—and spotted the hit man who had killed his partner. He was terrified. My guess is the staff wasn't too thrilled about it either.

They made a flight reservation for him that afternoon. They booked it under an alias and snuck him out of town. It was just like a movie, except I don't think this person had really understood the job description. Working third base in front of 56,000 fans in Yankee Stadium is probably not a really good hiding place.

There was absolutely no way to predict who would make it to the big leagues. They used to tell a story about one kid who seemed like he couldn't miss. He was big and tough, he had great judgment, he knew the rules, he could handle arguments—the whole package. At the end of the six-week course the very best graduates are offered jobs in the low minor leagues. Baseball was all set to offer him one of those jobs—until the St. Petersburg police found him at three o'clock one morning directing traffic in his underwear.

I knew the basic rules of baseball. Nine innings, three outs, three strikes, four balls. Baseball had always seemed like a pretty simple game to me. Hit the ball and run. Get the ball to the base before the runner. If a pitch crosses the plate between the batter's knees and chest it's a strike, if it's higher or lower or misses the plate it's a ball. The only thing I didn't know was how much I didn't know. What do you do about an obstruction? Give him the Heimlich? What call do you make if you get hit by a batted ball in fair territory? That one I knew: I call a doctor. What's interference? That's what you get on your television set when one of your neighbors is using an electric saw.

Baseball, we were taught, is a simple game made complicated by the existence of players and managers. Without them, no umpire would ever have a problem.

Most people go to umpire school because they love baseball. They grew up rooting for their home team, cheering for their favorite players, maybe even collecting baseball cards. My favorite player was the Dodgers' center fielder Duke Snider. I had a big card collection. But the very first thing taught in school—and maybe the single hardest thing to learn—is that as an umpire you can't have any favorites. You have to despise every player and manager equally.

From the first day, umpires are taught that players and managers are the enemy—the absolute enemy—and that on the field the best thing that can happen between a player or manager and an umpire is nothing. That players and managers aren't interested in forming meaningful relationships with umpires. As far as they're concerned, the real function of an umpire is to become an excuse for their mistakes. Most of the time, when a player screws up he knows there is only one courageous thing he can do to appease the fans: blame the nearest umpire.

The truth is that not all players and managers are bad. Some of them are much, much worse than that.

So, the first lesson an umpire learns is that the only thing to root for is a fast game.

After a few days of basic instruction the staff put us out on the field and let us call some plays. I had a close play at second base and called the runner safe. An instructor came out to me and asked calmly, "What'd you think?"

"Well," I explained, "I thought the runner beat the tag."

"Oh, that's very nice," he said, "you %$#@^%$! *You're not being paid to think! You never think! You KNOW!*"

That was the second lesson: Whatever call you make is the only right call. Never explain, never apologize. A great umpire named Beans Reardon was behind the plate in a World Series and a Yankee pitcher threw a fastball right down the middle. Reardon called it a ball. The Yankee catcher, Bill Dickey, complained, "What was wrong with that pitch?"

"Nothing," Reardon admitted, "it was right down the pipe."

"Then why isn't it a strike?" Dickey asked.

Reardon told him, "Because I called it a ball."

Young umpires have to learn that players and managers aren't interested in a debate. They don't want to hear a reasonable explanation. They only want one simple thing: They want every single call to be made in their favor. And they'll do just about anything to try to make that happen. They will make every possible attempt to intimidate an umpire.

I was tough, I didn't know the meaning of the word intimidation. Of course, I didn't know the meaning of a lot of other words either. But I knew intimidation when I heard it. There are only a few things in life that prepare a person to be an umpire: certainly a military career. And definitely Catholic school. And marriage. Places where people get right up in your face and scream at you as loudly as they can.

In umpire school the instructors don't start screaming at new students for at least the first forty or fifty seconds. Then they don't stop for the next six weeks. I don't think I ever realized that baseball was such a loud game. Pretty much everybody was a little stunned the first time an instructor stood about an inch away and screamed and poked us in the chest and cursed at us. The only thing we'd done is show up with a desire to be an umpire. Most students figure out pretty quickly that if they need to be liked or respected this is definitely the wrong field for them.

It was perfect for me. I knew my mother loved me, and I didn't spend too much time caring how anybody else felt. Where I grew up, people didn't believe too much in the new age philosophy of "tough love." It was more "tough tough." Respect was earned. You never backed down from anyone. Never. Take one step backwards, you might as well just keep going. This was the right attitude to bring with me to umpire school. I knew how to be tough; the rest I could learn.

When I attended umpire school the only thing I was really good at was being big. This is a profession in which size matters. That's why it's called the big leagues. I was about six-two and probably 250 pounds. My mentor and good friend, the late, great umpire Ron Luciano, used to tell people that God must have put me together in the dark. I'm built a little like a barrel with two arms stuck on—backwards. My hands seem to face away from my body. And when I walk my whole body sort of shifts from side to side—Ronnie used to tell people that if they watched me too long they would get seasick.

At the beginning I wasn't really a very good student. Umpiring did not come as naturally to me as, say, hitting my opponent over the head with a folding chair when I wrestled professionally. The instructors didn't seem to mind too much when I made a bad call, but what they objected to was my being out of position to make the proper call, or not knowing the right rule to apply. Whenever we screwed up, the instructors made us run laps around the field, screaming, "Safe, out, safe, out," and making the appropriate signals. I spent a lot of hours circling that field safe-ing and outing. I may still hold the school record for yelling safes and outs.

What surprised me was that one of the easiest things about being an umpire was making the correct call. It was all about being in the right position to get a good look at the play. Ron Luciano was one of my instructors, and he used to demonstrate the importance of positioning by holding his two index fingers in front of his body maybe an eighth of an inch apart and asking if they were touching each other. Hell, even I could make that call. I could see that they weren't touching. But then he would turn so that instead of both fingers being in front of his body, one was pointing directly in at his body and the other was pointing in the opposite direction. From that angle it was impossible to see if his fingers were touching. That's umpiring. Get in position to see the play and most of the time you'll make the right call.

Distance from the play didn't matter either. In school, the instructors would make everybody stand a few feet behind third base as a runner slid in. But because the third baseman was blocking the play, it was impossible to see if he tagged the runner, or if he dropped the ball, or even if the runner missed the base. It was impossible to make that call from only a few feet away. And then they would take everybody out into right field and let them make the call from there. Well, it was easy to make the correct call—even from two hundred feet away—because you got a good, clean look at the play. Most fans think that the umpire has to be right on top of the play to get it right, but the fact is that getting a good view is much more important than the distance.

So, making the right call was easy. The hardest thing about umpiring was everything else.

I didn't go to Al Sommers' school expecting to be offered a minor league job at the end of the course. At first I didn't even know that that was the way the system worked. I wasn't surprised when Long and McDevitt and a couple of other people got jobs and the rest of us got to go home. But what did surprise me was how much I enjoyed the whole experience. I hadn't really anticipated that. I liked being on the field, I liked being in charge, I liked being in the middle of the action—except at third base, when I was on the side of the action.

And the school staff was very encouraging. They told me they liked my aggressiveness. They liked my aggressiveness? Nobody had ever told me that before. That same personality that had gotten me into some tough situations throughout my life fit this job perfectly. My whole life people had been telling me, *Calm down, Kenny.* These people were telling me to be aggressive. I loved that. Just loved it. I'd gone to Florida to get a tan, and instead I found a profession. I was determined to become an umpire. And I never held another real job in my life.

I went back to Rochester and took a job as a bouncer in a club. A couple of months later Harry Wendlestat and Paul Nicoli, umpires who had been instructors at the school, came to Rochester to work an International League game. By the time they left my bar they had called a top minor league executive named George McDonald and gotten me a job in the Florida Rookie League. That was the lowest league in professional baseball. It wasn't even a real first step—it was more like climbing up out of the gutter onto the curb. The pay was $400 a month, and I was thrilled to get the job—which shows you how smart you have to be to become an umpire.

I packed my bag and went to Florida. McDonald had heard about my temper from some of the instructors and was a little nervous about me. But I told him that most of the stories he'd heard weren't totally accurate, and besides that, I'd changed. This was a real good opportunity for me to get my foot in the door—and I was pretty determined not to put my fist through it.

So what happened wasn't my fault. I mean, not completely my fault. My first professional game was scheduled for July 14, 1965. I arrived in Sarasota, Florida, the day before and had nothing to do. Nothing to do was always a problem for me. Across the street from my hotel was a pool hall. I could play pool—I mean, I could really play. Obviously, nobody knew me, so this one guy thought he could hustle me. Good luck to him.

We played a few games and I won $10 from him. That was a lot of money in those days, and he wasn't too happy with me. We started arguing and he smacked me in the chest with a cue. He cracked my rib. I wasn't too happy about that, so I picked up the pool table and hit him over the head with it. I trapped him against the wall and slugged him a few more times.

Then I went to the hospital.

The next day I went to home plate for the exchange of lineup cards before the game. It was opening day—my first game in professional baseball. The beginning of my career. It was a beautiful day—right up until the moment I got to home plate. Standing there was the kid I'd fought with—who turned out to be the catcher for the St. Louis club. I think he was just as surprised to see me as I was to see him. He had a black eye, his face was cut up and bruised pretty good. By the time I got back to my rooming house after the game, George McDonald was on the phone. "You $^%#%$#@!," he said. "That's gonna cost you $25, and if you get in one more fight I'm gonna send your ass back to Rochester." One game—I worked one game—and already I was being fined. This was some great start to my career in professional umpiring.

Actually, that wasn't such a bad beginning. An old-time American League umpire named Joe Rue began his minor league career in 1921 in Chickasha, Oklahoma. He was eating dinner the night before his first professional game when a guy named Bad Bill shot and killed the waiter. I mean, I've had some bad meals, but that seemed excessive to me.

The Rookie League consisted of eight teams, and everybody played in Sarasota. It was a beginner's league, for umpires as well as players. Teams assigned young players just out of high school and college to this league. They had four fields and played games every afternoon. I'd finish in time to get to the beach.

When the Rookie League season ended they fired me. Well, they didn't exactly fire me. At the end of the season they promoted one umpire and let the rest of us go. And maybe they said something to me about, "If you're ever again seen in the state of Florida. . . ." They just didn't think I was a very good umpire. Maybe I wasn't yet, but I loved the job. And it paid $400 a month, which to me was a lot of money!

I wasn't thinking about making it to the major leagues. That never even occurred to me. I just thought it was a great way of spending my life, until I had to deal with reality. And *that* I intended to put off as long as I could.

The only way to get a job as an umpire was to be recommended by the staff of one of the umpire schools, so the next winter I was back there safe-ing and outing all over the field. I didn't think of myself as having to repeat the course, I just considered it an extended second semester. Actually, a lot of people have gone through the school more than once. In fact, some people attended both schools several times and were never able to get a placement.

I had improved at least ten pounds. At the end of the course I met with George McDonald who told me sincerely, "You did a good job, son, so I gotcha moving up."

Technically, McDonald was absolutely right. He moved me from Florida all the way up to North Carolina. He got me a job in the Western Carolina League. Maybe it was the same classification as the Florida Rookie League, but it definitely was up—north. I was moving up geographically, if not professionally.

As I remember it, my first game in that league was a night game in Greenville, South Carolina. The pitcher for the Greenville Mets was a kid named Nolan Ryan. Nolan Ryan? Never heard of him. Didn't know anything about him. As far as I was concerned, he was just another young kid with a small chance of making the big leagues. I was working home plate that night. At that time umpires could use either a large inflatable chest protector—the balloon, we called it—which is what American League umpires used, or an inside protector which fit snugly inside a coat. I was using the balloon. I crouched down behind the catcher, my body safely behind the protector. Ryan went into his wind-up and threw his first pitch, a fastball, and . . . oh my goodness! I had never seen anything like that before. Didn't see it that night, either.

Until that night I didn't know a human being could throw a baseball that fast. I was just this kid umpire, and I was stunned. Nolan just reared back and threw it 150 miles an hour. The problem was that he had no control at all. He had no idea where the ball was going when he threw it. He could throw a ball through a brick wall, he just couldn't hit the wall. That ball was all over the place. What made the job even more difficult was that the lights were terrible. From home plate you could barely see the first baseman, which made it even harder to see Ryan's pitches. Wild doesn't even begin to describe him. When he pitched, people in the stands ducked. You could hear the fans screaming "Women and children first!" The batters were terrified and, admittedly, I wasn't too thrilled myself. Players would come to bat wearing catcher's equipment to protect themselves. I didn't stop them, I figured it was every man for himself. Normally, when an umpire uses the balloon protector he rests his chin on the top of it. That night I held up the whole protector just under my eyes. All you could see above the protector were my two wide-open eyes and the top of the mask. The truth is that I couldn't see pitches very well that way—but I didn't have a single complaint that night. Wherever the pitch was, *striiiike*. If I couldn't see it, I figured the hitters couldn't see it either. And believe me, they didn't care what I called. *Call me out, get me out of here—it's okay, I won't argue*. I remember wondering, *Whoa, if this kid is in the low minor leagues, how fast do you have to throw to get to the major leagues?*

The Western Carolina League was really my introduction to umpiring. I had been spoiled by the Florida Rookie League. In Sarasota we got small, quiet crowds. Nice people. All the teams in the league were the home team, so nobody got too upset about winning and losing. I thought that's what it was like everywhere else.

Now, I had heard some of the horror stories about what happened to umpires in the minor leagues. I'd heard about tires being deflated, cars being set on fire, fans beating up umpires. I'd heard about umpires being chased out of towns, but I just didn't think any of that applied to me. I was a good guy doing the best job I could, why would anybody get mad at me? And besides, I was pretty big, pretty strong, and I didn't scare easily.

I figured I was ready for anything. Yeah, right. Sure I was. About two weeks into the season I was scheduled to work a game in Spartanburg, South Carolina—the Spartanburg Phillies against the Rock Hill Cardinals. In those days minor league baseball was the only game in town, and those people took it seriously.

Turns out it was Rebel Day in Rock Hill. I didn't know what that was, but I found out pretty quickly. Rebel Day was the most important day of the year. It celebrated South Carolina's participation in the Confederacy during the Civil War. This was 1966, and a lot of these people weren't completely convinced that the war was over. They believed they were still in the middle of a long pause.

I had a little bit of a handicap, because my partner had quit baseball two days before. He hadn't even bothered to tell me he was quitting. We were working in Durham, North Carolina, I think. I just happened to be sitting on the front porch of the rooming house as the Greyhound bus passed by on its way out of town. As I watched the bus disappear down the highway all of a sudden I noticed my partner in the rear window waving good-bye to me.

I never did find out why he quit. Maybe he knew about Rebel Day.

I called George McDonald and told him my partner'd quit. McDonald told me not to worry about a thing, he'd dig up a new partner for me. Dig up? That certainly sounded promising. A day later there was a knock on my door and I heard a deep voice shouting, "Kiiiisa, open this door, boy!" I opened the door and I couldn't see any daylight. Then the biggest man I ever saw said, "I'm your new partner."

I looked up at him. He filled the whole door frame. "You bet," I said, "anything you say is all right with me."

"Pick up my bag," he said. He had one suitcase, and it looked like it had come out of the Civil War. As we drove to Spartanburg he told me about himself. Devo Butcher was his name and he came from, as he put it, "West-by-God-Virginia."

He was at least six-eight, 275 pounds and had arms that looked like elephant stumps. "I bale hay," he told me. "We get it together and tie it in a bunch and I toss it on the truck and that's what I do during the day. At night I umpire."

During the drive it became obvious that Devo wasn't too happy with life. He was a little militant about anything he disagreed with. That wasn't going to be a problem with me, soon as I saw him I knew that I was going to agree with everything he said. Even before he said it, I agreed with him.

The ballpark was jammed for the holiday. Spartanburg and Rock Hill are pretty close to each other, so it was a great rivalry. There were probably as many Cardinals fans as Phillies fans in the stands. The ballpark was segregated, and out in center field the Confederate flag was flying. A lot of people were waving little Rebel flags, and before the game, instead of playing *The Star Spangled Banner* on the PA system they played *Dixie*. Most of the people in the ballpark sang it. When I looked around the park and saw that, I started singing real loud. When the song ended some people took out guns and started firing into the air. Guns! I was scared to death. Nobody had ever told me that fans could bring guns to the ballpark.

We worked a two-man crew, one man behind the plate, the other man took the bases. "Where you want to work?" I asked Devo.

"I'm a plate man," he said.

"Good," I told him, "you got it."

We went out to home plate before the game to meet with the managers and exchange the lineup cards, go over the ground rules. One of the managers was Sparky Anderson, the other was a man named Bob Wellman. Wellman was almost as big as Butcher. Usually, the first time you see a team in the season you shake hands with the manager and wish him luck. It's tradition. Sparky shook hands with Wellman, then offered his hand to Butcher.

Butcher said flatly, "I don't shake hands with managers."

Uh-oh, I thought, *this could get interesting.*

The game was pretty uneventful until the ninth inning. With the score tied 3-3 in the top of the inning, there was a play at the plate. It wasn't really that close. The Phillies' runner was safe by maybe ten feet. Butcher called him out. We had a big argument. Wellman was furious. The Spartanburg fans went nuts. They had guns, I remembered, so I stayed as far away from Butcher as possible. I took my position behind second base—way, way behind second base.

Then, with two out in the bottom of the ninth inning and a runner on second the Cardinals' batter lined a base hit to center field. The runner came tearing around third base. The center fielder made a perfect throw to the plate. This time the runner was out by . . . a day and a half. It wasn't close—but Butcher called him safe.

The game was over. I guess that was when the riot began. Waves of Spartanburg fans were trying to climb the fence to get on the field. I could see my future in front of me, just about twenty-five feet in front of me, and, believe me, it wasn't all that promising. All I wanted to do was get to the safety of the dressing room.

I began figuring it might be the right time to make a career move. Maybe I could go back to Rochester and get a nice safe job, like running numbers for the mob in a really bad part of town. Whatever it was, it had to be more promising than being a minor league umpire.

The Phillies' third baseman, a good kid named Tommy Silicato, was the first player to reach Butcher. He stood defiantly right in front of him and started calling him every rotten name I'd ever heard. He just about came up to Butcher's chest. Butcher looked down on him and ordered, "Get yourself outta my way, boy."

Silicato didn't move. Instead he just screamed at Butcher. *"You no good son of a bitch!"*

"You best get outta my way, boy," Butcher repeated, "I'm gonna ask you nice just this one more time."

"I ain't moving," Silicato said defiantly.

That was probably a mistake. Butcher was holding his mask and his protector in his right hand. So he hit him with a left hook. Silicato was out cold before he hit the ground. His nose was smashed. There was blood everywhere. Butcher stepped over him and said to me, "I told that boy to get out of my way."

My eyes were the size of golf balls. Big golf balls. I couldn't believe I was seeing this. All of a sudden people were over the fence and running towards me. At *me*! Butcher and I were literally fighting our way to the dressing room. Some guy grabbed at Butcher's protector, Butcher whacked him in the face with his steel mask. Bam! The guy went straight down. I started thinking, if I get out of this I'm going straight home. I'll never complain about anything again. I'll be so good. Umpiring? Forget it, I was going to find another job. I didn't care what it was. Licking stamps. Driving dynamite delivery trucks. I didn't care.

We made it to the dressing room. As soon as we got inside

I closed the door and started piling everything I could find in front of it. Benches, suitcases, anything that wasn't nailed down. You couldn't get through that door with the Third Army. I looked at Butcher, "What are we going to do?" I asked. I was trying real hard to keep the panic out of my voice.

"I'm going to take me a shower," he said. "Those people got me all worked up."

"Hey, okay, that's fine," I told him. "I'll just stand right here and keep an eye on the door." As soon as he got into the shower someone started banging on the door. Opening it didn't seem like one of the options. "Who's there?" I shouted.

"It's Wellman. Open this door. I want Butcher. He hit one of my ballplayers."

What was I going to tell him? Go away, nobody's home? Meanwhile Butcher was still in the shower—and he was singing. But he must have heard Wellman shouting. "Open the door, Kiiiisa," he ordered.

"Yes sir, anything you say." I pulled down the suitcases and moved the benches and opened the door.

Smoke was coming out of Wellman's ears. "Where is he?"

"In the shower."

Wellman went over to the shower and ripped open the curtain and . . . and Butcher hit him with a right and knocked him out cold. I'm standing there in shock. I didn't know things like this went on in baseball. Three or four people came into the room—it was getting pretty crowded in there—and carried out Wellman. Meanwhile, Butcher got back in the shower and started singing again.

As soon as they got Wellman outside I locked the door and pushed the benches in front of it and piled up the suitcases. I could hear people outside screeching. Occasionally I'd make out words like "tar" and "too good for them" and "flat-bed truck," but mostly it was just screaming. Finally Butcher got out of the shower. I knew he'd been umpiring for a long time, so I figured maybe he had a plan. "You wanna take your shower now?" he asked me.

"Gee, I don't think so," I said. "What are we going to do? We can't leave."

As he pulled down his suitcase from the pile and opened it he said, "You're new at umpiring, aren't you?"

Not anymore, I thought, not anymore. "Yes sir, I am."

He casually dug into his suitcase and pulled out a gun. "Ah, don't worry, you'll get used to it," he explained.

The man had a gun! For a second I thought he was going to shoot me. He was going to put me out of my misery. Instead, he put two shots through the top of the door. Two big holes. "Pull them benches away," he told me, "we'll be leaving now."

I started ripping those benches away. "I'm right behind you." I opened the door and, so help me, there wasn't a soul standing there. "Grab those bags," he said.

"I got the bags," I said cheerfully. We walked out to our car and found five state police patrol cars surrounding it. Two troopers were standing there waiting for us.

"You boys those umpires?" one of them asked.

Yes, I wanted to shout, *yes, but I swear, just let me go this one time and I'll never umpire another game as long as I live. More than that, I won't umpire for ten years after I die*. I'd read all about the Deep South. I'd seen *Cool Hand Luke*. I'd seen *Deliverance*. I knew the kind of things that happened there. Let's see, I figured, a small riot, a brawl, just a few gunshots. . . . I was looking directly at fifteen years, maybe a few less, of hard labor.

"Tell you what we're gonna do here," the trooper explained. "I'm from the South Carolina State Police. This here's . . ." he told us a name, "he's from North Carolina. Y'all get your car between us and we're gonna 'scort you direct to the state line."

I looked at Butcher. "What are we going to do?"

He sighed and got into the passenger seat, leaned back, and closed his eyes, "Drive, boy, just like they told you." We took off. After a few minutes he opened his eyes and looked at me. Maybe he noticed I was getting nervous. The waterfall of sweat probably gave it away. "Don't worry about it, son," he told me, "those boys are just trying to scare us."

"Well," I told him, "it's definitely working."

There were two police cars in front of us, two behind us, and behind them maybe fifty cars. When we reached the state line the trooper leaned into our car and said, "All right boys, here's what I'm gonna do. I'm gonna give you a five-minute head start. Then I'm gonna let these people come."

I was pretty happy about being alive, so I said to him, "I just want to thank you for what you did for us."

"Don't thank me, son. I'm from Spartanburg and I was at that game. Those were two of the worst horseshit calls I have ever seen. I swear to God, if I wasn't working tonight, I'd be right there at the front of that crowd."

It turned out that the president of the league was also the mayor of a small town in North Carolina. The next day he fired Butcher—but got him a job as a turnkey in the local jail. And the mayor also got me a job in the New York–Penn

League. I was moving up in baseball pretty fast. If I kept working hard I would be in Canada before I knew it.

At the time I became an umpire it was possible for people to spend their entire careers umpiring in the minor leagues. Ten years, twenty years. That doesn't happen anymore. There are fewer minor leagues, fewer teams, and a lot fewer umpires. If an umpire doesn't make progress after a few seasons, if it becomes obvious that he's got no chance to ever make it to the big leagues, baseball will release him. There were legendary minor league umpires like Harry "Steamboat" Johnson, who spent thirty-seven years in the minors—and worked fifty-four games in the big leagues.

Johnson's autobiography, *Standing the Gaff*, was published in 1935. The legend is that he would stand outside the ballpark selling copies to fans before the game, then during the game, when he made a bad call, they would literally throw his book at him. He didn't care—he'd pick up the books and after the game sell them all over again.

Former National League umpire Dutch Rennart spent fifteen years in the minors. But former American League umpire Jim Honochik spent only two years. I spent thirteen years in the minor leagues—thirteen long, long years.

I saw a lot of umpires come and go during that time. Mostly go. It was a tough job. As many people have said, it may be the only job in the world where you have to be perfect the day you start, and then improve. The living conditions were terrible—in the old days, two minor league umpires often shared a $1-a-night room with only one bed—the pay was awful, even when you made the right decision, half the people in the game hated you, and you spent the entire season living on the road. So a lot of people quit or got run out of the game. The stress keeps building and you just never know when it gets to be too much. I worked with more than fifty partners in the minor leagues.

In the minor leagues you really get to know your partner. I mean, really get to know him. You room with him, you drive thousands of miles with him, you eat with him, you work with him. A good partner can make the season terrific, a bad partner can destroy your career. It's like a marriage. And like a marriage, eventually the little things get to be big things.

I remember one time when my partner and I got to our next town a day early. Sometimes when that happened, we would work a game with the two people already there. That gave all of us experience in the four-man system used in the major leagues. This particular game was halted by a rain storm in the sixth inning, so the four of us sat in the dugout waiting for the storm to pass. We were having a nice pleasant conversation—until one of the other umpires started talking about country music. He really loved country music, he said, his favorite country music stars were . . .

Suddenly, his partner stood up and started screaming, "*I can't stand to hear one more word about country music. That's all you talk about, country music. You make me listen to it hour after hour in the car—that same country music. I can't stand it anymore. I hate country music. And I hate you!*" With that, he sucker-punched his partner right in the mouth. Knocked him right to the ground. And while the guy was lying there on the dirt floor of the dugout he reached down and grabbed the car keys out of his pocket, turned around, and left.

He quit baseball in the sixth inning. He just got in the

car and drove away. The great thing was that as he drove away we could see cassette tapes being heaved out the window.

The most unusual partner I ever had was a man named Hips Hogan, who I worked with in 1967. At the end of my second season, the New York–Penn League did not renew my contract, which is much nicer than admitting they fired me. I wasn't fired, I just wasn't renewed. So I was out of baseball. My career was over. I was a has-been before I ever was. But, in July I got a phone call from a wonderful man named Barney Deary, who was the supervisor of minor league umpires. An umpire had quit in the Northern League and Barney needed a replacement immediately. Baseball wanted me. Baseball needed me. I accepted the job.

The Northern League was in northern South Dakota. The only thing I knew about South Dakota was that it had to be south of North Dakota. I figured it would be easy to get there. I'd worked in South Carolina and it had been easy to get there. So I flew to Chicago then transferred to a small plane. A real small plane. Four seats.

We landed in a field. It wasn't even an airport. It was just a landing strip. There was one car waiting there and a man was sitting on the hood. The plane pulled up right next to him. "Kaiser?" he assumed. "Hips here. I'm your new partner."

I got my bag and, as I started to open the car door, I saw a German shepherd that I swear to God was as big as a tank sitting on the front passenger seat. "He's all right," Hips said. "He won't bother you if he knows what's good for him."

That was reassuring. It was a dog. What if he didn't know?

Hips got into the car and grabbed the dog by the throat. The dog started choking. "It's okay," Hips said, "I got him."

"Maybe we could just put him in the back," I suggested.

"Nah, don't worry about him, he'll be fine." I got in the car slowly. The dog was sitting between me and Hips. "Just give him a little time to get used to you," Hips suggested, "till then, it'd probably be better if you didn't do anything to scare him, know what I mean?"

When we got to the ballpark, Hips put a muzzle on the dog and left him in the car. He told me, "I'll work the plate tonight 'cause it's your first night."

Fine with me. We walked out to the plate for the pregame meeting with the managers. One of them handed Hips his lineup card. Then a weird thing happened. Instead of looking directly at it, Hips held it up by the side of his head. He was facing the manager but reading the card he was holding by his ear. Hey, it looked pretty strange to me, but this was South Dakota.

When the game started the first batter got a base hit, so I moved into my proper position behind second base. I was looking straight in at home plate and, as the first pitch came in, Hips turned his head and looked directly into the dugout. Ball one! What the . . . ? The next pitch came in, he turned and once again he looked into the dugout. Striiike. Throughout the whole game he didn't look at home plate once. He was looking in both dugouts, the stands, everywhere but straight ahead. *Oh geeze,* I thought, *this is going to be a long year.* But nobody complained, nobody argued.

After the game we went back to our rooming house. The dog was still growling at me. "Don't worry," Hips kept telling me, "he'll get used to you." Hips took the bed closest to the bathroom, the dog settled down on the floor between us, and I was in the bed nearest the window. Maybe three o'clock in the morning I had to go to the bathroom. I very quietly got out of bed and put one foot on the floor.

Grrrrrrrrrrrrrrrrrrrrr.

"Hips," I said softly, "I gotta go the bathroom. Grab your dog." Hips was fast asleep. I tried again, a little louder. Still, nothing. Finally I yelled, *"Hips, I got to go to the bathroom!"*

He grabbed the dog by the throat and put the muzzle on him. I turned on the light and started to get out of bed . . . and on the table an *eye* was looking right at me. "What the hell. . . ." I looked at Hips and I saw an empty eye socket. *Oh my—geeze.* . . . Hips was blind in one eye! And his other eye didn't focus right—that's why he had to turn his head to the side to see straight ahead. I was working with a half-blind umpire. He was the only active umpire I ever knew who was legally qualified to park in a handicapped parking space. But, I'll tell you what, Hips was a good man and a fine umpire. He'd be working in the field, there would be a close play at third base. He'd be looking right at first base and make the call. The people in that league knew him and respected him.

After that first night, though, I did all the driving.

In the minor leagues a lot more time is spent in a car driving from one city to the next than on the field. Those drives get to be real long. Real, real long. In the Texas League, for example, some of those cities are hundreds of miles apart, Dallas to El Paso is six hundred miles, El Paso to Tulsa is eight hundred miles, and you had to make the trip in one night and work the next day. In the low minor leagues, partners were assigned based mostly on who owned cars. The leagues paid mileage, usually six cents a mile. Most of the time we'd leave right after the game and drive through the night. Minor league umpires know where all the 7-Elevens, Denny's, Burger Kings, and McDonald's are coast-to-coast. Nobody sleeps in the car, the passenger has to stay awake to keep the driver awake. When Teddy Barrett was in the Texas League for example, his partner would drive the minivan—and Barrett's job was to stay awake and keep the beer coming. Every time his partner finished a can of beer, Teddy had to be ready to pop open another one and keep him going.

One of the worst things that can happen is to be driving late at night and watching as the gas gauge goes down, knowing there isn't an open gas station for the next hundred miles. When National League umpire Jerry Layne was in the Southern League, he and his partner got lost going through Plains, Georgia. They tried a shortcut and ended up out of gas in the middle of a peanut field.

National League umpire Bruce Froemming had maybe the best partner in minor league history when he was working in the Midwest League. In his first year in professional baseball he was assigned a partner who flew his own airplane, a twin-engine Piper Apache. They would fly from city to city, usually landing in farmers' fields. I don't know if the league paid mileage on that one.

Every minor league umpire has had narrow escapes—and has gotten his share of tickets. One time in Double-A my partner, a good guy named Dave Smith, and I were driving from Redding, Pennsylvania, to Quebec City, Canada. We got up into the White Mountains in New Hampshire and we were making great time—until we got stopped by two New

Hampshire State Policemen. Smitty had a big sense of humor, but at times he said inappropriate things. So, as these troopers came walking up to our car I told him, "Just be careful what you say to these guys."

"You folks were going pretty good there," one of the troopers said.

"See," Smitty explained, "there's nobody on the road and we're baseball umpires."

"You work in Boston?"

Smitty was making friends with him. "No, we're minor league umpires." They started talking and eventually Smitty offered both troopers baseballs for their kids. We always carried extra baseballs with us. Brand-new white baseballs were better than currency. We didn't exactly use them as bribes, more like meaningful gifts. We traded them for food, gas, whatever we needed.

We used to steal them from the league. An hour before each game we were given two dozen baseballs, but by the time we got to home plate to start the game we had at best four left. We kept baseballs in the game as long as we could. We used a ball as long as you could read the league president's signature on it. Batters would complain that the ball was too dirty. *Too dirty? What are you talking? I can still see three letters on here, it's fine, get in there and hit.* Only once did I ever see anyone turn down a gift of an official major league baseball, and that was in New York City when Ron Luciano tried to give one to a doorman as a tip. The doorman looked at it and then handed it back, telling him, "I can't eat this."

But these patrolmen loved the baseballs. They loved

Smitty. They loved me. We definitely were not going to get a ticket. Everything was going just great, right up until the moment the trooper asked Smitty, "So what do you guys do in the off-season?"

"You know, not much," Smitty said, "I sell drugs and he drinks."

"That's it. Out of the car." They put us up against a fence and searched us. They went through the car. They checked under the hub caps, they went through the trunk. They kept us there two hours before finally giving us the speeding ticket.

The car was transportation, it was our office—in an emergency it was our hotel. Just about every minor league umpire has spent nights sleeping in his car on the side of a road. One night we got into town real late and the hotel had given away our room. They had no vacancies, the clerk told us. Sorry, they were completely booked. There was nothing he could do about it. Well, I thought there was something he could do about it. "You got a Presidential Suite?" I asked him.

"Yes sir," he said, "we do."

"Good," I told him. "He's not coming. We'll take his room."

Minor league umpires can't afford to stay in great hotels. Instead of the Motel 6, for example, we get the Motel 2½.

Every minor league umpire can tell you motel horror stories. When the late, great John McSherry was working in Florida, he stayed at Toffenatti's, a rooming house mostly for older people. It was fine, McSherry explained, except that during meals these people would take out their teeth and put them on the table. Then they would slurp up their food.

"Even that wasn't so bad," he said, "except that some of them couldn't see very well. So you didn't dare put anything down. Man, if you left a ring on that table for thirty seconds, whoosh, it was gone."

The strangest place I ever stayed in was The Aberdeen Hotel, in Aberdeen, South Dakota. I'll never forget it. That hotel had to be at least a hundred years old. It was built before the Civil War. My partner was a good guy named Doug Kosie, and when we checked in two men were sitting in the lobby chewing tobacco, spitting into big brass spittoons. Then there were these two sausage dogs, dachshunds, running around. It was like the old west. After we checked in the clerk told us to take the elevator to the third floor. "I'll be right with you," he said. I figured he must operate the elevator.

Doug and I got into the elevator. It was small, but as long as we didn't exhale at the same time we could both fit in. I'd never seen an elevator like this one. The clerk squeezed in and started pulling on a rope. This elevator was operated by a pulley. He pulled us up to the third floor. This is some hotel, I was thinking.

I swear, our room was no bigger than five-by-five. It had a bed and a cot. A pile of rope was coiled up in the corner. "What the hell is that?" I asked.

"That's the fire escape," the clerk explained. "If there's a fire you just throw it out the window and climb down."

I noticed that there was no lock on the door. "Oh, nobody'll bother you here," the clerk promised. "Just put your bags in front of the door and you'll be fine."

This was the life of a minor league umpire. Believe me,

to put up with all this you really had to love baseball—either that or you had to have absolutely no marketable skills.

Sometime after midnight Doug told me, "I'm thirsty, I'm going down to the lobby to get a soda." The walls were so thin I could hear every sound. I heard Doug walking down all three flights of stairs. And then I heard him start screaming. Then I heard him running back up the stairs. Real fast. Turned out the two dogs were attack dachshunds. The lobby closed at midnight and the dogs were left there to guard the place. They did a great job. They bit Kosie right on his little toe.

The next morning I decided to write a letter to my mother. In one drawer I found two sheets of hotel stationary and an envelope. The stationary had a little drawing of a sausage dog on the top and right below was written, "Stretch Them Hotel Dollars."

Stretch Them Hotel Dollars. You bet I did. We all did. In my best year in the minors I made $6,000. In 1970 umpires in the Triple-A Pacific Coast League were paid $600 a month, which came to about $20 a game—less than amateur umpires were making to work a high school game. I couldn't have survived without that occasional check from my parents. I guess they felt it was a good investment—it was a lot cheaper than putting up bail money. There were many times when I thought about quitting—many times. But then I tried to figure out what I would do when I got home. I never came up with an answer that was better than what I was doing.

There were a lot of fine people who spent a decade or more in the low minor leagues. I was luckier than most of them; I made it to the big leagues. But getting there left its mark. People who haven't done it can't imagine how tough it is. Maybe that's why I was such a strong member of our union. And it probably has a lot to do with my bitterness about what happened to me so many years later.

I learned how to umpire on thirteen years of minor league fields. I'm not exactly a Rhodes scholar, more of a dirt-roads scholar, but even I figured out pretty quickly how to survive as an umpire. To begin with, I had to throw out just about everything I'd been taught in school. And then I had to throw out a lot of players, managers, coaches—one time I even threw out a hot dog vendor and four sportswriters.

Minor league umpires are on their own. Once you get a job, baseball doesn't provide any supervision or instruction. There's no training, no teaching, nobody to tell you what you're doing right or wrong. When I was in the minors there was one scout in charge of the entire system. We saw him maybe once a season for a couple of days. If you happened to have a bad game it could cost you your job. If a manager didn't like you he could bury you. For example, like me, Bruce Froemming spent thirteen seasons in the minors. In the final game of the Texas League playoffs one year he called out a Tulsa Cardinals runner on an appeal play for missing third base—a call that almost ended his career because the Cardinals organization tried to get him fired. With the score tied, the runner missed third base by about three feet. It cost Tulsa the game and the playoffs—and Tulsa manager Vern Rapp tried to blame it on Froemming. It was an incredible gutsy call to make. It was the right call, and except for the riot it hardly caused a problem. The president of the league, who knew what a good umpire Bruce was, stood up for him and saved his career.

It always seemed ridiculous to me that a multibillion-dollar industry like baseball would have such little regard for such an integral part of the game. But you've got to remember that this is the same business that gave pitcher Steve Howe a lifetime suspension for his drug use—five different times.

In school they teach you the correct way to work. They teach you the rules, positioning, exactly how you're supposed to make all the calls. I had a problem right from the beginning: They taught us to do everything right-handed. To call a strike you raise your right hand, you signal an out with the thumb of your right hand. I'm left-handed all the way. I can't even open a door right-handed. For me, the most natural thing to do was use my left hand to signal. Umpires began using hand signals in the 1880s to communicate with a deaf-mute outfielder named Dummy Hoy. Since that time every umpire has used his right hand. Whenever I asked why I couldn't use my left hand I was told, "Because it isn't right."

Right, it was left. Nobody ever had a good answer to that question—except that if I insisted on using my left hand there was no way I'd ever get to the major leagues. The major leagues wanted everything done the right way.

So, when I had to make a call I had to pause for just a split second and think about it.

But I had been taught that umpires are not supposed to think. Umpires don't think, they react. Unfortunately, when I just reacted I used my left hand. For ten years in the minor leagues I forced myself to do everything right-handed. I'd make all my signals right-handed, I cleaned the plate with my right hand, I ejected managers with my right hand, and when I had to throw a new ball to the pitcher I'd throw it right-handed. And then, as soon as I threw it, I'd shout instructions: *Look out! Watch it!* Sometimes, *Jump for it!* Man, I was bouncing them all over the place—but I was doing it right-handed. It only took me ten years to discover the solution—I'd toss it back underhanded.

In baseball, that was considered revolutionary. Oh, an underhanded umpire! Interesting, very interesting. Sometime during my second season in the major leagues I stopped thinking. I started doing everything with my left hand. Calling strikes, outs, everything. Far as I know, I'm the only umpire to do that. Marty Springstead, a great umpire who became the American League supervisor, once tried to get me to change. It's just not right, he told me. "Marty," I said, "he's just as out with my left hand as he is with my right." Marty never bothered me about it again.

The most important thing I learned to do in the minor

leagues was how to control the game. Most umpires actually begin their careers suffering under the delusion that if they are fair and competent they won't have any problems on the field. Sometimes it takes as long as—oh, I don't know—the first three or four innings of their career for them to understand reality. Managers and players expect every call to go their way. To make sure that happens, they try to intimidate the umpire. They figure, ah, maybe this call didn't go my way, but if I scream at this guy and maybe spit on him and kick dirt on him and insult him then maybe he'll like me and I'll get the next close one—or else I'll have to do it again.

The only way to stop that is to stop that. You give a manager like Earl Weaver or Billy Martin or Lou Piniella one little inch and they'll take your house, your car, your next-born child. But you have to learn how to stand up to people like Earl Weaver. Well, actually, because Weaver was short, you had to learn how to lean down on him.

In the minor leagues you learn how to deal with people. Turns out that the very best way to maintain control of a game is to get rid of the problem as quickly as possible. Most umpires never forget their first professional ejection. I have. I just threw out so many so quickly that they all sort of blend together in my mind in a beautiful mosaic. But I do remember what surprised me: Ejecting your first manager or player is more difficult than I thought it would be. Throwing a person out of a game, or even out of a room, is just not a familiar or comfortable thing to do. Try to imagine getting in an argument with a person at your job and all of a sudden deciding, that's it, you're out of the office! You're done, get your behind out of here, you're not allowed to work here for the rest of the day! Or imagine being a waiter in a restaurant and getting so mad at a customer that you don't let them order—you toss them out of the restaurant and then you report them for being a bad customer.

You really have to work up to that first ejection. You have to be so angry, so upset you just can't help yourself. And you do it and then suddenly you realize . . . wait a second, this is pretty cool. It feels great. And pretty soon you start thinking, *Lemme understand this, I get to kick people out of the game if I don't like the way they're acting? And I still get paid?* Whoa! It was sort of like Columbus must have felt when he discovered the New World. *Has this been there all the time?* It is an extraordinarily powerful feeling. *You mean, I'm the boss? I'm the dictator? They have to listen to me?*

Believe me, it gets easier and easier to do. At first, you're willing to take all kinds of verbal abuse, so you let it go and let it go and let it go—but, after you get the rhythm, a manager comes out and says, "I . . ."

That's enough. "I don't have to take that from you! You're outta here!"

That's the way it starts, and by the time an umpire reaches the big leagues he knows how to handle managers and players. One time in the big leagues, for example, Dodgers manager Tommy Lasorda got ejected without saying a word. Terry Tata was behind the plate in Cincinnati and Lasorda was complaining from the dugout the whole game. Finally he couldn't take it anymore. He came out of the dugout and headed right for Tata. But before he got to the plate he must have remembered that managers couldn't argue balls and strike calls, that it was an automatic ejection. So he walked right past Tata and headed for the first base umpire, Dick Stello. When he got to Stello he said a few words and turned left towards second base umpire John Kibler. Just as he got to second base Kibler kind of shooed him away, meaning *don't you come near me*. Lasorda turned left again and headed for third base umpire Bruce Froemming. When he finally got to third base, before he could say one word, Froemming said, "That's it, you're done," and ejected him.

Lasorda couldn't believe it. "For what?" he demanded, "I haven't said one word to you."

"That's right," Froemming agreed, "but you circled the bases. You've run out of umpires. You got no place else to go."

Kibler walked over to see what happened, and Lasorda appealed to him, "John, honest to God, I never said a word and he threw me out."

"Come on Tommy," Kibler said, "you had to say something. He wouldn't chase you for nothing." And Bruce just stood there smiling innocently.

When I started, the minor leagues were very different than they are today. There were a lot more teams, they were playing mostly in old, dimly-lit stadiums, and the local fans were much more passionate about their hometown team than the nearest major league club. The game was their whole life. At that time, players stayed in the minors years longer than they do now. We had players who had spent ten years or more in the minors, but we also had a lot of former major league players just finishing up their careers and hoping for one more shot. These were guys who had played several years in the majors. It wasn't necessarily a love for the game that kept them playing as much as it was a need for a paycheck.

The minor leagues were a constant battle. Nobody wanted to be there. The career minor leaguers were angry, the kids on their way up were ambitious, and the former big leaguers were embarrassed. Everybody was always upset. I never minded people screaming insults at me—that just made me feel like I was home—but I did mind them throwing rocks, batteries, fruit, and glass bottles. One of the greatest things that ever happened in the long history of umpiring was the invention of the plastic bottle.

I didn't take nothing from nobody. I mean, nothing. The alternative to maintaining control was chaos. If somebody gave me a hard time, or even a medium time, they were history. I had the plate one night in Syracuse. It was my first game back after missing a few days with a broken toe, and I wasn't feeling that terrific. Richmond's shortstop, a kid named Pat Rocket, was batting. The pitch came in, I hesitated a second then decided, "Strike twoooooooooo."

Rocket stepped out of the batter's box. "Come on," he said, "I know it was a strike, but you got to call it quicker."

Quicker? He wanted it quicker. The pitcher went into his windup, he brought the ball back behind his head . . .

"Strike threeeeeeeee! That quick enough for you?"

With enough practice, minor league umpires get real good at ejecting people. In Pawtucket one night I called a runner out for interfering with the second baseman. After being put out on a force at second, it looked to me like he slid way out of the baseline to prevent the second baseman from completing the double play. I thought I had it right. Pawtucket's manager, Joe Morgan, who later would manage in the big leagues, was furious at the call. I folded my arms, stood rock-still, and listened to him. When he finished I told him the facts of life. Here are the facts of life: I'm the umpire. Whatever I say goes. Those are the facts of life.

That didn't satisfy Morgan. "You didn't even see the play," he insisted. "I'm gonna show you what the runner did."

"You don't want to do that, Joe," I said. He started backing up. "I'm warning you Joe, this isn't a good idea."

He came barreling down the line and made a nice hook slide into second base. Truthfully, it was the best slide I'd ever seen a manager make. "That's how he did it," Morgan shouted at me.

"You're sure it was just like that?" I asked.

"Absolutely," Morgan said.

"That's good then," I told him, " 'cause now I know I got the play right. So you're both out. He's out on the play and you're out of this game." I gave him a big good-bye.

But maybe the best response to an argument in the minor leagues came from Dick Stello, who eventually became a fine National League umpire. Stello was working the plate in a Texas League game when the batter hit a long drive down the left field line. He called it a fair ball. Fort Worth's manager, Alex Grammas, came out to argue. "How can you make that call from here."

"Well," Stello explained, "when the ball hit the ground I saw a little puff of chalk from the foul line go into the air, so it had to be a fair ball."

Grammas couldn't believe it. "Hold it a second. You're telling me that you can see a puff of chalk from more than 300 feet away?"

"You know what, Alex," Stello said sincerely, "on a clear day I can see the sun—and that sucker is 93 million miles away."

Grammas didn't know how to respond. He walked back to the dugout and sat down next to a coach. As Grammas later remembered it, the coach asked him what happened out there. And Grammas shook his head and said softly, "He said the sun was 93 million miles away."

One day in Toledo, Richie Garcia and I threw out fifteen people. Fifteen! I was throwing them out with both my right and left hands. Richie Garcia was a great partner, but he had a real Latin temper. By default I was considered the reasonable member of our two-man crew. He'd lose his temper and I'd go looking for it. Toledo's manager was Jim Bunning, and we both hated him. In fact, pretty much every umpire who worked a game in which Bunning participated hated him. He was like a whiny little kid when a call went against him. So Richie and I loved every minute of that particular game. Richie threw out two guys, so I got three. Three? I could see his mind working, you think three is something? Boom! Boom! Boom! Boom! Then I came back and got a few more. We were knocking them off, boom, boom, boom! *You, you're breathing on me, get outta here! And you, I heard what you were thinking, you're done!*

That wasn't even my all-time record. I got my personal best in the Carolina League, Lynchburg vs. Salem, when I threw out the entire press box. A close play at the plate went against Lynchburg. They came out of the dugout at me in waves. I started picking them off. I got a few players, a coach, and finally the fans quieted down. Well, I thought, that's done. But at the end of the inning the public address announcer boomed, "And at the end of four innings, the score is Salem 1, Lynchburg 1, Kaiser 1."

Bam! It started all over again. I turned around and stared at the PA announcer—and I saw that everybody in the press box was laughing. At me. So I pointed up at the press box and gave them my best heave-ho. I cleared it out. At first those people weren't sure who I was ejecting. But I made it clear to them: everybody except the official scorer. I got a hot dog vendor, sportswriters, media people, maintenance people, and I definitely got the public address announcer. They tried to tell me that I couldn't do it, I couldn't eject people who weren't in the game. Maybe not, I said, but this game isn't continuing until you leave, and I'll bet these fans aren't going to like that at all. I got them all.

Every argument, every ejection is a learning experience. At the beginning of my career I was inexperienced, I didn't know how to handle certain situations, so I'd get into trouble and solve it by throwing out people. But I got better, I learned how to do the job. I learned, for example, to think of the rule book as more of a good story than a Bible. Certain rules are not made to be followed: Batters like to stand as far back as possible, for example, but according to the rule book they must keep both feet in the batter's box. On-deck hitters are supposed to stay in the on-deck circle, but they like to get closer to the plate to time the pitcher. The shortstop or second baseman is supposed to actually make contact with second base while the ball is in his possession for the runner to be forced. The strike zone is defined in the rule book as that area over home plate stretching from the hitter's knees to the letters and any pitch breaking that plane is supposed to be a strike. Pitchers are supposed to deliver the ball within a specific amount of time.

Yeah. Right. There's only one equation that matters to umpires: The fewer calls you make the less chance you have to get in trouble. Even I understood that one. You don't make any calls, they can't criticize your work. Kaiser didn't make a single call the entire game; that means he didn't get one wrong.

It only took me a couple of years to learn that I was supposed to use the abridged version of the rule book. For example, just before the game began, after the groundskeepers had laid down all the chalk lines, I'd rub out the back line of both batter's boxes. I couldn't call a player out for being out of the batter's box when there was no batter's box. I rubbed out that line every time I had the plate for my entire career.

Umpires learn in the minor leagues that certain calls are absolutely guaranteed to start an argument, guaranteed. So, unless the violation is so flagrant, so obvious, they avoid making those calls.

The most important rule to any umpire is *Rule 8.96, Section XIL, Paragraph ii.* Or was it *Paragraph iii?* Or maybe it's *Section VIX.* It's known as The Bluff Rule, and it exists only on the Planet of the Umps. It's based on the fact that very few managers—particularly minor league managers—really know the rules of baseball. The best way to stop an argument is to quote the specific rule that you used to make a call, even if you have to make up that rule. The one rule that I was known for really enforcing was a balk. Basically, a pitcher can't alter his pitching motion to fool a base runner; he can't step towards home plate and throw to first. My interpretation of the balk rule was simple: I don't know what he did, but he fooled me. *Balk!* But as soon as I'd call the balk the pitcher's manager would come shooting out of the dugout screaming, "What'd he do? What'd he do?"

I'd laugh. "You got to be kidding me. Ask your pitching coach, let him explain the rules of baseball to you."

If the manager persisted, and some of them did, I would explain carefully to him that the pitcher's leg broke the imaginary plane towards home plate, but he threw to first base, "and geeze, Billy, you've been in this game long enough to know that's a balk." Imaginary planes? Most managers had no idea what I was talking about.

We were taught in school that the key to applying The Bluff Rule, or making any call, is to make it forcefully. Make it loud. Make it firm. Sell that call. Don't leave any doubt in anyone's mind that you know exactly what you're talking about. Right or wrong, you're always right. Managers had to understand that the call I made was the best call I could make at that instant, and, like it or not, they were going to have to accept it. When a manager or player was convinced that I knew—not thought, *knew*—that I was right he rarely pushed the argument. Didn't that runner leave third base too soon?

No he did not! Are you out of your mind, asking me a question like that! How do you have the guts to come out here and ask such a dumb question! Okay!

Okay, just checking.

Most of the problems I had in the minor leagues involved ground rules. A lot of the stadiums had been built in the 1920s and '30s, so they were old, cramped, and dirty. The lights were awful. I literally worked on fields that Babe Ruth had played on. Every field was different and had its own unique ground rules. One year I opened the Carolina League season in Salisbury, North Carolina. The manager of the Salisbury Astros, Jimmy Matthews, explained the ground rules. The seats were only a few feet behind the plate. I could stand at home plate and pretty much reach back and shake hands with the fans. Not that I would want to, of course. Against the rear wall was a mat, the same kind of wrestling mat used in high schools. "If the ball lodges back in there," Matthews explained, "just leave it. Don't let anybody reach in there."

"What are you talking about?"

"Last week one of our people found a diamondback by home plate."

"What's that?" I didn't know what he was talking about.

"You know, a diamondback snake. He killed the bastard with a bat, but they always travel in pairs. We're just waiting for its partner to show up."

You kidding me? I had some game that day. After every pitch I'd turn my head around so fast the people sitting behind the plate thought they were watching *The Exorcist:* Gee Maude, look at that umpire's head spinning around. Pitch. Call. Spin around. I could hear those people talking to each other, "What's wrong with him? Why does he keep looking at us?" By the third inning I had the whole crowd paranoid.

The worst ballpark I ever worked in was in Salem, Virginia. If they named stadiums for corporate sponsors at that time, this place would have been called Purgatory Field. For umpires, this was like North Hell. Center field was about 250 feet from home plate, right field was maybe 800 feet. The fences had big gaps in them and came out at angles. Telephone lines about twelve feet off the ground crisscrossed a portion of the field, and every wire required a different rule. They also played football on the field, so the outfield was covered with faded chalk lines. The field was laid out like a pinball machine. When a ball hit that fence it bounced around like a pinball. There were at least forty-five ground rules, and we were supposed to remember all of them. The popcorn stand was in foul territory about two feet behind third base. One time I asked them why they didn't move the popcorn stand. They looked at me like I was crazy. "You kidding? That's our big profit center."

At the beginning of the game it took Salem's manager forty minutes to go over all the ground rules. He had three pages of rules to go over—some of them had footnotes. I listened, but to me it all came down to the same thing: two bases. If the ball went through a hole in the fence, two bases. If the ball disappeared into the drainage ditch, two bases. If a fly ball landed in the beehive, two bases. If the ball rolled under the center field cow, two bases. The popcorn stand was in play, but fielders were not allowed to reach into the popper. The only thing good about that ballpark was that the lights were so bad that at night the fans couldn't see a ball hit into the outfield any better than I could.

Generally, if the visiting team manager disagreed with a ground rule the plate umpire was supposed to decide what rule to follow. When Earl Weaver was managing Aberdeen in the Class C Northern League, his team was playing the Minot Mallards. In right field a large tree hung over the scoreboard. Weaver and the Minot Mallards manager couldn't agree on the tree rule. As home team manager, Weaver wanted anything hitting the tree to be a home run, the Mallards manager wanted it to be in play. The umpire, Frank Dezelan—who later worked in the National League—decided, "Okay, I'll make the ground rule. The tree's in play."

Weaver probably leaped three feet off the ground. Okay, maybe six inches. But then he started screaming at Dezelan that *he* was supposed to make the ground rules, and no umpire had a right to tell him what the ground rules should be, and that he wasn't going to stand for it.

Dezelan waited until Weaver had finished screaming and asked, "Who's your manager?"

Weaver hesitated. He was standing right there with his lineup cards. "What do you mean," he asked, "I'm the manager."

"No," Dezeland told him, "no, no, no. You're scratched. You're gone. I mean, who's your new manager?"

Just about all minor league fields were in terrible condition. It really wasn't the owners' fault. Minor league teams weren't making any money, so they couldn't afford things like . . . dirt. Or grass. The infield consisted of clumps of grass and holes. The bases were old and ripped. But they had all the rocks they needed. The ground crew usually consisted of two guys who knew a friend of a close relative of the club owner, a high school kid trying to make gas money, and the town drunk who needed a quiet place to sleep it off.

But compared to the umpires' dressing rooms, the fields were beautiful. In the minor leagues, the umpires' locker room is always the worst room in the ballpark. Logically, it shouldn't have even been called a locker room because it didn't have lockers—we hung our clothes on hooks. They should have called it the hook room. Or maybe, in the low minors, the bent rusty nail room. It was always the room that was downhill from the septic system. The room that was so small that you had to go outside to change your mind. It was always hot, it always smelled terrible—and that was *before* the game! If it had a toilet, it didn't work. In Salem, for example, the umpires' locker room was on the other side of the wall from the popcorn popper. The locker room had no windows. Our side of the wall got so hot that the paint had literally melted away.

These rooms were filthy, bug-infested, rat-infested—just awful. Even today, I never put on a pair of shoes without shaking them out first to see if anything crawled in there. My first season I made a big mistake. I saw this big spider in the dressing room and I killed it. My partner was furious. "Don't you know anything about umpiring?" he shouted at me. "You never kill spiders—because they eat every other kind of bug in there."

We did make exceptions for poisonous spiders, and really big, really ugly spiders.

In addition to all the other irritations, I had to carry my balloon protector with me everywhere. In those days, there was a big difference between working in the American League and the National League. It had a lot to do with size; big guys went to the American League, the little guys went to the National League. The two leagues used different systems, wore different uniforms, had very different strike zones, and used different protectors behind home plate. National Leaguers wore form-fitting chest padding under their coats, and minor leaguers who used that armor could just roll it up after a game and carry it in a suitcase. Future American Leaguers had to get used to the big balloon protector. At one time these protectors were filled with air. They were pumped up before a game and could be deflated and rolled up, which made them pretty easy to carry. But the protectors we were using were filled with hard Styrofoam. They were solid. In the big leagues the umpires' gear gets shipped by clubhouse attendants. Not in the minors. In the minors we had to keep our gear with us. So I had to carry this big thing with me in and out of cars, in small hotel rooms—and it barely fit into some locker rooms. It was like a prop for a bad sitcom plot. No matter where I went, it was always just a little bit too small for me to squeeze in with my protector. And obviously, when people saw me carrying it they just had to make some clever remark, like, "Oh, are you an umpire?"

"No, I just carry this thing around because I'm a masochist. I like people to abuse me." Or, "No, I'm a gladiator and I just got a patent on this lightweight shield."

At times the life got to be too much for me. One day—I don't remember where this was, but it could have been in any town—I was sitting in the umpires' closet about an hour before the game. We'd driven most of the night to get there and I was exhausted. It was maybe 110 degrees and we had a ceiling fan with only one blade cooling the room. We were eating cold hot dogs left over from the night before; well, at least we hoped it was only the night before. An attendant poked his head into the room—there wasn't enough space for any other part of his body—and asked, "You guys want me to hold your valuables?"

I was a twenty-three-year-old low minor league umpire making $3,600 a season. I was living out of a broken suitcase, washing my clothes in sinks, driving a nine-year-old car on bare tires, eating leftovers, changing in a hot closet, and this guy wants to hold on to my valuables? Valuables? Who was he kidding? I handed him my socks.

It was tough. I wasn't exactly rocketing through the minor leagues. I had to fight for a job just about every year. And at the end of every season I would get fired. I got fired by the Florida State League, by the Western Carolina League, the Carolina League, and the Northern League. I could see a pattern developing. I'd been working three years and was still on the lowest rung of the minor leagues. In 1968 I got married and decided it was finally time to quit. I was done with baseball.

Barney Deary, who had just become supervisor of minor league umpires, called and asked me to come back. "Gee Barney," I said, "I don't know. I've got a good job at a bank." I told him I was in acquisitions. Technically, that was true. I was repossessing cars.

I think you'd have to search for a long time to find a profession where you get more abuse than being an umpire, and then you'd find being a repossessor. I worked for the Marine Midland Bank repossessing cars and furniture. It's not a particularly happy job. Nobody ever greets the repossessor at their front door with a smile; nobody in history has ever told a repossessor, "We're glad you're here, we've been waiting for you."

Most of the time I worked at night and as quietly as possible. Truthfully, except for occasionally being shot at, it wasn't that tough. You just broke into the car and drove it away. One time, though, I went to a home to repossess some furniture and the owner told me, "Mr. Kaiser, you can't get blood out of stone."

"Maybe not, Mr. Jackson," I told him, "but I sure can get that furniture out your front door."

When I told Barney Deary about my job he asked me, "Do you still love the game?" I had to admit that I did. "Come back and I'll do what I can to move you along." A season later Barney got me a job in the Double-A Eastern League, one notch higher. Everything was a little better, even the dressing room rats were fatter.

In 1972 the Eastern League sold my contract to the Southern League, which was also a Double-A league. At least when I was working in the Eastern League I'd get to go home a few times during the season; but if I took the job in the Southern League I'd be gone for the entire six-month season. So I decided to retire again. I told Barney, "I'll open up in Jacksonville for you, but then I'm coming home. You know, things are going good at the bank." I'd worked my way up to repossessing furniture, after all.

"Just hold on," Barney told me. "In spring training we might be able to make a move." That spring there was an opening in the International League when an umpire disappeared. One day he was just gone, and nobody ever found out what happened to him. So I was promoted to the International League, a Triple-A league. This was just one level below the big leagues. We had expense accounts, and we stayed in hotels that had real names.

I worked in the International League for five years. Other umpires around me were going to the majors, but I stayed there. Before I made it to the International League I had never thought about getting to the big leagues. It just didn't seem possible. And truthfully, I wasn't that unhappy about it.

I liked the International League. I worked a bunch of games in Rochester and Syracuse, so I was able to spend a lot of time at home. And I was making $600 a month plus $500 expenses—$1,100 a month. To me it was like I was earning $50 million.

In the off-season I took any job I could find. Because baseball was a full-time job only part of the year, there were a limited number of things I could do in the winter. In addition to working for the bank, I tended bar and did a little bouncing, I drove a truck delivering auto parts, and then there was my brief career in professional wrestling.

One time, I remember, I was working the bar in a disco named Spanky's when a group of about a dozen bikers strolled in and decided to take over the place. I don't remember the name of their motorcycle club, it could have been something like Kill Kaiser, but they were like tough Hell's Angels. Their leader was a guy named Patsy. They started tearing up the place a little bit, then they tossed the DJ out of his booth and started playing their own music. I thought, *This isn't good, I'm gonna get killed here.* What was I going to do, throw them out of the club?

We kept a sawed-off shotgun behind the bar. It was never loaded, we didn't even have shells for it, but it looked pretty scary. I went behind the bar and Patsy told me, "Set my boys up here."

I said, "You got any money?"

He sort of laughed at me. "Where we go we don't pay," he said. "How 'bout, instead of money I just come back there and kick the shit out of you, then we throw you out the window?"

Oh, so he was negotiating. I decided on my counter-offer. I picked up the shotgun and put it against his face, "I got a better idea. How about if I blow your head clear off your shoulders?"

Many years later I would become a participant in the labor dispute that cost me my job, my pension, and almost my house, among other things. The people involved were baseball executives, union lawyers, and leaders. All of them made a lot of money, wore really expensive suits, and had big expense accounts. And, while all the court documents were written in legalese, it pretty much came down to the same thing: How 'bout I kick the shit out of you? Oh yeah, how about if I blow your head off your shoulders?

The confrontation in the bar got settled a lot easier. We all understood that we had several things in common: None of us wanted to get hurt. They wanted to drink and listen to their music, we wanted them to pay for their drinks and use our disk jockey. We reached a compromise: as a peace offering I served them a few pitchers of beer—but they paid for all their other drinks. We put the club's disk jockey back in his booth and he played their music. It all worked out fine. They didn't break up the place and I didn't get killed.

My fight with baseball has already lasted more than than four years and is still in court.

I wrestled professionally for two years. This, too, was not part of a larger plan. I was in Norfolk, Virginia, sitting around a motel pool, and I got to talking to a man who turned out to be a wrestling promoter from Louisville, Kentucky. I told him I had wrestled in high school. "You know what," he said, "if you ever wanted a job in the off-season, you could be a professional wrestler."

Professional wrestling? I didn't know if I wanted to give up my exciting career in professional repossessing or bar bouncing. "I can't," I said. "If baseball found out about it, I could never umpire again."

"They won't find out, we'll put a mask on you!"

My partner that year was Nick Bremigan, a great guy who eventually became a fine American League umpire. "That's a great idea," he said.

I was a little insulted. "What? Me becoming a wrestler?"

"Nah," he said, "putting a mask on you."

Nick decided he would be my manager. I had never really seen the appeal in being kicked, gouged, or body-slammed. Then it was explained to me that I would get paid. Bremigan and I went to Louisville for a two-week training period, where I met people like Bobby "The Brain" Heenan and Mad Dog Vashon. I was taught how to get hit and fall without getting hurt, how to protect myself, and how to make it look real.

There were all kinds of tricks. For example, when you were about to get body slammed, you push up off the mat to help your opponent lift you up. And when you do get slammed there is a sheet of tin under the rubberized mat to amplify the sound.

It still hurt. When somebody lifts you up, then slams you down, it hurts.

To make sure baseball never found out about it, I was given a character to play. I became The Hatchet! I wore an all-black outfit, including a mask, and carried a hatchet into the ring with me. In wrestling there are the baby faces, who are the good guys, and the heels, the bad guys. I was a heel. Nobody knew who I was, I was just another masked face filling out the bill. I was a jobber. Nobody ever bought a ticket to see The Hatchet.

My first match was in Quebec City. I got paid $25. Nobody actually told me if I was going to win or lose. It wasn't like that. But it was understood that I wasn't going to win. The most important thing was to make it look good and not get hurt. I called my big closing hold the Steak Dinner, because after I put it on everybody went out for steak dinners.

When a team wins all its games it's undefeated; for my entire career I was defeated. I didn't win a match. I did wrestle some pretty well-known stars. I fought the legendary Haystacks Calhoun, 550 pounds of pure fat. I was doing great for awhile, then he bounced off the ropes and flopped on top of me. "The Big Splash," it was called. I felt like one of those characters in a cartoon who gets flattened by a steamroller. My face was literally smothered in fat. His fat just wrapped around my face. I was being blubbered to death. I couldn't breath and I couldn't get him off me. I was dying under there.

Mad Dog Vashon was the meanest wrestler I ever met. He was one of those backwoods lumberjack types that you just couldn't hurt. He was strong, and absolutely nothing bothered him. Backstage they used to say that if another wrestler hit him and he found out about it, no one could hold him back.

In Miami I wrestled the great Andre the Giant. There is no doubt in my mind that Andre was the strongest man who ever walked the face of the earth. He literally was a giant, maybe seven-five and at least five hundred pounds. I had a friend named Big John Studd. Big John was about six-nine and probably weighed four hundred pounds. For a time he held the record for bench-pressing six hundred pounds. He set that record on national television, on Johnny Carson's *Tonight Show*. But in the locker room one day Andre the Giant picked up Big John—with one hand!—and held him over his head. He carried him around the room balanced on that one hand.

You didn't actually wrestle Andre. I couldn't have hurt him with a real hatchet, so my strategy was to stay as far away from him as possible. New Orleans might be far enough, I figured. After the match we went out to dinner with a French-Canadian wrestler named Dino Bravo. Dino and I each had a steak, baked potato, and a salad. Andre—and I'm not exaggerating, this is absolutely the truth—had three sixteen-ounce steaks, twelve baked potatoes, a salad that was just a little larger than the Orange Bowl, all washed down with a quarter-keg of beer. Andre only spoke French, and toward the end of the meal he said something to Dino. I asked Dino what he said. "He told me to tell you that he's picking up the check."

I looked around the table at the pile of empty plates. "No kidding," I said.

Only one person in baseball ever discovered my identity. When it became obvious that I had a real shot at getting to the major leagues, I decided to quit before I got caught. One of my last matches took place at The Spectrum in Philadelphia. As I was locked in a death grip by my opponent, he accidentally ripped off my mask—and I found myself staring through the ropes directly at my fellow umpire, Eric Gregg. Eric was sitting in the front row calmly eating his popcorn when my mask came off and he realized The Hatchet was Ken Kaiser. He dropped his popcorn.

We were both in shock; Eric couldn't believe that I was a pro wrestler, and I couldn't believe Eric would drop food.

My pro wrestling career ended when I signed a contract with the American League. But in 1982 I was asked to mud-wrestle two women for charity. This was for charity, so how could I refuse? It was a big deal: Kaiser vs. the Gonzo Sisters. Without a mask. Naturally, when American League officials heard one of their umpires was mud-wrestling two women they felt it might not further the wholesome image they desired. It would be an understatement to admit that they weren't thrilled about this. I did have a gift for making my supervisors unhappy. But there wasn't much they could do to stop me. It was for charity—and it was two women.

In my wildest dreams I had never imagined two women like the Gonzo Sisters. These were two beauties. I'm guessing their combined weight was 385 but then again I've always been kind. And they really wanted to win this match. Just like Haystacks Calhoun, they used a smother hold—they tried to bury my head in the middle of their chests. But even a good thing had to come to an end sometime. Maybe not right away, but sometime. I pinned the two of them on top of each other and won the match, officially ending my wrestling career.

To some people, spending thirteen years in the minor leagues might seem like a long time. Me, for instance. To me, it seemed like forever. But I needed that time, or at least most of it. I was eighteen years old when I started. Thirteen years later I was . . . I was a lot older. I needed that time to learn how to control the game, but, more importantly, I needed it to learn how to control myself. By the time I reached the major leagues I had umpired more than a thousand baseball games. I had game experience. I'd heard all the arguments, all the insults. I'd seen all the fan promotions—cow-milking contests, lucky number car giveaways, Captain Dynamite, who got in a box and blew himself up. Believe me, if you spend enough years in the minor leagues nothing is going to surprise you. You've met all the characters. You've learned how to handle situations. You've seen all the plays and the misplays. You've learned how to get yourself out of trouble. And when you couldn't get out of trouble, you knew the fastest way to get to the interstate. If you spend enough time in the minor leagues you've seen just about everything—maybe with the exception of Kaiser wrestling the Gonzo Sisters.

For example, Chuck Cottier, whom I knew when he managed Seattle, started his managerial career in Clinton, Iowa. One of the most difficult calls for any umpire is a trapped fly in the outfield. There are times you really can't tell if the ball was caught on the fly or short-hopped into the outfielder's glove. Even in big league ballparks with great lighting, it's a tough call to make. In the minor leagues you don't have enough experience to make an educated guess. It's like a second-grade guess. One night, Cottier's Clinton team loaded the bases with one out. The runner on second was a player named Arturo Bonito. The batter hit a little blooper into left-center and everybody took off. In the two-umpire system used in the minor leagues, as soon as the ball was hit the umpire in the infield started running towards the outfield. The center fielder and left fielder converged on the ball. Baseball in action: one runner scored. Bonito scored. The third runner was about to score—when the umpire finally signaled the ball had been caught. The batter was out.

The action stopped. There was just a tiny little pause as everybody tried to figure out what to do. And then they took off again—in the opposite direction. It looked like somebody had started running a movie projector in reverse. All of the runners were trying to retrace their steps and were trying to get back to the base they started from. The problem was, some of them didn't remember real well where they had started. When the play stopped, the three base runners were standing on third base and the batter was on second.

I don't remember this being one of the plays that they teach in umpire school. But suddenly, Bonito, figuring out that there was a serious overcrowding problem at third base, took off—he took a shortcut, running directly across the infield over the pitcher's mound to first base. That probably wasn't as illogical as it might seem, first base was the only base that was unoccupied.

The fielders weren't any smarter than the base runners. When the shortstop saw Bonito heading towards first base he decided to make a play on him. But his throw to first was late and Bonito just beat the tag. So that left the batter on second with a double, Bonito, who had started on second, had made it safely to first on that double, and two runners were on third. The fielders were tagging everybody.

The umpires finally decided it had to be a double-play ending the inning. Had to be. They didn't explain it, but they didn't have to. Pretty much everybody else was in shock. Two outs were all they needed, but if there hadn't already been one out it probably would have been a triple play. They would have found all the outs they needed. And Cottier was absolutely right when he decided, "If they had needed four outs they could have found them somewhere, too." There was no argument on the play. Argument? People are still trying to figure out what happened.

The only player who seemed to have an idea of what he was doing was Bonito. As he explained later to Cottier, "I looked around. We had three men on third, one man on second, and nobody on first. I figured maybe they would forget where I started."

The strangest play I ever had in the minors took place in Durham. I was standing behind first base. In those days the bases were made a little differently. The bases used today are solid, they're rigid—like plastic rocks. But the bases we used in the minors were really bags filled with a soft substance. They were much more flexible, like pillows.

The batter smashed a hard line drive right down the first base line. The first baseman dived for it, kicking up a cloud of dust. I thought it was going to hit me, so I dived out of the way, and then I turned around, expecting to see the ball bouncing around in the outfield. It wasn't there. The ball was gone. I mean, just gone. And while we were looking for it, the batter circled the bases. Home run.

After he scored we finally found the ball—under the base. It was stuck under first base. There was no call to be made. It was a fair ball. It hadn't been caught on a fly. The runner circled the bases. Home run.

In addition to working in the minor leagues, umpires making progress towards the major leagues were invited to work in spring training and in the Caribbean leagues during the winter. I think I worked spring training for the first time in 1970. Later in my career, spring training would be a long paid vacation, but at that time it was thrilling. I umpired the first major league game I ever saw in person.

I took spring training very seriously. I knew I was being watched and that if I didn't screw up I might get a shot at the big leagues. I was behind the plate one night for a Washington Senators game. Jeff Burroughs, who would have a nice major league career, was still a kid trying to make the team. I was behind the plate. I called the first pitch a strike. Burroughs didn't like my call and stepped out of the box. He sort of shook his head in disbelief and stepped back into the box. Next pitch, same place. Strike two! Burroughs stepped out and started yelling at me. I yelled right back at him—that's all I knew how to do. The next pitch he popped out.

As I was leaving the field after the game, Senators' manager Ted Williams called me over. I assumed he was going to let me have it, but I really didn't care. This was Ted Williams. Growing up, I had his baseball card. And he wanted to speak to *me*. This was something that one day I could tell the kids I didn't even have yet: *Sure son, I knew Ted Williams, he screamed at me. He called me a $%#%%!*

He had Jeff Burroughs with him. "Look at the two of you," he said. "I'm gonna tell you something. I played in the big leagues for twenty years. If the umpire missed the first strike I knew I still had two left. If the umpire missed the second strike I still had one left. And in my whole career, I never had an umpire miss three."

Ted Williams never said one word to me. I didn't care. I was thinking, *You're absolutely right, Ted. You tell him. You are the greatest.*

I worked the winter of 1976 in Puerto Rico. In those days, Puerto Rico was considered an important stepping stone to the big leagues. You knew it was a stepping stone, because the fans threw steps, stones, and buildings at the umpires. I had heard all the horror stories about working in the winter leagues from other umpires. When Trujillo was in power in the Dominican Republic, for example, the army put machine guns behind first base and third base. Who knows, maybe they were worried a revolution might break out around second base. But truthfully, if you're looking to intimidate umpires, installing machine guns behind the bases is probably a pretty good way to start.

I didn't want to go to Puerto Rico for the winter. I was married, I had a baby boy, and I had been on the road all season. But being assigned there meant the big leagues were looking at you, and you couldn't turn it down.

I hated it. It was like going back to Single-A ball. Worse. The only people the fans hated worse than the umpires were other fans who threw things at the umpires and *missed*. These people took their baseball seriously; they dressed in the home team colors, they danced in the aisles to mariachi bands, and in one city, Santurce I think, before each game a woman sprayed each member of the home team with holy water. Some umpires claimed that after only one season in Puerto Rico they could identify the specific brand of rum being thrown at them by the sound the bottle made as it whizzed by their head. The long-neck bottles had more of a whiz. The truth is that Puerto Rico really wasn't that difficult for me—I was already used to being escorted from the ballpark by armed guards. One time though, I did get a little nervous.

In Ponce we were always escorted to our dressing shed out in right field by a policeman. One night we were walking across the outfield when somebody threw a rum bottle at us and hit the policeman in the shoulder. The policeman pretty calmly took out his gun and started shooting at the guy. Three shots. Bam! Bam! Bam! I couldn't believe it. It was like working as a repo man again. I wanted to work in the big leagues, but I didn't see how dying in Puerto Rico would help me get there.

Terry Tata had worked there a couple of winters before me. He warned me that the conditions were terrible, but that if you can go down there and survive the season you can umpire anywhere. The biggest hero on the entire island was Roberto Clemente. Clemente was one of the first great Hispanic major league ballplayers, and his countrymen worshipped him. To satisfy them, Clemente had to play winter ball for his old Santurce team.

Tata was behind the plate one night when Clemente hit a high pop-up into foul territory behind first base. The tarp used to cover the field when it rained was rolled up against the railing. The first baseman from the other team, George Scott, leaned over the tarp and tried to catch the ball, then fell into the stands. Scott climbed out of the stands holding up his glove with the ball in it. Tata couldn't tell if Scott had actually caught the ball, but he had no choice. He called Clemente out.

The fans went crazy. A lot of those people had traveled a long distance and spent more than they could afford to see Clemente hit. They certainly didn't want to see him foul out, particularly on a questionable call. Clemente was furious. He took off his helmet and hurled it about fifty feet through the air across the diamond. Tata reacted—he threw Clemente out of the game. That's when the fans really got upset.

One good thing about Puerto Rico was that the government was very tough. Nobody rioted without government permission. And they didn't have it that night. Eventually the fans settled down. However, as Tata was on his way home a car stopped next to him and the driver said something in Spanish. Tata asked his driver what the man had said. "It's nothing," the driver said, "just nothing. He just said, 'We know where you are living.'"

Guess who never got to sleep that night.

My wrestling "manager," Nick Bremigan, spent several seasons working in Puerto Rico. His second season there he worked with Dale Ford. On opening day two fans got into an argument and started shooting at each other. Shooting!

Everybody around them scattered. One of them was hit and wounded. Within seconds people had loaded him onto a stretcher and carried him out. The other fans went back to their seats. Watching this down on the field, Dale Ford was stunned. This was his first game in Puerto Rico. "Nick," he said nervously, "you see that? Does that kind of thing happen a lot down here?"

Nick was pretty cool. "You got nothing to worry about," he explained casually. "Don't even think about it. They got a city ordinance. It's against the law to shoot towards the playing field." Then he walked away.

When you spend thirteen years in the minor leagues you get to see a lot of players passing you—going in both directions. You really do get to see dreams come true, and dreams go up in smoke—literally, sometimes. One night, after a game in the Eastern League, I came out of our locker room and saw a player named Bob Taylor standing over a bonfire at home plate—he had decided to quit baseball and was burning his uniform, his glove, everything he owned.

After my first season in the International League I got pretty good at figuring out which players had a real shot at making it in the big leagues. I remember the day I saw two kids named Fred Lynn and Jim Rice playing at Pawtucket, the Red Sox club, and knew I was watching future big-league stars. I saw Tony LaRussa when he was a struggling player at Charlestown. He was a terrible hitter: some players couldn't hit the curveball; he couldn't hit the baseball. He couldn't hit *me* if I was standing in front of him—and even then I was a big target. Art Howe, who later would manage in Houston and Oakland, and the Mets, was at Charlestown. I worked with managers like Bobby Cox, Joe Altobelli, some really good guys. And Jim Bunning, who was trying to get back to the big leagues as a manager. He never made it, which broke nobody's heart. After he failed in baseball he went into politics and won election as a United States senator.

Every umpire who reaches Triple-A starts paying real close attention to the major league umpire rosters and tries to figure out if he really has a chance to make it. You look at the ages of the veteran umpires, you hear rumors about their health, and you start comparing yourself to the other Triple-A umpires. Sometimes it seemed to me that I wasn't exactly on the fast track to the major leagues, more like the dog track. After thirteen years I'd become a good tough umpire. I didn't just control a game, I kept it in a stranglehold. Nothing bothered me. The fact is that, once you've almost been asphyxiated by Haystacks Calhoun's stomach, a raving manager isn't going to affect you. On the field I had earned a reputation as an excellent ball-and-strike umpire. I was always in position to get a good look at a play and I knew the rule book. But each time there were openings in the big leagues I never seemed to be considered.

I accepted it. I knew that there was a lot of politics involved. If you had the right person pushing you, the right "rabbi," you had a good chance of going up to the big leagues. But I never had anybody pushing me. Nobody. Anything I got I earned because of my ability. At the end of the 1975 season, George Sisler, the president of the International League, told me, "I don't get it, Kenny, you're the best umpire I've had for the last three years. I don't understand why they don't look at you."

Two years later the American League expanded. They needed to add four more umpires. The league was very uneasy about that. Adding four rookie umpires in the same season? Who knew what was going to happen. (Of course, when baseball fired most of the umpires during contract negotiations in 1999, they had to bring up twenty-five new umpires—and claimed it would make no difference.)

In spring training, 1977, I was assigned to work with the future Hall of Fame umpire Nestor Chylak, a pretty good indication I was going to the big leagues. Near the end of the spring Dick Butler, the American League supervisor of umpires, told me he wanted to talk to me. We sat in the bleachers in Sarasota and he told me that the American League had purchased my contract. I was going to the major leagues. He said, "We're taking you to the big leagues for one reason only. That is because you're a good umpire."

I didn't exactly know how to respond to that. What other reason could there be? I was a good cook? They were trying to impress the people of Rochester? "Gee Dick," I said as nicely as possible, "I really appreciate the confidence you have in me."

A lot of people I knew growing up in Rochester figured that I had a real shot at someday going to the big house, but nobody predicted I would make the big leagues. I was hired with Stevie Palermo, Vic Voltoggio, and Durwood Merrill. I was thrilled and excited. I knew exactly what it meant: I wouldn't have to carry around that ^%$%$#-^&#! inflatable protector anymore.

No major league umpire will ever forget his days in the minor leagues, much as he might try. But, as bad as it was when I worked there, years earlier it had been much worse. Umpires took jobs and quit so rapidly that at times it was tough to find people to work the games. Supposedly, one time in the Florida State League, Red Jones, who later had a nice big league career, lost his partner before a game. The home team told him to find someone and they would pay him $2.50 to work the game. Jones hired a kid named Poindexter.

In the fifth or sixth inning there was a play at second base that wasn't that close—and Poindexter blew it. Just got it completely wrong. The runner he called out jumped up and started cursing at him. Finally he screamed, "What kind of %#^%# umpiring is that?"

Poindexter's answer endeared him to every umpire who ever worked a minor league game. He pointed his finger at the player and told him, "That's the best you'll ever see—for two dollars and fifty cents!"

I will never forget the day I held Roberto Alomar in my arms, looked into his eyes, and whispered sweet nothings to him. And he looked at me and cried like a baby.

Now *there* is a great chapter opening for a whole different kind of baseball book.

The truth is, he cried like a baby because he was a baby. It was after a game in Puerto Rico. I bumped into major league player Sandy Alomar and his family at a McDonald's, then I held Roberto in one arm and Sandy Jr.'s hand while their dad ordered the food. In fact, I'm one of very few people who can claim they struck out Sandy Alomar and both his sons, Roberto and Sandy Jr., both Ken Griffey and his son, Ken Jr., as well as Buddy Bell and his sons.

I spent twenty-three years as a big league umpire. Not long enough—not as long as I intended. Very few players in baseball history lasted as long in the big leagues as I did. During my career I saw at least two dozen present and future Hall of Famers do their jobs from a few feet away. I started my career so long ago that players actually believed a million dollars a season was a decent salary! It was a time that when baseball people talked about strikes they meant on the playing field. It was so long ago that Jesse Orosco was barely a rookie. It was a time when the Yankees had the highest payroll in baseball, and each year George Steinbrenner would buy whatever players he needed.

Okay, maybe some things haven't changed.

It was a time when an umpiring crew consisted of four men who stayed together pretty much the entire season. The crew I was assigned to in my rookie season consisted of three great veteran umpires—Bill Kunkel, Ron Luciano, and the crew chief, Bill Haller. We opened the season in Seattle. It was the first official major league game ever played in the Kingdome. I couldn't believe I was there. As I stood there proudly on the plastic grass, watching the American flag flapping in the air conditioning, I thought, *This is the real thing. I'm in the major leagues*. I just kept telling myself I'd made it, I was in the big leagues. I couldn't believe I was really there—and if I couldn't believe it, you can just imagine how all the people who knew me must have felt.

The Mariners opened up against the California Angels. Nolan Ryan pitched the opening game. Nolan Ryan? *Wow,* I figured, *this can't be that tough. I had him in the minor leagues.*

I was assigned to third base, feeling really comfortable. Then Ryan threw his first pitch. It was like a bullet, but faster. In only twelve years, Ryan had gotten bigger and stronger and faster. And he now had some idea where the pitch was going.

That was my introduction to the major leagues: everything was bigger and stronger and faster. I was so fortunate to have had Haller and Kunkel and Luciano break me in. In those days the veteran umpires really protected the new guys. They protected me both on and off the field. From Seattle we went to Kansas City. Our final game in Seattle had been a day game, so we landed in Kansas City after midnight. We got our rental car. At that time each member of the crew had specific responsibilities. Ronnie was in charge of all the cars. He couldn't see at all and he couldn't drive; but he was in charge of the cars. By the time we checked into the hotel it was after three in the morning. I knew I had to be in the big leagues, because the telephone was actually in my room, rather than at the end of the hall—and there were no sausage dogs protecting the lobby.

After getting settled, I got thirsty and went out to get a soda. I was halfway down the hall when I heard my phone ringing. Whoever it was had to be calling the wrong room, I figured. But a few minutes after I got back it rang again. It was Ronnie. "Where have you been?" he demanded. Just like that.

The last time anybody asked me that question I was eleven years old. "What are you talking about?" I said.

"Bill just called your room and there was no answer. He was worried about you. So he woke me up so I could worry too."

"I'm thirty-two years old," I told him, "it's okay if I get a soda, right?"

"Just do me a favor," Ronnie said, "call Bill and tell him you're okay."

We'd been in the hotel maybe a half hour. What did he think happened to me? But I called Haller and told him I was safely in my room, "and the door's locked."

Billy and Ronnie raised me. They taught me how to be a big league umpire. With four games left in my first big league season, the Yankees and Red Sox were battling for the pennant. They were one game apart and had a four-game series in Fenway Park. It was my turn to work the plate for the first game, which was televised nationally. Very few things have ever made me nervous on the playing field, but, truthfully, I was pretty nervous. The Yankees and the Red Sox, the pennant was at stake, national TV, a packed ballpark. In the locker room before the game, Supervisor of Umpires Dick Butler came up to me and said, "Remember what I told you in spring training? That I took you up because you were good. But you're still walking a thin line with us. I just want you to know we're watching you. And your career could go either way."

Gee, Dick, thanks a lot for your support. That was certainly a great confidence builder. This is what my boss tells me before I'm about to work home plate in the biggest game of my career? When Haller came into the locker room and heard about it he exploded. He was furious. Furious. He chased Butler down a stairway screaming at him, warning him to stay away from me. Then he came back and told me that, after working with me all year, he had great confidence in my ability and that, as long as I did exactly what I'd been doing all year, I had nothing to worry about.

One thing nobody could ever say about Bill Haller was that he was behind you all the way—because Haller was out in front. He was a leader.

Ron Luciano was the most controversial umpire in baseball. Ronnie did something baseball didn't like—he tried to have fun. Whenever possible, he tried to entertain the fans. So I could see why the baseball establishment disliked him. But the fans loved him. During my first season I was working third base in Toronto one day. We were in the fourth inning, there was one out and a runner on first base. Suddenly, I realized there was somebody standing next to me. This was the middle of a ballgame, I was on the field, working, there wasn't supposed to be a person standing next to me.

It was Ronnie. And he had this big grin on his face. "What are you doing here?" I asked.

"I'm lonely," he said.

"You're what?" I couldn't believe it.

"It's lonely out there all by myself at second base." And just as he said that the batter hit a line drive into the left-center field gap, meaning there probably was going to be a play at second base. Ronnie looked at me and said, "Go get it, kid." He made me take the play at second base.

That was Ronnie, and he made every minute being with him special. Another time in my rookie season I was again in the field and again Ronnie came up to me. This time, though, it was between innings. "What?" I said.

"You got any money on you?"

Do I have any money on me? We were in the middle of

a ball game. "Yeah," I admitted, "I got a couple of bucks."

"Loan me a dollar." I handed him a dollar and he trotted back to his position. Then I began wondering, *We're in the middle of a ballgame, what does he need money for?* Of course, I found out at the end of the half inning. I looked over and there was Ronnie next to the stands, buying a hot dog.

A lot of people assume that major league umpires get along very well with each other. It is a logical assumption—we are a relatively small group, we are all pretty much treated equally rotten by baseball, we all live with the same problems of life on the road. But, the truth is that a lot of umpires don't get along with each other. Members of the same crew would go the whole season barely speaking with each other off the field. There was a lot of jealousy, a lot of people afraid that somebody was getting more attention than they were, or making more money, or playing politics with league executives. And there were several umpires who didn't like Ron Luciano. Mostly, they were very jealous. He was making extra money doing commercials, he was invited to appear on television shows, and fans actually cheered for him. No wonder they didn't like him.

I heard all their complaints. Ronnie's a lousy umpire. Ronnie's making a mockery of the game. The fact is, Ronnie was a terrific umpire. In one of the first player polls ever taken, he and Haller were voted the only two "superior" umpires in the league.

Maybe I liked Ronnie so much because we had a lot in common. I remember my first game in Texas. I was at first base, Ronnie was at second. Jim Fregosi was playing for the Rangers. Fregosi and Ronnie were good friends. They had that Italian connection. That day, Fregosi called out loudly, "Hey Ronnie!"

Luciano looked over to him. "What do you want?"

"There are two things I need to tell you. First thing, you gotta start mixing in a little more salad in that diet of yours. And the next thing . . ." then he looked at me, "when did they hire your illegitimate son?"

The first thing any umpire absolutely has to do when he comes up to the major leagues is establish his boundaries. Let people know how much abuse he'll take, because he is going to take abuse. Believe me, if Gandhi had been an umpire he would have had to reconsider his belief in passive resistance. Managers and players are going to test a rookie umpire to see how much they can get away with. And that umpire's partners are going to be watching to see how strongly he responds.

It took me about two weeks to eject my first player. It was a Kansas City Royals infielder named Dave Nelson. He was easy. I threw him out of the game and he wasn't even in the game. I called a strike on George Brett, and the Royals dugout started screaming at me. "No wonder it took you so long to get up here—it's not a strike in the big leagues if you roll it across the plate." I was too inexperienced to know you weren't supposed to call strikes on George Brett. I looked over there, and Nelson was standing on the top step of the dugout waving a sign that read KILL THE UMPIRE. Gotcha! Good-bye. Number one.

It really didn't take me long to establish myself. A few weeks into the season I was working first base in Cleveland. Future Hall of Famer Frank Robinson was managing the Indians, who were playing the Red Sox. Frank wasn't exactly what you would call shy or quiet. He liked to share his opinions with umpires, even when he wasn't asked. George Scott was Boston's first baseman and he had a reputation for coming off the base early. Like just about every other first baseman, on routine ground balls to the infield he'd take his foot off the base an instant before catching the throw to avoid being stepped on by the runner. It was what's called a "neighborhood play," as long as he was in the neighborhood, usually nobody objected. Usually. All day long, Robinson was screaming at me from the dugout, "He's coming off too soon. Watch his foot. It's not supposed to be automatic. He's coming off too soon."

By this time I had pretty much learned how to block out the whining from the dugout. Only on occasion could they get your attention. For example, I think it was Jim Palmer who once shouted out at Ronnie, "You know what you are, Luciano?"

Now that got our attention. We all waited for the rest of it. There were so many potential answers to that question. A few of them might have even kept Palmer in the game. And we waited. Maybe we even started leaning a little closer to the dugout just to make sure we heard it. But Palmer never said another word. Just sat there. Grinning. And there wasn't a thing Ronnie could do about it.

But it was impossible not to hear Robinson, who just kept complaining. "You hear me? He's off the base. You gotta call that one in the big leagues."

Finally, I couldn't take it anymore. Andre Thornton was the Indians' first baseman. He "cheated"—came off the base before catching the ball—worse than anybody. A half inning later Dwight Evans hit a grounder to short. The play was close enough for me. Safe! Safe! Then I turned to Cleveland's dugout and shouted, "You're right Frank, he's coming off too soon." Haller and Luciano loved it. That's how I earned respect on the field.

Frank Robinson and I only had one more disagreement: He wanted every call to go his way, and I had to call them fairly. That disagreement lasted my entire career. We fought all the time, but none of the fights lasted very long. The one time I really got him upset didn't take place on the field. It was after a game in Kansas City. By that point Frank had become the Orioles' general manager. As I left the locker room to get our car, I walked right past the O's team bus. Frank was sitting in the driver's seat, waiting for the players. "Hey Frank," I said, "it's good to see you finally found a job you can handle. Driving a bus."

Now, why would he get angry at me for something like that? That was supposed to be a compliment.

The thing that surprised me most about the major leagues was the quality of play. If the difference between the lower minors and Triple-A was like the difference between a Motel 6 and the Waldorf, the difference between Triple-A and the big leagues was the difference between umpire Ed Hurley and Elizabeth Hurley. A lot of Triple-A players hit the ball as hard and as far as major leaguers, they just couldn't do it consistently. And some Triple-A pitchers threw as fast as big leaguers, and some of them could break off a great curveball. They just couldn't put it an inch off the plate every time like Catfish Hunter or Jack Morris.

Being a good umpire means anticipating the play and getting to the right place in time to make the call. After five years in Triple-A I had gotten comfortable. I knew the pitchers, I knew the fielders, and I knew the defensive plays they were able to make. So, when a ball was hit I had a pretty good idea what was going to happen—whether a fly ball would be caught, for example—and I could anticipate the play. It took me a little while to catch up to the big leaguers. Ground balls that would have gone through the infield in the minor leagues were turned into outs by big league infielders, fly balls in the gaps that would have fallen for hits in the minor leagues were caught. I had to raise the level of my game too. I had help though—there was always some manager volunteering to tell me where to go.

Later in my career I would be criticized for what appeared to be a lack of hustle on the field. That meant I didn't go running all over the place. But I always felt the object was to get the play right, not to look great getting it wrong. I'm not built like a sprinter, actually I'm more like a hurdle. Four steps to me was an outright sprint.

Baseball officials want their umpires to be runners. The basic philosophy seems to be that it doesn't matter where they're going, as long as they get there. As soon as the ball is hit they want to see umpires in motion. It used to be that the American League wanted its umpires running after the ball, while the National League preferred that its umpires first read the play to determine whether or not to take off running. Now that the two leagues have basically ceased to exist as separate entities, except in the standings, the supervisors want all umpires running somewhere on every play.

They want the fans to see that the umpires are hustling. Of course, they also make a point of reminding the umpires that the fans don't come to the ballpark to see the umpires.

Which means, basically, that they want the umpires moving so the fans don't see them.

Broadcasters don't help the situation. If anybody knows less about umpiring than managers, players, and league officials, it's the announcers. They are constantly praising umpires for hustling, even when they hustle themselves right out of the play. One night during my rookie year there was a play at second base in Chicago, and the White Sox radio announcer, Jimmy Piersall, just ripped me apart on the air. "That fat ass Ken Kaiser blew that play, he just butchered it. He was out of position and never got a good look at it."

The reason I heard every word he said was that I was in a car at the time. The game I was scheduled to be working in Milwaukee had been rained out and Haller and I were driving to Chicago, where we were scheduled to work the next day. Piersall was right about one thing, I was out of position. I was about 150 miles out of position.

The next day I cornered him in an elevator. I was polite about the whole thing. I very politely I told him I was going to kill him. Piersall had originally become famous for suffering and then recovering from a nervous breakdown. He really was crazy—and he could prove it. "Stay away from me," he warned me, "I'm certified. I've got papers."

"Good for you," I told him. "So does my dog."

To call a play, an umpire is supposed to be in a position to get a good look at it and be set. Not running, not moving around, set. I learned how to cheat on the field. I had to. I admit it, I didn't move too fast. I have always been a big man, it took me a few steps to put all my parts in motion. But I did learn to anticipate the play. I knew when a ball was hit where the play would probably be made, and I got in position. When the ball was hit I started moving. The way the league has young umpires running now, they are too often either out of position or still moving when the call has to be made. In three steps I could be in position. How do you hustle into position if you're already there? There was nowhere for me to hustle.

And then they want umpires running into the outfield on every fly ball. That is absolutely ridiculous. These are big league players, they are going to catch routine fly balls. And when you've umpired a thousand games you know as soon as the ball is hit if it is going out of the ballpark. Why does an umpire have to be in the outfield to determine that a ball is in the upper deck?

I was accused of being lazy because I didn't run after the ball. But I was never out of position. I used to challenge the supervisors to show me a video of a play in which I was out of position to make the call. Maybe I wasn't perfect, but I never saw that video.

When twenty-two veteran umpires lost their jobs in the 1999 strike, the leagues had to bring up twenty-five young umpires. Many of these kids weren't ready for the big leagues—they didn't have enough experience. But they could run. They could definitely run. So, now major league baseball has inexperienced umpires who want to show they're hustling, and as a result they miss plays because they're out of position.

As we were taught in umpire school, being too close to the play isn't necessarily a good thing. The angle matters. In the 1996 American League Championship Series between the Yankees and Baltimore, Richie Garcia was working the right field foul line. Richie has been a great umpire for his entire career, probably one of the most consistently excellent umpires in baseball history. But in this playoff game at Yankee Stadium the Orioles were leading by a run, when Derek Jeter hit a high fly ball to right field. The O's outfielder Tony Tarasco went back to the wall, reached up and . . .

. . . And the ball never came down. A twelve-year-old fan leaning out over the railing onto the playing field caught the ball. It was clearly fan interference. But Richie missed it, he was running out toward the wall and never had a good angle on the play. He called it a home run for Jeter. The replay showed that the ball would not have been out of the ballpark, although who knows if it would have been caught? The one thing it wouldn't have been was a home run. But that's what Richie called it. Tie score. The Yankees won the game in extra innings and Richie was blasted, just blasted.

Everybody criticized him. Every broadcaster and sportswriter, movie critics, restaurant critics, everybody wondered how he could have made the wrong call. That reminded me of one of the all-time umpire heroes, the president of the Appalacian League, Chauncy DeVois. He was from Bristol, Virginia. He'd sit in the stands during games and, if a fan really got on an umpire, he would go right over and sit next to him. He'd reach into his pocket and pull out a league contract, then say in a deep southern accent, "If you think you could do any better, son, why don't you sign this contract and go to work for me."

There have been very few umpires better than Richie Garcia. He took the criticism graciously. He admitted he got it wrong and didn't try to make any excuses. But he was just doing his job. He was hustling towards the play. That's why he never got a good look at it. You really can hustle yourself into tough situations. That's happened to me, it's happened to every umpire.

No umpire ever sold a call like Luciano. He wouldn't just signal for a home run, he'd leap in the air, he'd turn around twice, he'd stick his hand straight up in the air and twirl it to indicate circle the bases. And he'd shout loud. When Luciano called a home run, there was no doubt it was a home run. One afternoon he was working third base in Baltimore, Earl Weaver's Orioles were playing Dick Williams' California Angels. There were 48,042 people in the ballpark, the largest regular-season crowd in Orioles history. The Angels' Tommy Harper hit a drive down the left field foul line. Ronnie went tearing out to the outfield . . . well, maybe tearing is an exaggeration, but he went loping out there to see if the ball stayed fair or went foul. As he told me later, because he was running his eyes were jiggling. Trying to watch the ball or see a play when you're moving is like trying to take a real sharp photograph with a still camera while running. So he lost sight of the ball. He never saw where it went into the stands.

Another thing they teach you in umpire school is that you always have to make a call. It doesn't matter if you don't even see the play, you have to make the call. The good news is you have a fifty-fifty chance of being right. Ronnie didn't know what to do. But he looked at the Orioles fans. They were quiet, as if something bad had happened. It's got to be a home run, he figured. And just to make sure nobody doubted him, he sold his call big time; he leaped way up in the air, he screamed as loudly as he could, twirling his hand. No question about it, it was one of the greatest home run signals in history.

Except that before he came down the Orioles were attacking him like the Indians going after Custer at Little Big Horn. It was so bad that Orioles players who had retired years earlier were in the pack. He figured out right away that he must have blown the call. The reason the Orioles fans hadn't reacted was because the ball apparently was so far foul that no one could possibly have called it a fair ball. Well, almost no one.

Weaver was leading the pack. For Ronnie, this was the worst possible situation: Earl Weaver was finally right about something. Before Weaver could say one word, Ronnie held up his hand. "Don't do anything to get yourself thrown out of the game," he said, "I'm gonna get some help." What else could he have told him, I didn't see the ball because my eyes were jiggling?

Haller was working first base. Ronnie marched across the diamond. "I blew it, didn't I?"

Haller shrugged. "What's forty or fifty feet?"

Ronnie knew he had to change the call. "But if I do Williams is gonna go crazy, and I'm probably gonna have to toss him, right?" Ronnie had a serious decision to make. If he didn't change the call Weaver would go beserk and Ronnie would get to eject him, but if he changed it Williams would scream and have to be thrown out. In the dugout Williams was almost as difficult as Weaver. So for an umpire it was sort of like choosing between champagne or caviar. Toss Weaver or Williams? One of them was going. No matter what decision he made, he couldn't lose. He walked over to the Angels dugout. "Harper," he shouted, "that was a foul ball. You're still up." Then he turned and started walking away.

Dick Williams was the most sarcastic man I ever met in

baseball. When he came out to argue, he'd say things to me like, "Kaiser, you've been standing out here with nothing to do for two and a half hours. You finally get one simple call and you screw it up. Two and a half hours, and you still can't get it right. . . ." But with Ronnie he really couldn't argue the call, it was obvious the ball was foul, so he basically criticized Ronnie's entire career, "First you call it fair, then you call it foul. You're making a mockery of this game the way you jump up and down and scream, and you know you're gonna be doing me a big favor by throwing me out, because I can't stand to see you doing things like that . . ."

Ronnie moved closer to him. What could he tell him? "You wanna go now?" he asked.

"No, I do not, I'm gonna have my say and there's nothing you can do about it. And when I go I want you to throw me out of this game the same way you called that home run. I want you to leap into the air, I want you to make those funny circles with your hand, and I want to hear you scream it out so loud that the people back in Oakland can hear what a rotten umpire you are."

"Now?"

"No, not now. I'm not finished with you. I'll tell you when. Then I want you to start spinning around like some damn top." Finally, Williams wound down. "Okay," he told Ronnie, "now. Do it!"

Ronnie leaped into the air—okay, he got off the ground—he leaned way back, wound up and thrrrewww Williams out of the ball game.

As Williams departed he turned and said over his shoulder with satisfaction, "Not bad."

So that's what can happen when you overhustle. If Ronnie

had stood his ground at third base and watched the flight of the ball into the stands, he would have made the right call.

The first time I was working third base in Fenway Park, for example, Carlton Fisk hit a long fly ball down the left field line. I was a rookie umpire, I had enthusiasm, I had motivation, I had momentum, so I put my head down and went running down the line and I looked up and . . .

. . . Oh my goodness! All I saw in front of me was this giant green wall. The Green Monster. It was 37 feet high and only 315 feet from home plate. The closer I got to it, the less of it I could see. I couldn't even see the foul pole on top of it. Fortunately for me, the ball hit the top of the wall in fair territory and rebounded into play, so I didn't have to make a call. What was the sense in running out towards the wall? When the play started I was already about 110 feet down the foul line. All I had to do was turn around and watch it.

I don't deny that I missed a few calls during my career.

I said a few! A few! And if you don't like it I'm gonna throw you right outta this book!

The fact is that every umpire has blown calls. Every one of them. Nobody talks about that in school or in the low minors, but it's impossible to make every decision correctly. With good luck, though, you'll blow a call in a Brewers-Pirates game in late September, when both teams are streaking towards one hundred losses and the only fans there are having a nice outing from the home. With bad luck, you do it in a pivotal Yankees-Orioles playoff game. Or in front of the largest regular-season crowd in Baltimore Orioles history.

When I missed a play I just lived with it. There was nothing else I could do. I remember blowing a call at second base at Yankee Stadium when Billy Martin was managing the Yankees. As soon as I saw my thumb sticking up in the air I sort of looked at it and wondered, *How'd you get up there?* There was nothing I could do about it though. Billy and I always got along very well. So he was almost smiling when he came running out at me. He knew I kicked it, and he knew I knew I kicked it. So he stuck out his chin and said, "Is that right?"

"Well, Billy," I said philosophically, "it may not be right, but that's the way it is."

The league always told us that if we blow a call just admit it and nothing would happen. I believed that. To me, that was like telling a man on death row that if he admits he committed the crime they would use one less volt in the electric chair.

Umpire Terry Cooney once made sure he got the call right *and* wrong. He had a tag play at second base in Anaheim and he called the runner out while signaling that he was safe. The Angels manager, Buck Rodgers, came out to find out what had happened. Cooney told him what had happened, and that the call was against California. As Rodgers turned around to leave, he muttered, "You got it right the first time."

Actually no, he got it right and wrong the first time.

National League umpire Satch Davidson was behind the plate in Pittsburgh during a Pirates-Dodgers game. Two men were out, the bases were loaded, and there was a full count on the batter. The pitch came in, it was outside, and Davidson raised his right hand and pointed towards first base. Base on balls, take your base. The problem was that he didn't say a word, and his signal looked like he was calling strike three. Different players reacted differently. The catcher figured strike three, three outs, inning over, rolled the ball back to the pitcher's mound, and headed to the dugout. The runner on third base saw Davidson signal strike three so he headed to the dugout to get his glove. But Jimmy Wynn, the runner on second, realized the pitch was outside for ball four and took off running when the catcher rolled the ball back to the mound. As Wynn rounded third the runner who had been on third, who was just about to step into the dugout, saw what was happening and took off for home plate. The catcher came back from the other direction to try to get the ball. People were coming from all angles, from the dugouts, the bases. . . .

Second base umpire Lee Wyer was watching this whole thing with amazement. It was like Three Stooges baseball. When everybody finally stopped running Satch explained that he had called it ball four. It was a walk. The ball had remained in play. The runner on third was entitled to score, but if he had stepped into the dugout before touching home plate he was out. The umpires got together and decided he never made it into the dugout. But if Wynn had passed him on the base paths then Wynn was out. They decided that while the runner on third had made an exceptionally wide turn, he had beaten Wynn to home plate. So they allowed both runs to score. And then they ejected the world. They should have used the Kaiser defense, "It may not be right, but that's the way it is."

When I blew a call I accepted responsibility for it and then forgot all about it. It wasn't a life-or-death issue with me. What were they going to do, kill me? Well, there was that one fan at Yankee Stadium who threw a knife at me, but, other than that, I never had a problem. Some umpires let a missed call just eat them up inside. I can remember watching guys in the umpires' locker room after a game just agonizing over a missed call. Not me. As a lot of people I worked with would tell you, I got a lot more upset about missing a meal than missing a play.

That doesn't mean I didn't care about it. Believe me, I cared. But I'm a realist. In my major league career I made more than seventy-five thousand calls. Think about that, seventy-five thousand calls. I had to get at least one of them wrong. Maybe even two. Some umpires would make a point of reviewing tapes of close plays. I always wondered what good that did? Why watch it again? To make sure you were right that you missed it? To see if maybe it's changed since the game ended? To make sure you don't do it again? To make yourself feel bad? I didn't need to look at a replay to feel bad, I could just look at my paycheck for that.

So I absolutely never looked at replays, except for once in awhile. I certainly did look at a replay after making what might have been the most controversial call of my career in the fifth game of the 1997 World Series. The Florida Marlins were leading the Cleveland Indians by four runs in the top of the ninth. The Indians' Bip Roberts hit a routine ground ball to first baseman Jeff Conine. Conine flipped to the pitcher, Livan Hernandez, who was covering first base. I had a real good look at it, Hernandez missed first base. His foot never touched it. I called Roberts safe.

It was almost the exact same play—a routine grounder to the first baseman with the pitcher covering—that Don Denkinger had kicked in the ninth inning of the sixth game of the 1985 World Series, a call that resulted in him receiving death threats and having to have a police guard.

After I made the call, Florida manager Jimmy Leyland

came out of the dugout. "What happened there, Kais?" he asked me.

"He missed the base, Jimmy," I said, "he never touched it."

"Okay, that's good enough for me," Leyland said. He didn't even argue the call.

There were two big differences: After I called Roberts safe at first base, the Indians scored three times and got the tying run to second base, but still lost the game. In the '85 series the call allowed Kansas City to score twice and win the ballgame. The second difference is I got the play right. I did look at that replay, and Hernandez still hasn't touched first base.

After the game Hernandez admitted to reporters that he "might have missed the base," but that didn't stop the broadcasters and sportswriters from criticizing my "brutal" call. One sportswriter described the play as "it looked like he touched a corner of the base as he swiped at it." Now, who would know better, the player who was actually involved in the play or a sportswriter sitting up in the press box several hundred feet away? Naturally the correct answer is: the fans.

It must be the fans. They think they know everything.

When the writers finally saw the replay and realized I had made the right call they decided that Hernandez had missed the base because he been afraid of colliding with Roberts—therefore I still should have called Roberts out. It should have been one of those "neighborhood plays" they wrote. It was close enough.

In Kaiser's neighborhood, close wasn't good enough. If that play had been made on a Saturday afternoon during the season no one would have said a word. Or if the Indians had come back to win the game you wouldn't have heard the end of it. I was a lot luckier than Don Denkinger.

Several sportswriters suggested that this call at first base was an attempt to make up for a questionable call I'd made an inning earlier. In the eighth inning I'd called the Marlins' Moises Alou safe on a close play at first base. The fact that the replay proved I'd made the right call didn't seem to affect this theory. Here is the truth about that: There is no such thing as a make-up call. It doesn't happen. Making up a blown call on a subsequent play would require thinking, which makes it pretty much impossible for most umpires. Remember, umpiring is reaction: see it, call it.

I never cared who won a ball game. I never rooted for specific teams or players. I just didn't care. The only thing I ever rooted for was a fast game. Get the ball. Pitch it. Hit it. Catch it. Let's go home. Obviously, there were certain players I liked and others I disliked—umpires are human beings too. But after you've looked at ten thousand pitches and called them balls or strikes, it's impossible to suddenly decide that a pitch that has been a ball for seventeen years has suddenly become a strike.

Probably the nicest player I've ever known was Catfish Hunter. Catfish had the best control of any pitcher I ever saw. He'd give up ten hits, including two mammoth home runs, and yet he'd win the game 3-2. He just didn't walk batters. Once, early in my career, I was working home plate in Yankee Stadium on what definitely had to be the hottest day of the decade. Maybe the century. I was sweating worse than a CEO at a stockholders' meeting. At that time the American League still required us to wear a jacket when we were behind the plate, and I was holding up the balloon protector.

Between innings, Catfish suddenly came walking out of the dugout carrying a cup of cold water for me. I was shocked. A ballplayer bringing water to a sweltering umpire? This man was a future Hall of Famer, he was one of the most respected players in the game, but he cared enough about an umpire he didn't even know to bring me that water. So, when he was pitching and I was behind the plate I never consciously helped him, not that he needed my help, but he wasn't going to get hurt either. If you were in the league for fifteen minutes, Catfish would make a point of saying hello. Unlike Carl Yastrzemski, for example, who wouldn't say a word to an umpire until they'd been in the league ten years.

Truthfully, I never consciously helped a player or hurt one with a call. When I was behind the plate I never even knew who was hitting. Believe me, there were a few players I didn't like one little bit. The Orioles first baseman, Eddie Murray, for example. It was a toss-up between us who despised the other one more. I like to think I won, but I had the advantage; he was real easy to dislike. We didn't speak to each other for fifteen seasons. When I worked first base for an Orioles game it was so quiet I could have held High Mass there.

As it turned out, I was behind the plate for Murray's last at bat in the major leagues. He was finishing his career with the Angels. He fouled off the first pitch. Strike one. The second pitch was good enough for me. Strike two. He stepped out and turned around to look at me. I knew he wanted to complain, but he hadn't said one word to me for fifteen years. Finally, he got up enough guts to tell me, "That ball was outside."

"Hey," I said, "we ain't talked in fifteen years. Don't start now."

But he couldn't stop, "I've taken your shit for the last time," he snapped, "that's it, I've had enough."

"Just get in there and hit," I told him. The next pitch was right on the corner. Strike three! Murray tossed his bat way up into the air. "Soon as that hits the ground you're outta here." The bat landed. Boom. *You're gone!*

Murray was furious. "I want to fight you," he demanded.

Who was he kidding? "Tell you what Eddie," I said, "you're already gone, so here's what I want you to do. Go on downstairs and take a nice shower. On the other side of the stands is a parking lot. I want you to wait there for me when this game is over. I'll meet you there. And Eddie, you can even bring your bat with you, because the way you're swinging this year, you couldn't hit me with it anyway."

As far as I know, he's still waiting there for me.

I know I kicked some calls in my career. One time, for example, I was certain I'd missed a call on a tag play at second base. In my hotel room later that night I was watching ESPN, and they showed the play—to my surprise, I'd gotten it right. So, I was actually wrong about getting it wrong.

But for me, when the game was over it was done. No regrets. Once I left the stadium I didn't think about baseball until I went to work the next day. I must have been doing something right; in my twenty-three years in the major leagues, I never had a single protest lodged against a call I made. The fact is, there are only a few calls I made during my career that stand out. In April 1993, for example, I was at first base when Seattle pitcher Chris Bosio took a no-hitter into the ninth inning. With two out, there was a very close play at first base. The throw beat the runner by less than half a step, Bosio got his no-hitter. So I remember that call.

I was behind the plate for Gaylord Perry's three hundredth victory. He was with the Seattle Mariners in 1982. When the last batter struck out the catcher flipped me the ball. I palmed it and tossed another ball to Perry. This was years before baseball memorabilia became so valuable. I kept almost no souvenirs from my career, but I had that ball for a long time. Gaylord probably still believes he has it. He doesn't. So I remember that call.

One of the most unusual calls of my big league career took place in that game. Because Gaylord's pitches dropped suddenly, batters always hit a lot of balls into the ground. When he was pitching at home the grounds crew would soak the ground in front of home plate to slow down the ball. At one point the Yankees' Oscar Gamble hit a ball straight down in front of the plate and I lost sight of it. Gamble started running to first, the catcher went for the ball and I was completely blocked out. I couldn't see where it went. So I looked at George Maloney, who was umpiring at third base, and he was signaling foul ball. That was good enough for me. Foul ball! What I didn't know was that Maloney also had lost sight of it. That happens on occasion, you lose sight of a batted ball and pick it up by watching the reaction of the players. In this case nobody reacted. Since it obviously wasn't in play, Maloney assumed it went foul. Maloney said foul, I agreed with him. I never saw the ball. And once we called it foul, I didn't care what happened to it. Once an umpire calls a batted ball foul it is foul forever.

It was really strange. Each of us must have assumed that he was the only person to have lost sight of it. About an inning later, I walked out in front of the plate and stepped on something in the mud. It was the ball, just about completely buried—in fair territory.

Definitely one of the most bizarre calls in my career took place during a night game in Detroit in 1982. I had nine baseballs in play at the same time. Sparky Anderson's Tigers were playing Ralph Houk's Boston Red Sox. Larry Barnett was the home plate umpire, I was at second base. The Tigers' Kirk Gibson was on first base, and Chet Lemon was the batter. Lemon hit a shot into the left-center field gap and everybody started running. Center field in the old Tigers Stadium was about 440 feet from home plate, so when the ball rolled past the outfielders Gibson and Lemon kept running. Meanwhile, back at the plate, Barnett realized there might be a play at home and decided to do some housecleaning. He went in front of the plate to pick up the bat Lemon had flipped away.

Here's what was happening at home plate: Barnett was bending over to pick up the bat. Gibson was about halfway between home and third. Lemon was rounding third. And the throw from the outfield was coming towards the plate.

I don't remember the specific order in which everything occurred. It probably didn't matter. The result would have been pretty much the same. But I think it is fair to say that Barnett never saw Gibson coming. Gibson had been a college football star, and Barnett was the only obstacle between him and home plate. Gibson hit him full force and sent him sprawling, he knocked him out cold. Gibson hit Barnett with such force that, as Barnett flew through the air, the eight baseballs he was carrying in his ball bag scattered all over the ground.

Okay, so Barnett and Gibson were lying on the ground—that was when Lemon decided to try to score. He got tangled up with both of them and he went down. Just as the throw came in from the outfield to catcher Gary Allenson, Gibson and Lemon both recovered and went for home plate. Allenson caught the ball and started tagging people.

And then everything sort of stopped. The play ended. Allenson had nobody else to tag, and Gibson and Lemon had crossed home plate. Barnett was out cold on the ground and baseballs were lying all over the field. Allenson was holding one of them, but who knew for sure where it had come from? Nobody made any call. And Sparky Anderson and Ralph Houk came running out of opposite dugouts.

I looked at first base and third base. My two partners looked right back at me and didn't make a move. As I started walking in towards home plate the two managers came at me. I had stereo managers. Houk was shouting in one ear, Anderson was shouting in the other ear. "Hey," I screamed right back, "don't you think maybe we should wait until they carry Barnett off?"

The trainers were worried that Barnett had suffered a neck injury. They carried him off on a stretcher. While he was leaving I had a really bad realization: *I've got to figure this thing out.* At times, I got into trouble when there was only one baseball in play. This situation had the potential of being nine times worse. One thing I knew, I couldn't take a vote. So I took a shot. What the hell, I figured, I'll split the difference. I called Gibson safe and Lemon out. I couldn't defend that decision. I couldn't even explain it.

Houk went berserk. Ralph Houk always put on a great show. He yanked his cap off his head and held it in his hand

and started kicking dirt and yelling and screaming. *Yap, yap, yap, I've been in baseball twenty years and I've never seen a call like that yap yap yap!*

No kidding, Ralph. Do me a favor, huh? When you see another one just like it give me a phone call, okay?

Eventually I had to throw him out of the game. Barnett turned out to be bruised but fine. And the next day, when Houk came up to home plate to exchange lineup cards, he looked right at me and said with a big smile, "Boy, did I make an ass out of myself yesterday."

I hope he didn't expect me to disagree. That was Ralph Houk. Whenever he lost his mind on the field, he'd find it later, and whatever we'd fought about he would never mention again.

One of the things that always surprised me was that, no matter where the fans were sitting, they thought they could see the play better than I could. Maybe the only time in my career that I actually heard fans applauding an umpire was when Larry Barnett was being carried off the field. Most people thought the fans were giving him a hand for being alive, but there others who claimed people were applauding because an umpire was leaving the field.

On the field I almost never paid attention to fans booing me. I heard them, but it didn't matter to me. I had been a masked professional wrestler, so I was used to being booed. And most of the time I couldn't even hear individual fans shouting at me. Most of the time. Cleveland's old Municipal Stadium seated about a quarter million, but usually only about thirty-five people showed up for the games. And the only reason those people were there was because they'd lost some bet. Believe me, nobody wanted to be there. In Atlanta, the Braves always had a fan playing the tom-tom; in Cleveland the fans played solitaire. That place was awful, the crowds were so small that the public address announcer used to welcome the fans by name, "Hey, Jack Smithlin, thanks for coming." There were so few people in the stands that you could overhear personal conversations. So, when a fan yelled, you could hear him. When a fan took a deep breath, you could hear him.

The old Toronto stadium was just the opposite, it was really small, so the fans were close to the field. Close enough to be heard. One night in Toronto, admittedly, a fan really did get on my nerves. He had a high-pitched, shrill voice and he just wouldn't shut up. I hadn't even made a call, he was just all over me. I love Canadians, especially all the really smart Canadians reading this book, but I finally couldn't take it anymore. Between innings I walked near the stands, pulled a dollar out of my wallet, and waved it at him. "Here, pal," I said, "here's an American dollar. Go buy yourself a house."

Occasionally the fans would get to a player. George Brett was one of the really good people in baseball, besides being a Hall of Fame player. A lot of times, Brett would come into the umpires' dressing room before a game just to say hello to his "favorite umpire." And, amazingly, his favorite umpire always turned out to be the guy working the plate that day. Everybody was George's favorite—until the next game, when you were working at third base. Then he'd turn around, wag his index finger and admit, "You're not my favorite umpire today."

George Brett probably had the worst temper of any player I knew—but most of the time he kept it under control. If he had a bad at bat he would jog back into the dugout and go right down the runway—and seconds later you'd hear bats flying, helmets flying, walls breaking, sirens wailing. I mean, the man had a temper. I was at third base in Kansas City one night and Brett the third baseman. He was in the middle of a bad slump. He probably was only hitting .340. The Royals fans were all over him though. During the game a batter hit a hot shot down the third base line. It was foul, but before I could make the call Brett fielded it and fired towards first base. His throw sailed, it took off and went into the stands behind the base. It was a foul ball, so it didn't matter. As George walked back to his position he kind of lowered his head so no one would see him speaking to me, and said, "Hey Kais, you know what the worst thing about that throw was? I only hit one of those %$#@^% fans."

Fans never bothered me, they never bothered most umpires—as long as they stayed in the stands. The problems began when they came onto the field. One time, Doug Harvey was working third base and Shag Crawford was behind the plate when the Cardinals' Lou Brock tried to score from first base on a single. That's a play you don't see very often in baseball—and the main reason you don't see it is because it doesn't work. The catcher had the ball by the time Brock rounded third. Rather than trying to knock the ball out of catcher's hand, Brock just slid into the plate. He never even touched it. The third base coach, the man responsible for sending Brock in, came running down the line to argue that the catcher had missed the tag. Brock was arguing because he looked so foolish. The Cardinals manager came out to protect his player. They had Crawford surrounded when Harvey decided to even the odds. And as he got closer to home plate he saw a man dressed in a white T-shirt, red slacks, and red-and-white tennis shoes join the argument. *That's strange*, Harvey thought, *what's the trainer doing on the field in the middle of an argument?*

The guy was standing right behind Crawford. Suddenly he doubled up his fist, drew it back, and was about to slug Crawford in the back of the head. Harvey couldn't believe it; he wondered, *What's the Cardinals trainer doing slugging Crawford in the back of the head?*

Then it dawned on him: that wasn't the trainer! Before the man hit Crawford, Harvey smacked him across the nose with his forearm. Broke his nose. Blood started gushing out all over everybody—but it didn't stop the argument. The guy went down, and they had to step over him to argue with Crawford.

See, that's what happens when a player tries to score from first on a single—and when a fan comes on the field. In the 1980 AL championship, Mike Reilly was at third base and I was behind the plate at Yankee Stadium. I just happened to glance at the stands behind third in time to see this little guy hop over the fence, run onto the field and attack Reilly. Within seconds, Graig Nettles had grabbed the fan and was holding him. I confess, I hit him. I got a clean shot at him, and I really let him have it. I gave him my best shot. I put my weight behind it and hit him square—and it barely slowed him down. I broke his nose, but it still took three cops to hold onto him. Mike Reilly was in shock, he didn't have any idea why the fan attacked him—until the fan, who was fighting to get at Reilly, screamed, "Lemme go, I'm gonna get that Kaiser."

Talk about adding insult to injury, this guy thought Reilly was me.

Actually, it was pretty common to have fans run onto the field. They'd run around for a few minutes, trying to avoid the security people chasing them. What I never understood is why the 31,567 fans who stayed in their seats cheered for the one fan who didn't? What were they thinking—*boy, I wish I had the guts to make a fool out of myself and get beaten up by security in front of all these people?*

I never minded it too much when people ran onto the field. Ronnie used to try to borrow money from them. In the White Sox's old Comiskey Park I watched a fan run in from center field and make a long slide into second base. He missed the base completely, but I called him safe anyway. The fans started booing me for blowing the call.

National League umpire Eddie Montague was working a game at Chicago's Wrigley Field when a fan ran on the field between innings. Rather than trying to evade security, the fan stopped on the pitcher's mound, dropped his trousers, and mooned the entire crowd. They later discovered that this person had psychological problems and had been brought to the game by his older brother. This older brother had left him sitting in their seats when he went to the men's room. And when he returned he asked people sitting nearby if they had seen his younger brother. "Yeah," one of them said, "he's the one standing on the pitcher's mound with his pants off."

The fact is that it could get dangerous on the field. For most of my career the ballparks had no security checks. Fans could bring in anything they could hide under their coats. Supposedly, at the turn of the century there was a sign hanging in a Chicago ballpark reading, "Please don't shoot the umpire, he's doing the best that he can." It was a joke, I hope. But just about every umpire who has been in baseball for a few years has received death threats. In the 1997 Championship Series between Baltimore and Cleveland, I ruled that a ball hit by the Indians' Eddie Murray had been caught rather than trapped. The next day I was in my hotel room in Baltimore when someone called and threatened my life. "You better watch out, Kaiser," this stranger said, "the next time you go out on the field we're gonna get you." He hung up before I could reply.

It was a long-distance call. The number couldn't be traced. At least the person making the call was smart enough not to try to call collect.

Of course, not every fan is that smart. Umpire Jerry Layne was working third base at Dodger Stadium one night. In the first inning, the Padres' Tony Gwynn tried to check his swing on a high fastball. The plate umpire looked down at Layne for help, and Jerry ruled that Gwynn had swung. Strike three! Gwynn was really angry. He walked back to the dugout, threw his arms up in the air, and he flung his bat over his head. Layne ejected him.

Padres' manager Jack McKeon came out to argue. "How could you do that, Jerry," he screamed, "forty-five thousand bleeping people come to the ballpark to see Tony Gwynn hit, and you threw him out of the game." Like it was Layne's fault that Gwynn had tossed his bat.

After the game Layne found a note in his locker with a phone number and the message "Please call." Jerry figured it was an old friend or classmate trying to get some tickets, so he called the number. When the phone was answered he could hear a lot of noise and loud music in the background. Somebody's having a good time, he thought. He told the person who answered the phone who he was and that he was returning a call. "Hang on a second," that person said, "I'll get him for you."

A few minutes later another man got on the phone. "Listen Jerry," he said, "we're gonna get you." And then he threatened to kill him. As soon as he finished making the threat he hung up real fast, maybe to prevent Jerry from having the call traced. Trace the call? The man had left his phone number! Jerry immediately called major league security and told them he had just received a death threat. He was asked if he had any idea who might have made the call. "Well yeah," Jerry said, "actually, he left his home phone number."

Even in a crowded field, this has to be the dumbest fan in history.

When you've almost been smothered by Haystacks Calhoun's stomach, a telephoned threat isn't that scary. Most people don't know it, but baseball has security people in every major league city to handle a variety of situations for both players and umpires. After being threatened, I contacted this police officer who did as much as possible—which, basically, was to warn me: *Hey, be careful when you leave your hotel room.*

I never remembered to be worried on the field. Way in the back of your mind, way, way back there—probably behind the lyrics to bad country songs—there is the knowledge that somebody could sneak a gun into the stadium. But, even if they did, actually hitting whatever they were aiming at would be very difficult. From a few hundred feet away, even *I'm* not that big of a target. I was always a little more concerned about people throwing things on the field. During my career I found all kinds of objects on the field, everything from lipstick cases to ball bearings. The one time I did get a little bothered was during the same playoffs in which Mike Reilly was attacked.

I was at third base at Yankee Stadium and I heard an unusual *thump* sound behind me. I turned around and saw a knife sticking in the ground. It had about a four-inch blade. I looked around. I knew it had to have been thrown by one of the 55,000 people in the ballpark. I figured it had to come from the upper deck. But that was the closest I came to narrowing it down. At the end of the half inning I gave it to security. For my own sense of well-being, I assumed that this was the only knife that the guilty fan was carrying. I mean, nobody was going to carry thirty-five knives with him.

Under the circumstances I did the only thing possible—when I pulled it out of the ground I showed it to Nettles. "Hey, Graig," I said, "look what somebody threw at you."

Only once in my career was I attacked by a fan. This took place off the field, in the stadium parking lot at Kansas City. I really was surprised—this was in Kansas City! The nicest people in the world, outside of Rochester, live there. It was after a game, I hadn't even had any close plays, and I was walking to my car with umpire Mark Johnson. A young tough guy, probably in his mid-twenties, approached me. "Hey Kaiser," he said, "see those guys?" He pointed to three men about his age leaning against a fence. "They bet me ten dollars I couldn't kick your ass."

When I was younger I would have warned him, *That would be the toughest ten bucks you'll ever earn.* Instead, I turned my back to him and continued towards my car. And when I did, he kicked me right in the ass.

I proceeded to give him my autograph. Well, actually the

doctors had to stitch it in. I lost control. I picked him up and tossed him on top of a car, and then I ripped into him. I banged his head. I rammed his back into the big tail fin of an old Cadillac. I don't know what I might have done to him if Mark Johnson hadn't pulled me away. My guess is that the fan was thrilled to be safely arrested.

So, maybe there are a few things about the job I don't miss.

In umpire school we were taught to always refer to managers, players, and coaches as "rats." They weren't good guys or bad guys, they were rats. All of them—rats. But, after my first few years in the big leagues and really getting to work with them, I thought that it was a pretty unfair comparison—unfair to the rats.

The relationship between umpires, players, and managers is sort of like that of dieticians to overweight people, or dentists to kids, or IRS agents to pretty much every working person: Umpires are the authority figures who ruin all the fun. However, I think most players and managers have found that umpires do perform at least one very important function—if they didn't have umpires they wouldn't have anyone to blame for their own mistakes. Mostly, though, being a major league umpire is sort of like being a playroom monitor for really, really well-paid babies. For playing a kids game, these people get paid millions of dollars—and they don't even have to build houses or hotels on Park Place.

Here's an example of the way the relationship between players, managers, and umpires used to work. In the opening game of spring training one season, I was assigned to work a Dodgers-Rangers game in Pompano Beach. My plane landed, I drove directly to the ballpark, put on my gear, and got behind home plate. The first pitch of the first game of spring training to the Dodgers' leadoff hitter, Steve Sax, looked pretty good to me. Strike one. Sax whirled around and screamed, "The ball was outside."

I told him calmly, very calmly, "Get back in there and hit."

He stepped out of the batter's box and took two steps closer to me, "Don't tell me what to do. If you can't get it right don't blame it on me. . . ."

I'd been on the ground for less than an hour. The spring training season was about thirty, forty seconds old. "You're done," I told him, "I don't have to listen to you." I pointed to the Dodgers team bus. "Go get on the bus."

Before I finished throwing him out, Dodgers manager Tommy Lasorda was standing next to me. "What's going on?" he asked. "It's the first pitch of the season."

I'd been in the big leagues about ten years, but I don't think I'd ever met Lasorda. I'd certainly heard about him, though. "Hey Tommy, that's exactly what I just told him," I said, "but he didn't want to hear it from me. So I told him to go get on the bus."

Lasorda didn't believe I'd thrown him out. "You can't

throw him out," he told me, "this is spring training. I ain't putting him on the bus."

That started it with Lasorda. So I had to throw him out too. "You go get on that bus too." But he refused to leave, he wasn't going anywhere. I kept thinking to myself, *This is going to be some year.* One pitch and I've already thrown out two people. But Lasorda was adamant, nobody was getting on the bus. Even the bus driver. "Tell you what, Tommy," I said. "See those two umpires out there. You either take Sax and get on that bus or I'm taking those two guys and we're leaving."

"Oh no," Tommy challenged me, "you can't do that."

"Try me," I suggested. Eventually Lasorda and Sax walked across the field and got on the bus. That's the way baseball used to be—they would fight you on every single pitch.

That's not the way it is anymore. The fact is that life in the major leagues changed a lot during my career. Things got a lot quieter. Managers, players, and coaches definitely did not argue as much. The dugouts got much quieter. There was less noise on the field. Maybe the level of play got worse, but the managers and the players definitely got more intelligent. It only took them most of the twentieth century to figure out that it was better to stay in the game than get thrown out.

In the old days people just didn't care if they were ejected. It was a constant battle on the field. No more. The level of hostility has been dramatically reduced. It's rare to see a good, old-fashioned, hat-throwing, dirt-kicking, home-plate-covering tantrum. Who knows why, but, on the field, the game now has all the color and passion of a corporate board meeting. It might have something to do with the fact that more players have attended college, but in the last five years of my career I couldn't find an ejection. I couldn't throw out the garbage. I barely had an argument. I was supposed to be the big, tough guy who liked throwing people out of games. But nobody wanted to argue with me. For a time I was a little concerned about my reputation, maybe people thought I was getting soft, maybe they were feeling sorry for me. Kaiser has lost his thumb. Then I realized that it wasn't just me, it was the game itself. It was as if the rats had finally got the cheese.

The change started with managers like the Twins' Tom Kelly. In my entire career, Tom Kelly was the finest manager I saw, as well as a very decent person. Everybody respected him. Every umpire knew that when Tom Kelly came out of the dugout, you'd better start rerunning the play in your mind, because there was a pretty good chance you might be wrong. Certain managers, not to mention any names like Earl Weaver, came out to argue all the time and, with them, you knew that even if you were wrong you were right—but not with Kelly.

T. K. rarely came out to argue; most of the time he came out to discuss the play. Two gentlemen having a bit of a disagreement over the proceedings. That's the way he was for his entire career. One night in Boston, Mark Johnson was working first base when he called out a Twins runner for interfering with the second baseman. Kelly kind of ambled out, like a professor thinking about a lecture he was about to give, and asked Johnson, "How'd you see that?"

"Tommy, he interfered."

"Yeah," Kelly agreed, "I know he did, but the guy at *second* base is supposed to make that call."

"Well, he was probably looking at the ball. He didn't see the runner."

Kelly nodded his head. "Look, I know you got it right. I appreciate that. But it's against me." And then he left.

During Ted Barrett's first big-league season he was at first base for the last game of a four-game Twins-White Sox series. On a close play, Frank Thomas had to come off first base to catch a bad throw, then took a swipe at the base with his foot. Barrett called the runner out. It was the kind of play that other managers, not to mention any names like Earl Weaver, might have tried to use to bury a young umpire. To intimidate him—to test him. Instead, Kelly complimented him: "You missed that one, but you had a great series. I think you're going to be a really good umpire. A good addition to the staff. Just keep working hard."

When they heard that, people in Hell had to be putting on overcoats, because there was a deep freeze coming. Bears were relieving themselves in cities. The Pope wasn't Catholic. The sun didn't come up the next morning. Believe me, nothing in Barrett's training, nothing they taught him in school, nothing he learned in the minor leagues had prepared him for that encounter. If life came with theme music, an aria would have started playing in the background. It was the kind of scene that old-time Hollywood movies ended with. Barrett just stood there looking at Kelly, maybe even brushing away a small tear, and said nicely, "Thanks, Tom."

What umpires liked about Tom Kelly was that he maintained control of his team. At times I'd get into it with one of his players. Not that I was about to lose my temper. I said I don't have a bad temper and you'd better pay attention. I would simply be so angry that lava would be ready to flow. But, before I exploded, I'd hear the voice of reason, Kelly telling me, "Hey Kais, don't worry about it, I'll straighten him out." And I'd see him in the dugout screaming at the player.

Kelly was one of those managers who actually had to ask to be thrown out of a game. Managers really do that. They do it to motivate their team or get the fans involved. I had that with Tony LaRussa one night. The White Sox had been going bad, and he needed to shake things up. One night in Chicago LaRussa came out to discuss a play in the outfield. I think I called the batter out, but he insisted that the ball had been trapped. He yelled at me for a while and when I told him, "Come on Tony, that's enough, you had your say, so let's go." He stood there defiantly and told me, "You have to run me."

I didn't want to run him. "I'm not gonna run you, Tony. Come on, let's go."

"No," he said pointing a finger at my chest, getting the crowd going, "I want you to run me. You don't run me, I'm gonna have to throw my hat."

"Come on, don't do that. If you throw your hat I'm gonna have to run you."

He grabbed his cap and flung it on the ground. "Now, you go ahead and run me," he challenged. I did, but I didn't even know whether to count that as a real ejection.

There are managers who want to be ejected because they just can't bear to watch their team anymore. When Terry Collins was managing Anaheim he came out one time and told me that he needed to be ejected. *Needed* to be.

I don't like to do any favors for managers. A manager has to earn his ejection. I told him I wasn't going to throw him out. "Come on, you gotta. This team is playing so badly I just got to get ejected. I got a second baseman who can't catch the ball, I got a third baseman who can't throw it, I got a cleanup hitter who can't hit, I got a relief pitcher. . . ."

I started laughing.

That got him upset. He got right up in my face and warned me, "Don't you laugh. Don't you dare laugh. If you laugh they're gonna know what I'm doing out here. I'm supposed to be out here chewing your ass. . . ."

I did him a favor and kicked him out. But as he left he was still muttering, ". . . coaches who can't coach, runners who can't . . ."

When Jackie Moore was managing Oakland he was having a terrible year, and one day he came out and begged me to eject him, *begged* me. I didn't want to do it—Jackie Moore was one of the nicest people in baseball. Besides, I just couldn't go around throwing people out of baseball games. The league frowned on it. I told Jackie he had to earn it. But, the more I resisted throwing him out of the game the angrier he became. He was furious that I wouldn't eject him. It was ridiculous, the angrier he got about not being thrown out the more determined I was *not* to throw him out. Meanwhile, fans were on their feet, screaming, supporting him. When I turned around and started to walk away he circled in front of me, cut me off. "You're gonna throw me outta this game or I'm not leaving this field. . . ."

Finally, I really had no choice, I had to boot him. I don't remember if he thanked me.

Managers do put on an act for their players or fans. There are times when it takes preparation to be spontaneous. Doug Rader, "The Rooster," could put on a great show. I liked him;

he was a tough guy who ran his ball club and never tried to show up anybody. Some managers just press buttons—use this guy in this situation—Rader had more of a wing-and-a-prayer style. I remember one time when his Angels team was in Baltimore. Jim Joyce, who was then in his first season in the major leagues, was working third base. In the bottom of the ninth an Oriole hit a fly ball into the seats right down the left field foul line. Joyce didn't get a real good look at it. It was close, real close, and he called it fair, a game-winning home run. I couldn't tell, I had a real bad angle, but if he called it fair, as far as I was concerned, it was fair, and would always be fair. Rader came shooting out of that dugout faster than a groupie chasing a rock star. But all four umpires were going in the other direction. The game was over. Time to eat. See ya tomorrow, Doug.

Rader stood there desperately looking for someone to argue with. Supposedly, at times, Rader would get so frustrated after a game that he would walk back to his hotel from the ballpark. My guess is that this would have been one of those days. My guess is that if he was walking miles for a charity, he would have raised enough money to cure cancer. But we knew he was eventually going to get his say in.

I knew we'd hear about it the next day. Rader rarely brought his lineup card up to home plate. He usually had one of his coaches do it. But, before the next game, I looked over at the Angles dugout and here comes Rader, a little cloud of steam hanging over his head. I asked our crew chief, Jim McKean, "Who's gonna handle this? You can't let Joyce handle it." That was a time when veteran umpires really protected the new people, when umpires weren't worried about losing their jobs.

"I don't know," McKean said.

I looked at Joyce, "I'll take care of it."

We were absolutely silent as Rader reached the plate. He knew exactly what was going to happen. "All right," he asked, his first words flowing in a very friendly fashion, "which one of you guys is going to run me?" It was like he was picking his executioner.

I nodded at Joyce, "It ain't gonna be him."

"Who's it going to be? You?"

"Yeah. You wanna put on a show?"

Rader laughed, "You bet I do."

"Okay then," I said, "go ahead." And here we go. He yanked off his hat and started screaming at me. He got up close to my face, screeching that it was a horseshit call, and how could we let a call like that decide the game when his team was out there breaking its collective behind, and we had no right to walk off the field, and who did we think we were, and he had been taking that crap from us for so long, and couldn't anybody give the kid help and. . . .

His head was bobbing up and down so furiously he looked like he was modeling for a bobblehead doll. The veins in his throat were popping. This was no act, he really was furious.

Naturally, I gave it right back to him, explaining to him, Mr. Rader, this is no way to speak to people in authority, and should you persist in this behavior I would make it my duty to ensure that there would be repercussions. Something like that. Maybe I threw in a colorful word or two hundred. I let him blow off steam, then told him, "Okay, Doug, it's time for you to go," and I ran him.

A lot of managers will argue to protect a player, even when they know that player is wrong. A manager who won't protect his players loses the respect of his team pretty quickly. One night in Texas, Rader came out to protect his player, I don't remember who it was—he pushed the player out of the way and inserted himself between me and the player. He started screaming and yelling, veins popping, and it took me a few seconds to realize that Rader didn't even know what the original argument was about. That didn't stop him though. He's a big outdoorsman, and when he finally finished, as he started to walk back to the dugout, he stopped and added angrily, "And your fishing sucks, too!"

Meanwhile, 25,000 people in the stands were supporting him. That's right, Doug, you tell him Doug, don't you let him get away with that, Doug. And they gave him a big ovation as he walked off the field. That Doug, he sure told that umpire what's what.

Tommy Lasorda prided himself on protecting and motivating his players. One time, in Cincinnati, there was a play at second base that wasn't really that close, but when Eddie Montague's call went against the Dodgers, the base runner started arguing. Instantly, Lasorda came trotting out of the visiting dugout. He pushed his runner away and turned on Montague. "Eddie!" he screamed.

"What do you want, Tommy?"

"I heard you were at the Montgomery Inn last night." The Montgomery Inn was one of the better restaurants in Cincinnatti—and Montague had eaten there the previous night.

"Yeah, so what?"

"So what? So how were the ribs?"

"They were great, Tommy."

"I'm glad, that's all I wanted to know." And he turned around and jogged off the field.

I never minded an argument—if the manager had a legitimate point to make. But I liked Sparky Anderson's philosophy. When he came over from the National League to manage the Tigers we were warned that he could be very tough on umpires, but for the first couple of seasons he barely said a word. Geeze, I thought, this guy's not that bad. It didn't make sense.

So I asked him about it. "I don't argue because we're not good enough yet," he explained, "but just wait, when we get good enough to win I'll be out there." And that is exactly what happened.

Just about every umpire has one or two managers or players that he just doesn't get along with. No matter what happens, they just can't get along. It's like a feud. And when the Tigers finally became competitive enough for Sparky to argue, he started making up for lost opportunities. One umpire he didn't get along with was Mark Johnson. In Johnson's first season he had to run Anderson three or four times. The first time Johnson ever spoke to Sparky was in Minnesota's Homerdome. He was at second base and Don Denkinger was at first. Kirby Puckett hit a long fly ball over the right field wall that was just barely fair. Sparky argued with Denkinger that it was a foul ball. After losing that argument, instead of trotting off the field he went up to Johnson and asked him, "What'd you see?"

Johnson told him, "I thought it was a good call."

"Yeah," Anderson said to this person he had never met before in his life, "you probably would lie for him." Boom! Johnson had his first ejection.

This feud created a real problem for Johnson, because his mother was a rabid Cincinnati Reds fan, and Anderson had managed the World Champion Big Red Machine. Having problems with the American League and the commissioner's office was one thing, disappointing your own mother was another—*that* was serious. It got to the point where Johnson's mother told him not to bother coming home.

One afternoon Johnson was working in Milwaukee and his parents were coming to the game. Just before going onto the field, Johnson looked out from a dugout to make sure they were in their seats. And he was stunned. Sitting there talking to his mother was Sparky Anderson! That mother-talker! Johnson was livid. None of us had ever heard of a manager complaining about an umpire to that umpire's mother!

But, right after the game Sparky grabbed Johnson and told him, "Young man, you have a very nice mother and father there. Now you and I have had our differences in the past . . ." Johnson absolutely agreed with that, "but I want to tell you one thing. I want to promise you right now, never again in your career will you have to run me."

And that's exactly what happened.

A similar kind of thing happened to me with Don Zimmer. There is no one more knowledgeable about baseball than Zimmer. But he also loves the horses. Sometimes he'd come out to argue and we'd end up talking horseracing. Through the years I also got to know his wife, Soot, real well. The day after I threw him out of a game in Texas he came up to home plate and told me, "Now you've really done it, Kaiser. Soot got so angry at me for yelling at you that now she isn't talking to me."

The late, wonderful National League umpire Lee Wyer just didn't get along with a player named Alex Johnson. One day, when Johnson was with Cincinnati, he tagged up on a fly ball, but left the base too soon. The Cubs appealed, and Wyer called Johnson out. The Reds manager, Dave Bristol, charged out of the dugout and Wyer charged right at him. Lee was a big man and he never backed down. Bristol was fuming. He started screaming at Wyer, "What's your problem with him? You just got a hard-on for him."

"Who are you kidding?" Wyer responded, "I wouldn't waste it on him."

Bristol took off his hat and threw it at Wyer, then told him, "I oughta punch you."

Wyer later admitted that that was the only time in his career when he came close to hitting a man on the field. He didn't, instead he laughed and said, "You haven't got the guts." And that was the end of it.

Wyer's longtime partner and close friend, Eddie Montague, actually did hit a player, the St. Louis Cardinals' Vince Coleman, in San Francisco one night. When Montague called Coleman out on an attempted steal of second, Coleman butted him just above the nose with his helmet. He opened up a big gash and blood started gushing. Without consciously thinking about it, Montague smacked Coleman on the side of his head with his left hand, while throwing him out of the game with his right hand. Giants second baseman Robby Thompson was stunned. "Eddie," he said, "do you know that you just hit him?"

Montague was just as surprised. "I did?" He definitely did.

Cardinals manager Whitey Herzog came out to see what was going on. Montague had his back turned to Herzog. "Eddie," Herzog began, "what's your prob . . ." Montague turned around and Herzog saw the blood all over his shirt. "Oh," he finished.

National League president Bill White suspended Coleman for a week. When White asked Montague for an explanation. Montague said he didn't remember hitting Coleman. "But if he hits me with his helmet again," he admitted, "I'll probably react the same way. I'm not going to take that kind of crap on the field."

Of course, the most memorable feud I ever saw was between Earl Weaver and—and just about every major league umpire—but especially Bill Haller and Ron Luciano. And Don Denkinger. And Marty Springstead. And certainly Steve Palermo. And, of course, me. Among others. There were so many reasons not to like Weaver, but the primary one was that he complained about every single pitch that went against him. At every pitch, that shrill voice would come out of the Orioles dugout. *Where was it? Where was it? Ball was high. Ball was low. Pitch was inside. Pitch was outside.* Every single pitch. There is no question that Weaver was an outstanding manager. He won, and that's how he should be judged. But as far as umpires were concerned, he was nothing more than a walking headache. He believed that the more he complained, the more calls he would get. He believed wrong.

He was always griping about something. People used to say that Earl wasn't happy unless he wasn't happy. When I made speeches I would tell people that he was the only person I knew who could end Happy Hour just by showing up. Nobody got along with him. Umpire Lou DiMuro was the nicest man who ever walked the face of the earth. He was a good, decent person, he liked everybody.

Okay, everybody in the world with one exception. Lou

DiMuro hated Weaver. In the World Series one year he was working home plate. He got so mad at Weaver and Frank Robinson for screaming at him from the dugout on every single pitch that he snapped. He took a baseball out of his ball bag, turned towards the dugout, and threw it right at them. He definitely tried to hit them. He got in a lot of trouble with the league for that, but he didn't care. The umpires all supported him. We would have walked off a cliff to support him—either that, or we would have pushed Weaver off.

Haller and Weaver hated each other. In addition to all of Weaver's normal complaining—every single damn pitch—Weaver publicly questioned Bill Haller's integrity by stating that Haller couldn't be fair when he worked Detroit Tiger games, because his brother, Tom, was catching for the Tigers.

Haller and Weaver were just a fight waiting to happen. Haller had the plate one Saturday afternoon in Baltimore, and he looked over into the O's dugout and immediately called time—Weaver was down on his knees on the top step of the dugout, his hands clasped in front of him. This was an easy one—Boom! *You're gone, Earl! You're finished here today*. This time Weaver thought he was too smart for Bill. "What are you throwing me out for? I'm praying. You can't throw me out for praying."

That was probably the first time in baseball history that a manager claimed a religious exemption. My guess is that Weaver wanted Haller to ask him what he was praying for? And I'll bet he had a real good answer prepared for that question. Earl always had an answer. One time, for example, Richie Garcia had thrown him out of the game, but found out he was hiding in the bathroom just behind the dugout, watching the game and managing through a hole in the door. "Just what do you think you're doing in here, Earl?" Richie demanded.

"I'm in here throwing up because I'm sick of your calls."

Haller didn't fall for it, he didn't even bother asking Weaver what he was praying for. Instead, he asked, "Hey Earl, you Jewish?"

Weaver paused. A trick question? "No," he told him.

"Oh, that's too bad, Earl. Because it's Saturday, and if you're not Jewish you don't pray on Saturday. You're outta here."

It's no surprise that the best argument I ever saw on the playing field was between Haller and Weaver. This was probably in 1980. Baltimore had lost the 1979 World Series to Pittsburgh, and Weaver had been criticized for some of his moves. This argument began when Haller called a balk on the Orioles' pitcher. Weaver came out and went right at him. All the animosity these two had for each other was released. I don't how long it went on, ten minutes at least. The whole thing was filmed and taped. Weaver followed Haller all over the field. Finally, Weaver said, "That's all right, big-nose Haller, I'm going to be in the Hall of Fame."

Haller didn't even pause to think about his answer. "For what Earl," he said, "screwing up the World Series last year?"

I guess that's probably when the argument really got started.

Ron Luciano got into trouble with the American League for saying out loud what most umpires thought privately, that he didn't care which teams won the division pennants, but that he hoped it wouldn't be Baltimore. The league made him apologize to Weaver at a press conference and made sure he didn't work any more Orioles games. In other words, they arranged it so that he didn't have to listen to Weaver complaining. That was some terrific punishment. There were long lines of umpires trying to sign up for that one.

I don't know how many times Ronnie threw Earl out of games. Whatever the number, as far as Ronnie was concerned, I'm sure the correct answer was: not enough. The Orioles used to have a betting pool when Luciano worked one of their games, guessing how many innings Weaver would last. One time, Ronnie threw him out then looked in the O's dugout—Jim Palmer was so excited he was jumping up and down. We knew Palmer and Weaver didn't get along, but that seemed a little excessive. We discovered later that he'd won the pool! I think Weaver believed that Ronnie was somehow hurting the game of baseball by having fun on the field and entertaining the fans. He often complained that Ronnie didn't take his job seriously enough. That wasn't exactly true—Ronnie was very serious when it came to ejecting Weaver.

One time Ronnie got him both games of a doubleheader, a two-fer. In the first game, Weaver came out to argue a call at first base. Ronnie saw him coming and started laughing. He knew Weaver was about to leave the premises. "That's the problem with you," Weaver screamed at him, "you think everything's a big joke . . ."

That wasn't true. Weaver was too small to be a big joke.

". . . All you care about is jumping up in the air and throwing your arms all around."

To demonstrate what he meant, he did a poor imitation of Ronnie. "You can't throw your arms in the air," Ronnie told him, "you're not an umpire. Here, let me show you how to do it." With that, he wound up and, in a great, big gesture, threw Weaver out of the game. That was the first game.

Before the start of the second game Weaver came to home plate with his starting lineup. "Okay, Ron," Weaver said, "I want you to take this game seriously. I want to see you call balls and strikes the way they're supposed to be called. None of that other stuff you do. . . ."

Ronnie listened politely. Then he sighed and said, "I have some bad news for you, Earl. It doesn't matter what you want, because you're not going to be here to see it." Then he wound up and gave Earl an even bigger ejection than the first game.

Weaver was furious. He didn't want to let Ronnie start the game. He refused to hand over his lineup card, telling him, "You're not serious about this game, so I'm not going to let you be the umpire."

"Oh yeah?" Ronnie said, and then he just grabbed the lineup card right out of Weaver's hand. The lineup consists of two copies, the home plate umpire keeps one, the official scorer gets the other. Ronnie handed a copy to the ball boy and told him to take to it upstairs to the scorer.

Weaver told the ball boy, "Don't you touch that."

The ball boy didn't know what to do. He was caught between a rock and a hardass. "You can't tell him anything, Earl," the Rock said. "You're not even here anymore. You're already out of this game."

Working with Haller and Luciano and Kunkel, maybe I didn't get too many shots at Weaver. I don't know what the problem was, but I really didn't have that many arguments with him. For some reason I never seemed to have problems with physically big managers, guys, like Rader, who were nearly my size. Most of my real arguments were with the little people. And no one in baseball seemed smaller than Earl Weaver.

Earl had this trick he used to use when arguing with umpires. He'd get up real close in their face and start bobbing up and down, hitting the umpire with the bill of his cap. That way he had the umpires backing away from him. I guess it looked impressive from the stands: he had the umpires on the run. But people got wise to him. He came out one night and an umpire named Hank Morgenweck not only stood his ground, he intentionally stepped on Weaver's foot with his spiked shoe, preventing him from bobbing up and down. Earl limped off the field.

From that point on, when Weaver came out to argue he'd turn his hat around. So, one day as he came running towards me, I turned *my* hat around. We really went at it, and he said to me, "I'd like to hit you."

Now, that was a funny thought. I looked down at him and asked, "Where, Earl? On my knee?" He didn't like that at all. Not at all, so he kicked dirt on me. And, in response, I kicked dirt on him. As I was following through I was thinking, *This is crazy, what am I doing?* In my entire career that was the only time I ever did anything like that. But, truthfully, it felt great.

One of the few managers who was possibly worse than Weaver on the field was Billy Martin. On the field—but off the field he was a terrific person. Billy had a Jekyll and Hyde personality, as opposed to Weaver, who was more like Hyde and Hyde. When Billy put on the uniform something happened to him. He turned into Charlie Manson's cousin, Billy Manson. But I remember leaving Yankee Stadium one night after a long game and seeing him standing there patiently signing autographs. I don't know how many he signed, he just stood there signing. "What are you doing?" I asked him. "How come you're still here signing?"

"The Old Man," he told me. The Old Man was Casey Stengel. "When I was coming up he told me to sign all the autographs you can, because someday you're going to wish they were still asking you for it."

I loved Billy, loved him. I thought he was a great manager; he was always three moves ahead of his opponent and got the most mileage possible out of players. But I was definitely in the minority. There were a lot of umpires who hated him. Dale Ford hated him. Larry McCoy hated him. Billy had absolutely no sense of fair play. The only thing that mattered to him was winning, and he would do anything to win. He really believed that if an umpire wasn't cheating to help him, he had to be cheating to hurt him. One time in Oakland, Dale Ford made a call against Oakland and Billy went berserk. The writers called his type of managing "Billy Ball," but for us it was more "Billy Brawl." Dale threw him out of the game. Actually, that was more of a beginning than an end. When the game was over we were going to our locker room and Billy was waiting at the top of the ramp to confront Dale. I don't know if I've ever seen two men more angry with each other. I stopped that fight. I stood between them and tried to keep them apart, but I couldn't keep them apart forever.

A few weeks later we were in Chicago on a hot day. I mean, it was one of those sweltering Chicago days when people doing the weather on TV issue advisories like, *Anybody who goes outside today dies*. Dale was working home plate, meaning he had to wear a heavy mask, shin guards, and the chest protector—but we were *all* drenched in sweat. From the first inning Billy was screeching at Dale. He just wouldn't let up. And finally there was a disputed play, I don't remember what it was, but Billy came out of the dugout and went right for Dale. I came running in—and I'm not a big runner on *cool* days—and got between them. I was holding onto Billy's belt buckle and Dale's shirt under his chest protector, trying to keep them away from each other. They were screaming right through me. Suddenly, Dale tried to slip around me and, as he did, I ripped the shirt right off his body. He still had the chest protector on, but I was left holding his shirt. He just kind of looked at me holding his soaking wet shirt in my hands. I think that shocked him back into reality. He suddenly realized that he wasn't allowed to beat up managers. There had to be some rule against that. And I'm sure there was no Billy Martin Exception to that rule.

Some time later Billy asked me why I'd done that. I looked at him up and down, up and down, and started laughing. Billy was tough, but he was about as much a match for Dale Ford as I was for Andre the Giant.

I don't know why Billy and I got along so well. Maybe he figured I was as unpredictable as he was. But when the Yankees retired his number I was the only umpire invited to his banquet in New Jersey. On the field I don't think I ever had to eject him, although we did have our times. When he was managing Texas I had a bang-bang play at first base that I knew I got right, but Billy still came out at me. *Here we go,* I thought, *what does he want?* He got right up in my face and told me, "Kais, let's put on a show for these people."

"What?"

"Let's give 'em a good show." He started waving his arms in frustration, "Come on, let's wake these people up." I was a little surprised. "What's the matter with you?" he screamed, throwing his hat. "You always have something to say." He did his whole act, and as he left the field he nodded and decided out loud, "That was a good one."

There was one time I would have thrown him out, but I couldn't, because he wasn't there. I was working third base in Oakland. He had been suspended for bumping umpire Terry Cooney. He wasn't even allowed inside the ballpark. For some reason, the game was moving unusually slowly. Then I noticed that the A's third base coach, Clete Boyer, was getting signs from a pitcher named Matt Keough, who was sitting in the corner of the dugout. I saw that Keough was spending a lot of time on the dugout telephone. It was pretty obvious what was going on—either Billy was watching the game on TV in some roadhouse and giving instructions to Keough to relay to Boyer, or Keough was ordering takeout and wanted to know if Boyer wanted the wonton or the hot and sour.

I let it go for a while. In the bottom of the eighth Oakland was trailing 2-1, but had runners on first and second with one out. That's when Billy made his mistake—he took too much time. There is nothing an umpire hates more than a long game, and this game was getting longer and longer. Finally I called time and started walking toward the dugout. Clete Boyer got in front of me, so I had to walk over him. When Keough saw me coming he took off, leaving the receiver dangling. "Get over here," I told him. I handed him the phone, "Get Martin on here."

A few seconds later he handed me the receiver. The first

thing I heard was Billy asking, "Hey, what's going on down there?"

"Hey Billy," I said, "this is Kaiser. You've just been disconnected." And with that I ripped the entire phone right out of the wall and handed it to Keough. "Here," I told him, "now it's a portable."

The next day Billy walked into our dressing room before the game. He was laughing—as he handed me a bill for the telephone.

I honestly don't know how managers like Billy and Weaver would have adjusted to the way the game has changed. I don't mean strategically—the game hasn't changed that much in that regard, but, rather, with what seems to be a lack of passion on the field. I think they probably would have fought that lack of passion passionately.

Some veteran managers have been able to adjust. There was no one, absolutely no one, who threw a better tantrum when he disagreed with a call than Lou Piniella. Piniella would throw his cap down in the dirt, stomp on it, kick it around, his whole face would turn red, the veins in his neck would bulge out, then he'd start kicking dirt on home plate—and if he couldn't get it completely covered he'd get down on his hands and knees and cover the plate with dirt. He would pick up a base and walk away with it, screaming and yelling how he was being cheated the whole time. Piniella would lose it completely. One night in Cleveland he got into it with Larry Barnett. When Barnett threw him out, Lou threw his cap on the ground and tried to kick it—but he missed completely, slipped, and fell backwards, almost breaking his back. That made him even angrier. He called Barnett every nasty thing imaginable, but—when he was finally done, when he was finished—as he was leaving the field he walked by me and said, "I love you, Kais."

Then Barnett got mad at *me!* "What the hell have you got on him?" he demanded.

"I didn't say anything," I told Barnett, then added, "I can't help it if he doesn't like you."

If throwing a tantrum was an Olympic event, Lou would have been a world champion. But that was then. Now he says, "I don't take it personally anymore like I used to. When we lost I would take it personally." Piniella really learned how to keep up with the times. Now instead of whining about balls and strikes, he actually got into a fight with an umpire over whether his pitcher had to remove his diamond earrings.

One time I saw Piniella get so angry after losing an argument that he went back into the dugout and tried to kick the water cooler—and he missed that, too—and fell down. As a lot of people have learned, arguing with an umpire can be dangerous. One time, Steve Palermo was working first base and he threw Dave Kingman out of a game when Kingman argued about a checked-swing strike. After the game Kingman wouldn't let it go. He told reporters, "Tell Palermo he's got the worst case of bad breath I've ever seen. He's got to cut down on his garlic." The next day Palermo was behind the plate. Kingman singled in his first at bat and, as he started running to first, he turned to yell something at Palermo—and stumbled and fell, straining a muscle. He was out for a week. The only thing that Palermo was upset about was that it was only a week.

Maybe I was one of the few umpires who got along with Billy Martin, but I was also one of the few umpires who did not get along with Whitey Herzog. Most umpires thought

Whitey was a very good guy, but we never got along. I think there was probably a pretty good reason for that: He hated me. Several people gave me nicknames during my career; for example, when *The Incredible Hulk* was a popular TV show the Yankees' Thurman Munson started calling me The Incredible Heap. It was Whitey who gave me the nickname Dr. Strange Call. Truthfully, he was a pretty funny guy. When he was managing a bad Texas ball club he told the writers very seriously, "This club needs just two players to be a contender. And those two players are Babe Ruth and Sandy Koufax."

My guess is that Whitey didn't like me because he wanted umpires to call only the basic six: fair, foul, safe, out, strike, and ball. He didn't want umpires to make any other calls—balk, interference, obstruction. Whenever I made a call like that he'd come out to discuss it. For some reason, I probably had more arguments with him than any other manager.

In those old days, I admit it, I was a little quick on the trigger. But that was the only way to retain control. Just like managers used to test young umpires, I immediately established myself with young players. The first time I met Jimmy Leyritz, who had a nice career, I was working the plate in Cleveland. He swung and missed at the first pitch. The second pitch was good enough for me. Called strike two! Leyritz stepped out of the box and shook his head in disbelief, a nice, subtle way of telling everybody in the ballpark, *This $#^% is screwing me. That pitch was a strike like I'm Father Teresa. I happen to be a great hitter, so great that I only swing at strikes. Since I didn't swing at that pitch, it couldn't have been a strike.*

Meanwhile, I'm thinking, *Who does this kid think he is? He's been in the big leagues five minutes and he's trying to use me for an alibi?* The next pitch was right down the middle of the plate. A perfect pitch and he took it. Strike three! See you, kid. Don't forget to write!

I watched Leyritz walk back to the dugout. I watched as he slammed his bat into the bat rack and stood next to the manager, Stump Merrill, and indicated with his hands that the pitch had been about six inches off the plate, and that ^%$# had called it a strike. *Blaming me? You blaming me, punk? I don't think so.*

I walked toward that dugout like King Kong stomping a city. I wasn't exactly Dirty Harry, I was more like Unkempt Kenny. Somebody must have warned Leyritz, because he turned around in time to see me coming. The chase was on. He started walking up the ramp towards the clubhouse. Man, I was furious. I walked right down into the dugout and followed him, screaming at him, "Don't bother to come back. You're a late scratch."

Stump Merrill, who I knew pretty well from the minor leagues, must have educated him, because the next day I was working third base and Leyritz tried hard to make up with me. But every time he came near me I'd just turn around and walk away from him. One thing I absolutely guarantee, he never used me as his alibi again.

I had a similar thing happen with the Minnesota Twins' Kirby Puckett. Kirby was one of the greatest clutch hitters in baseball. I hated to see him coming to bat in a clutch situation. The Twins might be losing 9-1, with the bases empty and two outs in the ninth, and I still hated to see him come to bat. I was afraid he'd figure out some way of tying it up. I was behind the plate for his first major league at bat. The first pitch was a fastball over his head—but he swung at it and missed. The next pitch was a slider in the dirt—he swung at that one, too, and missed it. The third pitch was maybe two inches off the plate. I called it strike three. He whirled around and looked at me. "That ball was outside," he complained.

"Hey kid, look. The first pitch you swung at was over your head. The second pitch you swung at was in the dirt. You ain't gonna hit the son of a bitch anyway, so just get out of here." The way that kid swung, I knew I'd never see him again.

I didn't walk away from too many arguments. In fact, there was only one time I walked away on purpose. When Harvey Kuenn was managing Milwaukee he came out to argue one night, and I walked away from him. The problem was that Kuenn had lost a leg, to diabetes I think, and had a wooden leg. So every time he got close to me I'd walk away from him. I made him chase me. Eventually I wore him out.

Baseball has never had a specific rule about how to handle arguments, or when to eject a manager, player, or coach—or, in my case, a press box. Each umpire has to decide how much abuse he can take. It was very much a personal decision. Legendary umpire Bill Klem supposedly drew a line in the dirt with his foot and warned players and managers that if they stepped over that line they were gone. Steamboat Johnson carried a doctor's letter in his pocket confirming that he had 20/20 vision, and sometimes during an argument he'd take out his pocket watch and stare at it, meaning you've got a few more seconds and then you're done. The old National League president Warren Giles said, "I don't believe an umpire should descend to the player's level. . . ." According to Giles, a person could be ejected for "reflecting on an umpire's honor, ancestry, or morals—in any kind of language." While supposedly it was permissible to call an umpire "four eyes," or ask if he is going blind—players weren't allowed to tell him that he was already blind.

My own personal rule was a little more basic: Based on my experience and my previous encounters with the specific individual with whom I was engaged in this debate, taking into consideration the relevant facts of the situation and the perversities of human nature, I would weigh all factors and then, if I felt that person had made personal aspersions against me, rather than endeavoring to focus on the controversy, I would respond appropriately.

In other words, when I felt like it. Technically that can be summed up as, enough is enough.

You throw out people to keep control. For most of my big league career there was usually a lot of noise coming out of the dugouts. It seemed like somebody was always complaining about something. Players or coaches used to hide in the corners where they couldn't be seen and scream at the umpires. After a while it got to be too much. The only way to stop it was to stop it. One time Haller basically cleared an entire bench, he got everybody, the whole team. One of the coaches, a good guy, came out to plead his case. "Come on, Bill," he said, "I've been in this league nineteen years and I've never been thrown out of a game. How can you do it to me?"

Haller was sympathetic. "See, it's like a raid on a whorehouse," he explained, "the good go with the bad."

At times it was tough to identify the guilty party. That's when we did a little baiting. After someone shouted from the dugout I'd take a couple of steps towards the dugout and shout, "What'd you say? I can't hear you? Come on out here and talk to me."

That heckler in the dugout usually was surrounded by his teammates. There was no way he could back down from that challenge. *Yeah, go ahead, you tell him. We're behind you.* But the minute he took that first step out of the dugout, *bang, gotcha.*

When that didn't work and you couldn't figure out who was actually doing the shouting, the only thing to do was pick one guy out and make an example out of him. Bill Haller did that to pitching coach Art Fowler one afternoon. He walked over to the dugout, pointed at Fowler, and told him it was time to leave the premises. Fowler came out of the dugout and started complaining, "Oh, come on Bill, that's not right. I didn't say a word."

"Well, Art, if that's true maybe you should think about hanging out with a better crowd," Haller told him.

I cleared a whole press box once, so two or three warm bodies in a dugout was nothing for me. One time, when Hall of Famer Larry Doby was managing the White Sox, somebody was on me the whole game. *Kaiser! If you missed as many meals as you have pitches you'd probably disappear.* Or—*Kaiser, shake your head, your eyes are stuck.* I kept looking over to the dugout, but I couldn't figure out who it was. *Kaiser, that ball was so low it hit a Chinaman.* Finally, I had enough. I walked over to the White Sox bench. Doby was sitting at the very end. I got him first. Then I got the guy sitting next to him. Doby came out to complain. "You can't do that," he said, "I didn't say a thing."

"I don't know who did," I admitted, "but I'm working my way down the whole bench. Eventually I got to get him." And that was the end of it.

I admit that there were times in my career when I was the instigator. For example, one night the Indians were beating the Twins, something like 9-2 in the ninth inning in Minnesota. Believe me, that game was over. The Twins' Kent Hrbek was on first with either one out or no outs. Lefthander Dennis Cook was on the mound for the Indians. Cook started throwing over to first to keep Hrbek close to the base. Hrbek was a slow runner. Believe me, Hrbek wasn't going anywhere unless there was a steak sandwich at second base. It was a reasonable play the first time. And the second time. And maybe the third time. And, I suppose, even the fourth time. But, by the fifth time I was getting a little tired of it. Hrbek was nailed to first base. There was less room between him and the base than between my stomach and my belt. The sixth time he threw over I began to get a little irritated. Maybe I clapped my hands, *Come on, let's go*. This had all the drama and charm of a stirring rendition of the song *A Hundred Bottles of Beer on the Wall*. The seventh time he threw over I was getting hot. After the eighth time I told him, "Hey, you throw over here again I'm gonna balk you." Fair warning, right.

Cook laughed at me. "I'm not kidding," I told him, "try me." He did. He threw to first base. That was the ninth time. I had one word for him: *Balk!* Cook came running at me, screaming, "What'd I do? What'd I do? You can't call that a balk!"

"Oh no? Well, I just did." As I had learned in the minors, the balk is the umpire's friend. Nobody understands the rule, so they can't really complain about my interpretation of it. Cook wouldn't quit arguing, so I finally had to dump him.

When manager Mike Hargrove came out to calmly discuss the situation he said, "I can't believe you balked him."

"Hey, I warned him, Mike," I said.

"Yeah I heard that," Hargrove agreed.

Then I added, "And his right leg was moving towards the plate." Maybe it wasn't really fair of me, but my job is to keep the game moving. And that game had come to a halt. It was moving slower than roadkill. If I hadn't tried to force Cook to pitch he might still be throwing to first. And I'd never get to see my grandchildren grow up.

Actually, there are very few mandatory ejections in the rule book. The one that seems to make the most sense is ejecting pitchers who intentionally try to hit a batter. That rule seems to make sense, but, in fact, it doesn't. The problem is it forces umpires to become mind readers. In situations when a pitcher might throw at a batter, in retaliation after one of his teammates has been hit, for example, the umpire is supposed to warn the pitchers and managers of both teams that they will be ejected if the pitcher throws at a batter—and then it's up to the umpire to decide when an inside pitch is actually an attempt to hit a batter. The problem with that rule is that I'm not a mind reader; I barely read my mail.

I understood the intent of the rule, it was the application that bothered me. It's like the old joke: Dangerous Dan burns down the ranch, steals the cattle, and runs away with the rancher's wife. The rancher searches for him for thirty years and finally finds him. "Did you burn down my ranch, steal my cattle, and run away with my wife?" he asks. Dangerous Dan admits he did. "Well," the rancher says, "don't do it again!"

The only real problem with the rule was that it didn't do what it was supposed to do. Basically, the way the rule is written, each pitcher gets one shot at an opposing player without being penalized. One shot. It's definitely a hit-or-miss opportunity. Don't do it again. A baseball thrown at ninety miles per hour is potentially a very dangerous weapon. In 1992, umpire Terry Cooney got hit accidentally on his left knee by pitcher Frank Tanana. By that point in Tanana's career he couldn't even throw very hard—but that injury ended Cooney's career. He never worked another major league game and has had trouble even walking ever since.

So, one night I passed the Kaiser Amendment to that rule. Mike Heath was hitting for Oakland. I'm pretty sure Ed Whitson was on the mound for the Yankees. The batter before Heath had hit a home run to put the A's ahead by a couple of runs. Whitson's first pitch to Heath went behind his back. Understand now, the pitch went behind him. Calling that bad control is like calling George Steinbrenner shy. Intent? To me, that was practically an assault. It's a judgment call and, believe me, even Judge Judy would have thrown out Whitson. There were maybe 30,000 people in the stadium, and probably the only person who didn't know that it was intentional was this little old lady standing in the restroom line who thought she was waiting to go into The Johnny Carson Show. I didn't wait. I didn't issue any warnings, I just threw Whitson out of the game. That was the Kaiser Amendment. It was so obvious that even Lou Piniella, the Yankee manager, didn't bother to come out and argue.

I had the same situation in Seattle during the brief period Maury Wills was the manager. His pitcher, Paul Abbott, gave up three consecutive home runs, back-to-back-to-back, then hit the next batter in the ribs. I threw Abbott out of the game. Now, Maury Wills, who has to be a leading candidate for the worst manager in history, came out and he was furious. "What are you throwing him out for?"

How long you been in the game, Maury? Oh, about a hundred years. And you can't figure it out? You got a big future in this game. "It's pretty obvious, isn't it?" I told him. "Three guys in a row hit home runs, the next guy gets drilled? You think maybe it's just a coincidence?"

"I wouldn't let my pitcher hit somebody intentionally," Wills claimed.

"You may not allow it, but that's what happened." Eventually, I had to throw out Wills too.

The warning rule was ridiculous when it was passed, and nothing has changed. It puts the umpires in an impossible situation. It's a judgment call, and making that judgment depends so much on experience. To know enough to understand the situation, it helps if you know the participants. During the 2002 season, for example, the Dodgers' closer Eric Gagne took a 4-0 lead over Cincinnati into the ninth inning. The Reds' Aaron Boone hit a two-run homer to cut the lead to 4-2. Gagne then hit the next batter, Adam Dunn, in the back of his left arm. Dunn had done nothing except bat after Boone. Rookie umpire Dan Iassogna immediately ejected Gagne. Gagne charged him and had to be restrained. They had to pull him away. Dodgers manager Jim Tracy also got thrown out. With Gagne out of the game, the Reds tied the score, then won it in the thirteenth on a Ken Griffey Jr. home run.

After the game Tracy said, "That was the grossest error in judgment in quite possibly the history of the game." Don't hold back, Jim. You have something to say, go ahead and say it.

"Everybody knew it was unintentional," Gagne said. "You don't bring up the tying run. Where's he been? It's a joke. Has he been umpiring before? It's like it was his first game or something."

You want to know how much baseball has changed? Adam Dunn, the batter who got hit, sided with the pitcher who hit him. "The ump thought it was intentional," he told the writers. "I didn't. He didn't want to hit me in that situation. I know him. I know how he thinks."

Let me see now, that's the batter who was hit siding with the pitcher who hit him against the umpire. That's like the mugger and his victim blaming the cop. If Pete Rose heard that he'd be turning over in his Mercedes. I'm glad that Dunn was so certain he knew what Gagne was thinking, because I don't think anybody else did. Maybe he should have told Iassogna: *It's okay Dan, he didn't mean it.* One thing I know for sure, Iassogna basically had no options. Baseball has instructed the umpires to cut down on beanballs by ejecting pitchers, and one of the situations they cited as an example was the batter being hit right after the previous batter has hit a home run.

My philosophy about this situation has always been pretty simple: when in doubt, throw 'em out. Well, admittedly, that was my philosophy about all situations. The real problem is that major league baseball executives replaced too many veteran umpires at the same time, forcing them to bring up a lot of people who may be talented umpires but lack the necessary experience to handle certain situations. You spend thirteen years in the minor leagues like I did, you learn at least one very important lesson: Don't do it again.

Certainly, one of the best responses to an argument was given by Emmett Ashford, who became major league baseball's first black umpire in 1966. In spring training one season Ashford was working a Giants-Cubs game in Arizona. A batter took a half swing and Ashford called it a strike. Cubs manager Leo Durocher came running out to argue. He demanded that Ashford check with first base umpire Billy Williams. Ashford pointed to Williams, who signaled it was a strike. Then Ashford looked at Durocher and told him, "Okay Leo, it was a strike—and now you got it in black and white."

There really is no place like home plate. For an umpire, it is definitely the most difficult assignment. Major league umpires work in four-man crews, rotating clockwise around the diamond: third to second to first to home. That means you work the plate every fourth game, then you get three games off to recover.

The responsibilities for each base are different. When you're working third base, for example, the one thing that you have to be really careful about is that you don't fall asleep. After the problems of home plate, in which you have to make about 250 calls, third base is like a vacation. I've always believed that if I had worked third base my whole career I would have been in the Hall of Fame. If all of life was like umpiring third base, the manufacturer of Prozac would be out of business. I had a lot of games at third in which I had two or three fair-or-foul calls and that was it.

There just aren't too many plays in which you're involved at third base. Appeal plays on half-swings. Sometimes you have to cover for another umpire who left his position to make a call in the outfield. Occasionally you get a tag play at third base. And every once in awhile a team will make an appeal that the runner left third base before the outfielder caught the ball on a sacrifice fly.

The real problem at third base is boredom. Umpires aren't fans. We don't care who wins the game. Umpires don't care if Randy Johnson is pitching or Roger Clemens is going for his 267th win. Umpires don't care if A-Rod breaks his team's record for doubles in a season. Being a major league umpire is incredibly exciting—for at least the first thirty or forty games of your career. After that it becomes a job. And after you've just flown coast-to-coast, you haven't had much sleep, and you're standing behind third base on a very humid night with absolutely nothing to do, it's a difficult job. Sometimes you really have to fight to stay alert. Obviously that's not a problem if you're working a big series in the heat of a pennant race in a crowded ballpark, but when you've got a Milwaukee-Texas game in September with six thousand people in the stands you have to concentrate real hard not to start yawning. I would talk to anybody who would talk to me—coaches and third basemen, fans, the grounds crew, but generally those conversations don't last long. I mean, let's be honest, what kind of conversation can you have with members of the grounds crew while they're dragging the field? *Nice plastic lawn you've grown here. That's a great tarp to cover the infield, you buy it at Wal-Mart?*

Most of the time at third base you just stand there looking into the stands and the dugouts thinking. When you're working third base, umpires generally think about the game, for example: *When is this game going to be over? How can I speed up this game?* And when I wasn't thinking about the game, I was thinking about the same things everybody else thinks about—paying my bills, where am I going to eat after the game, family problems, winning the lottery, my feet are killing me, what am I going to eat after the game, who was the first president of Mauritania, all the usual things, and nothing in particular.

Maybe the biggest thing that ever happened to me at third base was that I sat down. Throughout the entire history of baseball, umpires have never sat down between innings. No matter what was going on, no matter how long a game lasted, the umpires stayed standing on the field. It was a matter of great pride: during a game umpires don't sit, don't leave the field, and don't take a drink. But Jim McKean and I were in Chicago on a cold day in late September. I was at third, he was at second. It was raining, snowing, and the hawk—the icy wind—was sweeping across the field. We were freezing. When they built the new Comiskey Park they included a little alcove, basically a hole, where the ground crew and camera crews would sit during the game. And in that little area they had installed heaters. McKean and I were among the first umpires to duck in there between innings to warm up. We sat down on the job.

Believe me, that was a pretty daring thing to do. A lot of

veteran umpires didn't adjust real well to change. I'll give you an example: In 1967, at a meeting of all the American League umpires, after a long debate it was decided that the umpires on the bases could take off their dress coats on hot days and work in long-sleeved shirts. By then National League umpires were already working in short-sleeved shirts, but American League umpires wouldn't even consider that, supposedly because several veterans had hairy arms and were afraid fans would call them apes. Believe me, this story is absolutely true. But the big decision they had to make in 1967 was how hot it would have to be for the umpires to remove their jackets? It was finally decided that the three umpires on the bases would take a vote to determine if it was hot outside—and the majority ruled.

At that same meeting they also decided—by a majority vote—that Emmett Ashford would be allowed to wear French cuffs on the field.

So, you can just imagine how some veteran umpires accepted the concept that between innings umpires would be allowed to sit down or get warm or even drink a glass of water. *Hey, if you wanted to sit down you should have become a bank president*. But it made sense to me. I may be tough, but I'm not stupid.

You have to work at second base. Second base required covering more ground than the other positions. Granted, I cover a considerable amount of ground when I'm standing still, but at second base I really had to move to get in the proper position. This was not my favorite slot. At second you had steals, force plays, double plays, you had to go into the outfield to call catches, trapped balls, and home runs, and you had to cover first base if that umpire went out on fly balls. Basically, you had to keep moving. Probably more than any other place on the field, second base is where you most often heard those two terrible words: instant replay.

Most umpires will tell you that they don't mind instant replay, because it almost always proves they got the call right. Even those very few times when it appears to show that the umpire blew the call it doesn't really matter, because as the National Football League has proved, the same play looks very different from different angles. So most umpires will tell you they don't mind it. And when they do they're probably lying.

Umpires hate instant replay. There is no benefit to it for them. You know what happens when the instant replay shows that the umpire kicked the call? Nothing is what happens. The rules of baseball are very clear: Umpires can't change the call. A lot of umpires have "magic words" that result in an instant ejection if a player uses them. For some umpires it's any kind of personal reference, for others it's being called certain curse words. For me, the magic words were "instant replay."

"Kais, just look at the replay . . ." Boom. Gone.

For a time most teams had TV monitors in or near the dugout. After a close play, if I saw players moving towards that monitor I told them to keep moving all the way back to the clubhouse. Allowing managers and players easy access to TV monitors would have caused endless arguments—usually without being conclusive. So we made sure there were no TVs in the dugouts.

But there is still a television set in the clubhouse, and when there is a debatable play you can see people running back into that clubhouse to look at the replay. I had a play in Toronto one night when Joe Carter came running straight towards me to try to catch a line drive. And I was running right at him to try to get a good look at the play. At the last second he dove for the ball and came up with it—but I saw a speck of white hit the grass and ruled it no catch.

Carter came running in to make his case. Manager Cito Gaston came out of the dugout. I've known Cito for a long time. We were in the low minor leagues together so long ago that he was still known as Clarence. "No, Kais, no," he started telling me, "that was a good catch, that was a good catch." As I explained to him that I saw the ball hit the grass he started maneuvering around me, so that I had my back to his dugout. *Okay,* I thought, *I'll dance with you.* But while I was talking to him he was looking over my shoulder. I knew what he was doing, he was looking into the Blue Jays dugout for a signal. Obviously someone finally gave it to him, because he said, "Kais, on the replay he caught it."

That just made me furious. Just livid. The TV station had at least three cameras and all kinds of sophisticated equipment that enabled them to show the play from different angles in slow motion, while all I had was me. And while there are people who would claim I moved naturally in slow motion, in fact I had one look at the play and less than a second to make my call. "Well, Clarence," I said calmly, "let me ask you this. You ever see *Perry Mason*?"

He admitted that he had watched it on occasion.

"You think it's real?"

No, he knew it was fiction.

"Exactly right. See, that's proof that you can't believe everything you see on TV. Now, if I were you," I continued, and perhaps I did raise my voice just a little bit here, "here's what the ^%$ I would do. I'd turn myself around and get back in that dugout and change the $%$#@ channel—because I got it right, and that ain't changing!"

There was one occasion in which even I looked at the replay. It was real early in my big league career and I was working second base in Chicago's Comiskey Park. The Yankees' Mickey Rivers hit a long fly to right-center and I went racing out. As outfielder Chet Lemon leaped for the ball a fan stuck out his glove to try to catch it. I'm moving, Lemon is leaping, and the fan is leaning. This was very similar to the play that practically buried Richie Garcia in the Yankees-Orioles playoff game. The rule is clear: The fan can catch any ball after it goes over the wall. But if the fan reaches over the wall onto the playing field to catch the ball, it's interference. When you're moving directly towards the play it's impossible to determine if the fan is reaching over the fence. I had no idea what really happened, but one thing I knew for sure—the ball ended up in the stands. I figured it had to have gotten there somehow. Home run!

White Sox first baseman Jim Spencer led the charge. "It's interference," he was yelling, "that guy interfered with the play."

"The ball went out of the park," I said. Technically, I was absolutely correct. Of course, I never said how it got out.

Bob Lemon was managing the White Sox, and he was generally pretty fair. He came out and got his players away from me, then asked, "You get it right?"

"Lem, that's the best I can do," I admitted. That was enough for Lemon. That night I watched the replay on ESPN. It showed Chet Lemon leaping and the fan leaning over the railing onto the field trying to catch the ball—and missing it completely. Both Chet Lemon and the fan missed the ball! The ball hit the top of the fence and bounced into the stands. We were all wrong. But the rules state that if a ball hits the top of a fence and bounces into the stands it's a home run. So I got it right, but for the wrong reason.

I had a similar play at Yankee Stadium. The Yankees' Mickey Rivers hit a long fly ball down the right field foul line. Tigers outfielder Mickey Stanley went into the corner and leaped for it, and, as he did, a fan leaned over the fence. I was concentrating on whether it was fair or foul. I pumped it fair. I thought I saw it go into the stands, so I began signaling that it was a home run. The next thing I saw was the ball lying on the ground, Stanley was running towards me to complain that the fan had interfered with him, and Rivers was circling the bases. Once again I really couldn't tell if the fan had interfered with Stanley. It didn't look that way to me. But Stanley insisted that he had caught the ball and the fan had taken it out of his glove, which would have been interference and Rivers would have been out. What I eventually discovered was that Stanley had misplayed the ball; it had hit off his glove and bounced right into the fan's hands. Then the fan misplayed the ball, dropping it onto the playing field. Instead of a home run, this should have been a judgment call. What I should have done was called it a dead ball and then placed Rivers on the proper base, probably second. So Stanley missed it, the fan missed it, and I missed it.

I definitely had one of the toughest calls of my career at second base. We were in Anaheim late in the 1997 season and Larry Barnett was behind the plate. With the Angels trailing Seattle by a run in the bottom of the ninth and a runner at second, Jim Edmonds lined a single to right field. Jay Buhner's throw to the plate was a little up the third base line. The catcher had to move a few feet to get the throw, partially blocking Barnett's angle on the play. He just didn't get a good look at it. But the throw beat the runner, the catcher tagged him as he slid by, and Barnett called him out. Game over. The Mariners were running off the field.

The problem was that when the catcher short-hopped the throw he fumbled it—then picked it up quickly and held it up. I had a perfect view of it. There was no question that he lost possession of the ball and the runner was safe. Barnett didn't see him fumble it.

There is a question they supposedly ask students in business school: A customer walking out of a store drops a hundred-dollar bill. You see it and pick up the money. The moral dilemma to be decided is—do you tell your partner?

If I didn't do anything the game was over and we were going home. But if I opened my mouth we could be there for the rest of the night. Obviously I had no choice. I came running in from second base signaling safe, and telling Barnett, "He dropped the ball. He dropped the ball."

There wasn't much of an argument. There was no question that the catcher dropped the ball—apparently it was pretty clear on the instant replay. We ended up playing fourteen innings—fourteen long innings. Four hours and forty minutes. Four long hours and forty long minutes.

At first base you get a lot of close plays on infield grounders, you get some fair and some foul, a lot of appeals on half-swings, and balks. I liked working first base because a lot of first basemen would talk to me. The only third baseman who really liked to talk was George Brett, who liked to tell me dirty jokes while the pitcher was warming up. But first basemen liked to talk. Like George Scott, for example, who I got to know towards the end of his career. The Boomer would talk to anybody. He would be just chattering away. And I can honestly say that in the three seasons I knew him I never understood a single word he said. Not one. Mumble, mumble, mumble, mumble, hmm?

Anything you say, George.

Mumble, mumble. Grunt, mumble.

You got that right, George.

One of the best people I ever met in baseball was Don Mattingly—Donnie Baseball, as he was nicknamed. Mattingly was another guy who loved to talk, although he usually talked about baseball. I'd be at first base, and when he got out in the field after batting the first thing he would do was ask me questions about his swing. This guy is hitting .330 in the major leagues, I couldn't hit a rubber ball in Rochester, and he's asking me about his swing?

Didn't stop me from answering him though.

Each November I hosted a charity dinner in Rochester to raise funds to help kids, and Mattingly was one of the first players to almost volunteer to attend. In 1986, the year after he'd won the American League's Most Valuable Player Award, I was standing behind first base one night and explained to him, "Donnie, I have this little sports dinner up in Rochester for these kids. I'd love to have you come to it."

"Oh, Kais," he said, "I'd really like to, but ever since I won this MVP thing I haven't been able to spend time with my family. I've had to go here and there and . . ."

"That's fine, it's okay, either you want to come or you don't. That's all."

The next night I was behind the plate when Mattingly came to bat. The first pitch was a borderline strike—but definitely a strike. Strike one! As always, I wasn't going to hurt him, but I sure wasn't going to help him. The next pitch was a big breaking ball that dropped into the strike zone. Strike two.

Apparently Mattingly didn't like my calls. He stepped out of the batter's box, took a couple of practice swings, and asked me, "So, Kais, what's the date of that dinner?"

Actually, it was at my dinner that he got his nickname, Donnie Baseball. Kirby Puckett gave it to him. Kirby got up to speak one night and said, "One thing I don't understand. How come every time I want to use the limousine to get around town Donnie Baseball's got it?" Donnie Baseball? That name stuck.

Ed Montague was working first base the night Pete Rose broke baseball's all-time hit record by lining a base hit to center field. It was an incredibly dramatic, emotional moment. The game was stopped and Pete's teammates, his son, and dozens of photographers rushed onto the field. Pete got a huge standing ovation. His eyes filled with tears and it looked like he was crying. Like everybody else, Montague was really moved by Rose's tears. At the end of the inning, when Pete came back out to play first base, Montague went over to congratulate him. As they shook hands Eddie said, "Boy Pete, you got us all a little emotional out here."

"Well, you know," Pete said, "I was thinking about my dad."

Eddie said the gracious, sentimental thing, "Well, you know he's here today somewhere."

Pete looked at him like he was crazy. "No he's not," he said, "he's dead."

First base is pretty much the only place on the field where

you have to rely on your hearing as well as your vision. The way you call close plays at first is to watch the runner's foot as it hits the bag while listening for the sound of the ball hitting the first baseman's glove. And, just like counting the seconds between seeing lightning and hearing thunder is a way of figuring out how far away a storm is, the time between the runner's foot hitting the bag and the sound of the ball being caught is a way of determining how fast the manager would come running out of the dugout. One night in 1987, for example, the Yankees were trailing the White Sox by a run in the late innings, but had a runner on third with two out. Rickey Henderson hit a ground ball to deep short. Ozzie Guillen went into the hole and made a great stop and throw. It was going to be one of those bang-bang plays. If Henderson's safe, the tying run scores. This is a play I'd called hundreds of times. A thousand times. Watch his foot, hear the throw, watch and listen. Here comes Rickey, the throw, Rickey and heeeeeeee . . . slides? He slides into first base? I'd seen players slide into first a few times, but I hadn't been expecting it at all. He raised a big cloud of dirt. In that cloud I couldn't really see his hand touch the base, although I did hear the ball hit the glove. I still had to make some kind of call, though. Again, I just reacted. Out! I gave it the big call. Out! Out!

And herrrrrrre comes Lou Piniella. "No," he was screaming as he jogged towards me, "no way. How can you make that call?"

What could I tell him, that he sounded out to me? "The throw beat him," I shouted right back at him. "I was right on it." And I did want to add, *And you can tell him not to slide into first base anymore!*

No matter where you are in the infield you have to be ready to move fast enough to avoid being hit by a batted ball. If the umpire is hit by a batted ball in fair territory while standing in front of the fielders the ball is dead and all runners who are forced to advance get one base, but if the umpire is standing behind the fielders he is considered part of the playing field. The ball is in play. According to the rules, the umpire is no different than a rock. If the umpire is in foul territory and is hit by a batted ball, the ball is dead and the umpire is still in pain. At first base and third base those line drives would come shooting by me like heat-seeking missiles. They seemed to follow me: I went left, they would curve left. If anybody ever asks you, the answer is yes, you can hear line drives whizzing by your head. There were times when big, strong pull hitters like Dave Winfield, Don Baylor, or Mark McGwire would come to bat against a hittable pitcher and I'd hear people warning from the dugout that all the players who hadn't had children yet should get off the infield. I called those guys three-cup hitters—because, if you got hit in the groin by a line drive hit by one of those people, two protective cups weren't going to be enough.

The hardest-hit ball I ever saw in my career was hit by Don Baylor. I was working third base in Anaheim, the Angels were playing the Yankees. There was a runner on first with no outs, the Angels trailing by a run at home in late innings, a definite bunt situation, and Baylor was the batter. If there was one thing certain in baseball it was that Don Baylor does not bunt. The Yankee third baseman, Graig Nettles, was playing on the grass just behind the infield dirt. Baylor whaled a rising line drive right down the line. Nettles leaped for it, it tipped the top of his glove—it started rising and went over the outfield fence. Home run! Nettles and I were both sort of stunned. I said to him, "I thought you touched that ball."

Nettles nodded, "I did." I turned around and looked into the stands with admiration.

I have to admit that I was always amazed to see fans reach out with bare hands and try to catch line drives just blasted into the stands. I mean, don't you think it might occur to these people that there is a reason fielders wear gloves? Sometimes fans catch a ball, or knock it down and pick it up, then they stand up, hold it over their heads, and show it proudly to the crowd. Or they hand it to a little kid. The other fans applaud. The person who got the ball sits down and we go on with the game, and his catch is forgotten.

My guess is that's about the time the pain usually starts to kick in. I can just imagine these people at home later that night, soaking their swollen hand in an ice bucket as their wife or girlfriend says, "So tell me again what you were thinking when you stuck your bare hand in front of a line drive?"

In the major leagues I never got hit by a batted ball, but I had a lot of near misses. Once, when Dave Winfield was with the Twins, I was at third base in Minnesota. I was in position, my legs planted apart, my hands on my knees—and he hit a line drive right through my legs. It was hit so hard I didn't have a chance to move. I wouldn't have moved anyway, because I never saw it. This is the God's-honest truth, I never saw that ball. A few inches higher and I'd be writing in a higher octave. If that ball had hit me in the head I still wouldn't have seen it.

In the minor leagues I did get hit once, just brushed in the arm, by a line drive. Getting hit is just a matter of bad luck. Dale Ford liked to talk to people on the field, and one day he had his head turned to the side just for a second and somebody smashed a line drive that got him right in the gut. It just bent him in half. But in our locker room after the game he insisted that it didn't hurt. I think his exact words were, "Nobody can hit a ball hard enough to hurt me. Please pass me another ice pack and a few more aspirin and I'll just be sitting here a spell until I start breathing again."

Working the bases is just preparation for a plate job. When you're working the plate you've got something to do every pitch. From the moment you walk onto the field to start the game—and in Kansas City, when Brett would come into the locker room to remind whoever was working the plate that he was his "favorite umpire"—until you're done filling out forms in the locker room after the game, you are in complete control of everything that takes place. You're the boss, the manager, the judge, and the lighting director, you're the captain of the ship, you're even the housekeeper. Each umpire prepared differently when he had the plate. Some umpires reviewed the starting pitchers so they knew what kind of pitches to expect, others would be very quiet and withdrawn, a lot of umpires wouldn't eat before working the plate. Me? I went out there and did the job. Not eat? Trust me, you put me behind a plate, I'm going to eat.

Plate jobs begin with the pregame meeting at home to exchange lineup cards and go over the ground rules. The first time I worked in Fenway Park, Don Zimmer was managing the Red Sox. Fenway has an odd shape and there are a few things about it you need to understand. Zim was telling me all about the Green Monster, the ladder hanging on the wall in play, and finally he looked at me and said, "And then there's the two cockatoos who have a nest on top of the wall. It's pretty amazing, they come back every year and live up there. Mr. Yawkey . . ." the Red Sox owner, "really likes them, so we've had to put in a ground rule."

As Zim is explaining this to me he's pointing to the top of the wall. I looked out there but I couldn't see any birds. But I was a big league umpire and here was a big league manager giving me instructions, and I didn't want him to know I didn't have the slightest idea what he was talking about. So I nodded in agreement.

"See, if a batted ball hits the male cockatoo, that's the one with the red tail feathers, the ball is dead and it's two bases."

He stopped, and I just fell right in line, asking him, "What if it hits the female?"

Zim looked at me, "It's all you can get."

Usually the pregame meetings are professional and cordial—it's a baseball business meeting. There's nothing very interesting about them. But in 1996 I had the plate for a Mariners-Indians game in Seattle. These two teams just didn't like each other. That happens, and every time they played it felt like we were always one tight pitch away from a brawl. So, before one of the games, I told umpire Joe Brinkman, "I'm gonna loosen up these guys."

I waited until the three other umpires, Piniella, and Indians manager Mike Hargrove were at the plate before I joined them. I kept my head down until I got there, so until that moment nobody knew I was wearing a pirate's black patch over one eye. For a few seconds nobody reacted. Then Piniella looked at me and asked, "What is that thing? You okay?"

I told him, "It's nothing. Don't worry about it, it's just an eye patch."

Just an eye patch? Don't worry about it? Piniella's problem was that he knew me well enough to know that maybe I was serious.

"I'm telling you, it's nothing. It's just temporary," I added. That's when Hargrove started laughing. It really did reduce the tension.

When I came up to the big leagues, umpires were still required to wear a blue sports jacket when they worked the plate. That was the tradition. I never knew why, maybe so we could be properly dressed if a dinner party broke out. At least we didn't have to wear the ties that had once been part of the uniform. But we did have to wear caps. Most of us wore regular baseball caps, but some of the veterans still wore those silly caps with the very small brim. I hated those things; they made grown men look like little boys, like the Cub Scouts.

In the American League we were still using the mattress protectors, but one of the greatest benefits of being in the big leagues was that we didn't have to lug it around with us from city to city. In the minors I'd lived with that thing. But in the majors they kept them in the ballparks. When we worked the plate we wore special pants with extra large legs to allow room for shin guards, and most umpires carried a pencil to make changes on the lineup cards, a whisk broom to clean the plate, and an indicator to keep track of balls, strikes, and outs. Most umpires. I didn't exactly march to a different drummer, I walked to a different trombone player.

I did carry the little whisk broom, but I didn't use it too often. I did the things that had to be done my own way. It's true that some umpires were a little more immaculate than I was. When they worked the plate it had to be cleaned of every speck of dirt. I didn't feel all that strongly about it. I'll be honest, when I was growing up my room at home wasn't that clean—and I had to live there. Most of the time when there was dirt on the plate I used my foot to sweep it clean. There were some umpires who thought that was scandalous behavior. They used to complain about it: Kaiser's lazy, he never cleans his plate. Kaiser doesn't bend over and clean the plate with his whisk broom. I didn't grow up expecting to hear the commissioner of baseball telling me to clean my plate.

As long as I could see the plate it was clean enough for me. And when was the last time you heard someone commenting about an umpire, *He really cleans his plate well?* And now just about everybody cleans it the Kaiser way.

The indicator is a little piece of plastic shaped to fit into your hand. It has three rotating dials that allow an umpire to keep track of balls, strikes, and outs. Most people think it can't be that tough to remember how many balls, strikes, and outs there are. All you got to do is be able to count to four. But too many things happen during a game to disturb your concentration. For example, you've got a 2-2 count on the batter and the runner tries to steal third on a low outside fastball; he gets caught in a rundown. The shortstop overthrows the third baseman and the runner goes for the plate. He collides with the catcher, who manages to hold on to the ball for the out. You make the call.

Everything calms down. What's the count on the batter again? The correct answer is 3-2—the pitch on which the runner took off was ball three, but in the confusion it got overlooked. Umpires do lose count. Believe me, there is nothing more embarrassing to an umpire than calling a batter out on two strikes. It happens to players, too. Hey, the only thing the players in the field have to remember is how many outs there are. The most there can be is three, so that's a tough one to get wrong. But at least once in every season of my career a batter struck out for the second out of the inning and the catcher would roll the ball back to the mound and start to go to the dugout, or an outfielder would catch a ball for the second out of the inning and start running in. These people are being paid a million dollars a year and can't get one-two-three right. One time Larry Walker caught a fly ball for what he believed to be the third out and flipped it into the stands to a fan—and when he saw the base runners take off he realized that it was only the second out and that he had just tossed a ball still in play into the stands. He had to grab it out of the fan's hands and throw it back in.

I used an indicator in the minor leagues and when I first came up, but I hated it. After every pitch you're supposed to click it to record the pitch, and I did; but there were too many times when I looked at my indicator to get the right count and it read: Balls 4, Strikes 3. I had completely lost the count. When that happened the first thing I'd do is hope like hell that the batter hit the next pitch. If he did I got to start over. If he didn't I'd check the scoreboard, which most of the time had the correct count. And when I really got desperate, I'd ask the catcher for help. But I'd try not to let him know I'd lost it, saying things like, "Hey, you got the same count I do?"

"Three and one?"

"Yeah, that's right. Three and one." The truth is that, for the last fifteen years of my career, I didn't even bother carrying the indicator.

Just about every umpire has lost track of balls, strikes, or outs at some point in his career. Jerry Layne was behind the plate in San Diego on the night of September 9, 1999—9/9/99. The Padres were playing the Expos. In the seventh inning Reggie Sanders struck out for what Layne thought was the third out of the inning—but none of the players acted as if the inning was over. Instead of rolling the ball back to the mound, for example, catcher Chris Widger threw it to third base as if there were less than three outs. The Expos didn't run off the field, and the next Padres batter, Phil Nevin, stepped into the batter's box. Layne checked his indicator—which read Outs 2. So much for the value of an indicator. Layne thought, I've got to be wrong. It's not possible that I'm right and everybody else is wrong.

The count on Nevin went to 2-1. Finally, Layne realized that in fact he was wrong to assume that everybody on the field couldn't be wrong while he was right. It was a moment of mass insecurity. Obviously, when nobody moved, everybody must have assumed they had lost track of the number of outs. Phil Nevin had an interesting theory. "I thought there were three outs, but the Expos stayed on the field, so I went up to bat. I figured maybe they do things different in Canada, because of the exchange rate."

The one position player umpires really do get to know is the catcher. Catchers can help you or help bury you. The catcher controls the manager, the manager controls his players, the managers and players can get the fans on you. So, if you don't get along with the catcher you can end up with the whole world against you.

Catchers can help or hurt an umpire a lot of different ways. When a pitch comes in every catcher tries to move his glove into the strike zone. The announcers call it "framing the pitch." What they really mean is trying to steal a strike. The best ever at that was Bob Boone. Boone was so smooth that he could be sitting in the dugout and still move an outside pitch into the strike zone. When Boone was behind the plate I'd watch the pitch coming in and it would start out off the plate and then break maybe two feet outside, but somehow, by the time Boone caught it, that ball would look like it just nipped the corner.

There were also some catchers who would take strikes away. Instead of just *eaaasssssing* the ball into their glove, they'd take a smack at it. Cliff Johnson, for example, would just knock down pitches rather than catching them. I nicknamed him "Steel Hands."

A catcher or pitcher can incite the dugout and the fans by their reaction to a call. I hated catchers who tried to show me up by catching the ball and then holding his glove perfectly still. The message is clear: *I just want you and every person in the ballpark and those people watching on TV to get a real good look at it, because you blew that call.* One guy who did that all the time was Rick Dempsey. Most umpires would have disliked Dempsey even if he wasn't wearing an Orioles uniform—that was just a little extra incentive. He'd set up his target a foot outside the plate and Jim Palmer would throw a pitch right into his glove. Dempsey would jump up, start to roll the ball back to the mound, and head for the dugout. From the dugout and the stands it looked like it had to be a perfect strike—the catcher didn't have to move his glove. Sure, Dempsey set up off the plate, Palmer's pitch was a foot outside—and everybody screamed at the umpire.

There are some pitchers who would try to intimidate the umpire when they had two strikes on a hitter by throwing a pitch then starting to walk off the mound. Doug Harvey was behind the plate for a Cubs-Phillies game in the late 1960s. Larry Jackson was pitching and Dick Bertell was catching. The count was a ball and two strikes on the Phillies' Wes Covington. Jackson's next pitch was a hard slider on the inside corner. Doug's strike zone was exactly as it is described in the rule book: the ball had to cross the plate to be a strike. This pitch was a little bit inside. Ball two! Bertell caught it and held it still. Jackson leaped straight up into the air about a foot. "Why Doug," Bertell complained loudly, "what was wrong with that pitch?"

"The ball's inside," Doug told him.

Jackson's next pitch was even closer. For some umpires it probably would have been a strike, but not for Doug Harvey. Ball three! Again Bertell caught it and held it perfectly still. This time Jackson leaped at least two feet into the air. "Come on, Doug," Bertell screamed, "that's a good pitch."

"Ball's high," Doug told him flatly.

The next pitch in the sequence was a pretty good pitch. It was close, very close. "Ball four, take your base!" Doug shouted. Jackson leaped three feet straight up into the air. Bertell couldn't believe it. "Doug, Doug," he screamed, "what was wrong with that one?"

Doug leaned over his shoulder and told him. "Not too much, but I just wanted to see how high Jackson could jump."

Some catchers like to talk to umpires and batters, others never say one word. Occasionally, Gary Carter would try to confuse the hitters by telling them exactly what the next pitch was going to be: "This one's going to be a fastball away, get ready for it." And that's what the pitch would be. Then he'd do it again: "Slider away." You could hear those hitters thinking. And as Yogi Berra once explained, you can't think and hit at the same time.

Apparently Yogi would talk to everyone when he was catching. He'd comment on every call. Good call. Or, what was the matter with that one? One day he got into a conversation with a veteran umpire named Red Flaherty. Yogi complained about a call and Flaherty told him, honestly, "Hey, Yog, I'm not infallible."

Yogi asked, "What the hell does that mean?"

Flaherty explained, "It means that I'm not perfect, that every once in a while I miss one."

"Hey," Yogi said in a complimentary voice, "you're the most infallible umpire in the league."

A lot of batters will ask the umpire after swinging and missing: Was that a good pitch? Where was it? Was it a strike? The correct answer was: Hey, if it was good enough to swing at, it was good enough for me to call it a strike. What did they expect me to say? *Good enough to fool a hitter like you.*

There are batters who will ask that same question to the catcher after a called strike. Eric Gregg was behind the plate when Carter was catching for the Expos, and several hitters asked Carter about the call. Carter didn't answer, he didn't want to get in an argument with Eric. Instead he would hold his hand up to indicate that the pitch was a little too high, or down to indicate it was low. The second base umpire saw that and told Eric that Carter was trying to stick it to him.

The next time Carter came to bat the first pitch to him bounced in the dirt. That was good enough for Eric. Strike one! Carter whirled his head around, his mouth was open, "Eric! Come on, where was it?"

Eric looked right at him—and held his hand about waist high.

There were some really good people back there. The Rangers' Ivan Rodriguez has more ability than any catcher I ever saw, and he's also a really good kid. He wasn't much of a conversationalist, but on occasion he would warn me, "Better stay loose today, this guy is wild. Be careful, you could get hurt."

Mike Scioscia was great at defusing a situation. He was always in control. If his pitcher started complaining or showing up the umpire, Scioscia would tell the umpire, "Don't worry about it, I've got him. He just doesn't see very well from the pitcher's mound."

And nobody was a better guy than the Kansas City Royals' Mike Macfarlane. There are catchers who will stick up for the umpire when he's right, but on occasion Macfarlane stuck up for me when I was wrong. When you're calling 250 pitches a game, a lot of them thrown at more than ninety miles an hour—which means it takes slightly more than half a second to get from the pitcher's hand to the catcher's glove—and then the ball is curving or dropping or rising, and maybe the batter is in a crouch. Admittedly, there are times when you're not going to get every call quite as right as you would like. There were a few pitches every game that I knew I missed. But once I made a call I lived with it. Macfarlane was the only catcher who protected me. I called a pitch a ball, the Kansas City dugout started screaming it was a strike—and in rare instances they were probably right—and Macfarlane yelled into the dugout, "It was outside."

There is a kid whose parents raised him right.

One time Phillies catcher Darren Daulton protected umpire Joe West. Maybe. When Jim Fregosi was managing Philadelphia, West was having a tough game with him. The whole dugout was complaining. Finally, Fregosi came out to talk to his pitcher. Daulton joined him on the mound. After a minute or so West went out there to break up the meeting. As he walked back to the plate with Daulton, the catcher started shaking his head. "What's the matter?" West asked him.

"Well, Joe," he replied, "the things that they were saying about you out there were so bad it even pissed *me* off."

Unfortunately, umpires also have to deal with some pretty unpleasant players behind the plate. Some people have off days, these are the kind of people who have off lives. There was a journeyman catcher named Duke Sims who was angry when he woke up in the morning and never recovered. The Mets' Jerry Grote was a similarly wonderful guy. Eric Gregg said, "He was the kind of guy that when the game started I'd say to him, 'Good afternoon,' and he'd growl, 'What's so ^&$^#% good about it?' "

Legendary minor league umpire Augie Guglielmo spent only a single season in the big leagues. One day he got into an argument with a catcher, supposedly it was future Hall of Famer Roy Campanella. Augie told Campy, "I feel like chewing your head right off your shoulders and swallowing it down to my stomach."

To which Campy replied, "If you did that, Augie, you'd have more brains in your gut than you do in your head."

But, once again, the award goes to . . . the Baltimore Orioles' Rick Dempsey. Dempsey and I never got along, never.

He was with six different big league teams, although his best years were with the Orioles. We knew each other from the minor leagues, and in 1976 he told a reporter, "If Kaiser ever goes to the big leagues I'll retire."

Talk about an incentive! A year later I was working the plate at Memorial Stadium in Baltimore. When he came out to start the game I didn't say a word to him, I just smiled. And the first time he whined about a call I didn't say a thing. The second time he complained about a call I still didn't respond. Finally he said something like, "What's the matter with you, can't you hear?"

I looked right at him: "Hey, Dempsey," I said, "I guess I'm just surprised to see you here. I heard you were going to retire." He just wasn't fair behind the plate. He was always doing something to get Weaver started, framing a pitch, jumping up, shaking his head. I don't know a single umpire who liked him. But as proof that there is some justice in the world, for most of his career he had to play for Earl Weaver. No two people have ever deserved each other more. And they didn't get along at all. Several times they had to be held apart—and one thing I guarantee is that no umpires did any of the holding. One time Weaver took Dempsey out of the game, Dempsey was furious. He took off his catcher's equipment and threw it on the ground. Weaver was shouting at him the whole time. Then Dempsey started walking up the ramp into the clubhouse. Weaver followed him up the ramp into the clubhouse, still shouting at him every step of the way. Dempsey walked into the clubhouse, ripped off his uniform, walked into the shower and turned it on—and when he did Weaver was standing right behind him in the shower still shouting at him.

What made Dempsey even angrier was the fact that Weaver would never let him call the pitches. One day the two of them got into another shouting match and Weaver was just all over Dempsey. Finally Dempsey turned to Dale Ford and appealed to him, "You gotta help me with him."

Dale looked right at Dempsey and spoke for me and a lot of other umpires when he replied, "Help you? Are you kidding me? I %$#$#@ hate you."

After I'd worked a few seasons in the league I got to know the veteran pitchers, too. And just like the batters, after seeing them work a few times I got to know what to expect from them—from their pitches and their mouths. Most pitchers were smart enough not to try to show up the plate umpire, because eventually they were going to see him back there again. If you're not born stupid you want to have a good relationship with the home plate umpire. But, occasionally, some pitcher would react to my call by staring into the sky or shaking his head.

Instead of complaining on the mound, what they would do is talk to me at the end of the half inning, on the way to the dugout. They'd stop and ask seriously, "Isn't that ball breaking?" "Is that pitch really missing the corner?" Obviously, what they really mean to say is, *Listen you $^%$#, what the ^&$# is wrong with you? Those are good pitches and you're killing me out there. Sir.*

Several times, I had pitchers who tried to show me up stop by the plate at the end of the half inning to explain, "Hey, I'm mad at myself. Not you." Sure they were. That was fine with me, it meant we had something in common: I was mad at them too.

Some pitchers were what is known as surveyors, which means that the instant they released a pitch they were already glaring in at me. These were the pitchers who believed every pitch they threw should be a strike. The Yankees' Ed Figueroa was a complainer. He'd break off a curveball that bounced four feet in front of home plate, and when it was called a ball he'd stand on the mound muttering and kicking the dirt. The Tigers' Jack Morris complained about everything. Everything was bad, the plate wasn't clean enough, I missed a pitch, I was wearing an ugly belt, everything. The Orioles'—what a surprise, right?—Jim Palmer complained all the time. But there is one thing I will admit about Palmer. He beat me once. Just once.

After a ball was fouled out of play, or if a ball got dirty, or even if a pitcher just didn't like the feel of a baseball, I'd put a new baseball in play. The pitcher would look at the new ball I'd given him and most of the time keep it. But, every once in a while a pitcher would decide he didn't like the new ball and toss it in to me to be exchanged for another new ball. I am now about to reveal, for the first time, my big secret. When that happened I'd put the first ball in my ball bag—and then I would take out the same ball and throw it back to the pitcher. The same ball! I did it a thousand times. Two thousand. Only once did a pitcher realize what I'd done. Jim Palmer. One afternoon in Baltimore I tossed him a new ball and he looked at it, rolled it over in his hand, walked a few steps towards the plate and flipped it back to me, telling me, "This is the same ball I just gave you."

Guilty. But, you know what Palmer, I'm mad at myself for doing that. Not at you.

There were a few pitchers who really gave me a hard time. When Toronto's Dave Stieb didn't like a call, for example, he'd look up at the sky as if praying for a new umpire. Of course, there are some people who would have suggested that if he really wanted a new umpire he was looking for help in the wrong direction. But, sometimes when a pitcher did that, I'd walk out in front of the plate and ask them, "What's happening? Something wrong?" *No, you kidding me Kais, everything's great. You're beautiful, love you big guy*. "Oh, okay, just checking."

If I really got angry at a pitcher, when he needed a new ball I'd roll it or bounce it out to him. I used to love doing that on Astroturf. I'd try to short-hop it right into his shins. In fact, I was fined $500 for rolling the ball to the mound. I was working the plate in Chicago and the White Sox brought in a rookie pitcher. His first pitch, this might even have been his first pitch in the big leagues, hit me square in the mask. I knew it wasn't intentional, I knew it wasn't his fault, but it was just one of those days when every little thing had gone wrong. So I got angry—and I rolled the ball back to the pitcher.

Here comes White Sox manager Terry Bevington. "That's real nice," he said, "you showed a lot of class." Bevington and all umpires had a mutual dislike for each other. Bevington didn't even like the color blue. So we got into a real good one. I'd had a bad day. The coffee was cold, the lines were long, the luggage was late, it was one of those days. And it was really nice after having a completely frustrating day to have such a perfect opportunity to get out all my anger, all that frustration. Standing in front of me was the only good thing Terry Bevington ever did for me. We got into a hellacious fight. I tossed him and then I undressed him. If he came too close to me I'd try to step on his feet. He'd back off. We were doing the umpire-two-step. Eventually I was fined $500 for the offense of rolling the ball. Worth every penny.

I was only fined one other time in my entire career. The American League fined me another $500 for cutting off the sleeves of my uniform shirt and wearing a long-sleeved jersey underneath it. They asked me why I did it. I told them I wore the jersey because it was cold outside. Now, admittedly, I didn't take a vote to find out if it was officially cold. Some people get in trouble for wearing too little in public, I wore too much.

Hall of Famer Gaylord Perry would complain once in awhile. Gaylord was always looking for an advantage. Everybody knew he was putting some substance on the baseball to make it move erratically, but nobody really wanted to catch him doing it. There was no advantage to it. The league office never pushed very hard to stop him. In reality, if they had come down hard on him they would have had to do the same thing to a lot of other pitchers who defaced the ball; it's just that Gaylord got tremendous publicity for doing it. There never was any doubt that he threw a spitball, or a Vaseline ball, or a vodka and tonic ball, whatever it was he put on the baseball to make it drop suddenly—but it wouldn't have made any difference if he wasn't a very good pitcher. Believe me, I could have put mustard, ketchup, and mayonnaise on a ball and it wouldn't have made me a major league pitcher. One time, I remember, on a really hot day in Texas, Luciano was behind the plate and Gaylord was on the mound against the Yankees. From the first pitch Billy Martin was screaming at Ronnie, "Look at the ball, look at the ball."

Every pitch, "He's loading it up." Finally Gaylord threw a pitch that dropped straight down like it had been hit by a hammer. Martin insisted Ronnie search Perry. Just imagine this: it was about 130°, Gaylord was drenched in sweat, and Ronnie was supposed to frisk him to find out where he was hiding the Vaseline. This was not a real enviable job. Ronnie looked in Gaylord's glove, on his wrists, on the back of his neck, in the band of his cap and finally Perry said to him, "Don't look under my armpits."

There was one thing we all knew for sure. One place Ronnie was not going to search was Gaylord Perry's armpits. When Ronnie finished his search Martin was shouting at him from the dugout, "You didn't look under his armpits."

Ronnie looked at Billy and nodded knowingly. Then he grinned.

Only one time did I have a problem with Gaylord. In addition to everything else, he threw the puff ball. He would cover his hands and the baseball with rosin, so that when he released his pitch a white puff of rosin would explode into the air. It was really distracting for the batter, not to mention the home plate umpire. A couple of umpires had tried to stop him, but there was no rule against it. So I said, "I'll show you how to stop him." The first time I saw him loading it up I told the batter, I think it was Don Kessinger, who was then with the White Sox, "Don't swing at this pitch." It was a good pitch, had a lot of the plate. Ball one! Gaylord looked at me but didn't say anything. But he loaded it up again. This time the pitch split the plate. Ball two! I asked the catcher for the ball and threw it out. As I stepped in front of the plate and tossed a new ball to him, I warned, "You keep putting that stuff on there, I can't see the pitch. It's distracting, you know what I mean?"

He never threw another one when I was behind the plate.

Eddie Watt, a relief pitcher who had a pretty good major league career, actually went a little further than Gaylord when he was finishing up in the minors. One year in the Pacific Coast League playoffs his team was getting clobbered, so Watt went into his wind-up—and threw the rosin bag.

In thirty years working behind the plate I pretty much saw everything a pitcher could do to make a baseball move in and out, up and down, fast and slow. Pitchers would throw anything up there that would make it harder for a batter to hit the ball, but the truth is that there still is nothing better than an old-fashioned great fastball. A lot of pitchers can fire it up there for a few pitches. For an inning Goose Gossage threw as hard as anybody I ever saw, but the only pitchers I ever saw who could sustain it for nine innings, thirty times a season were Nolan Ryan and Randy Johnson. And in Ryan's case, for twenty-seven years. Think about that, twenty-seven years. Gilligan wasn't even on his island that long. Three different teams retired the number Ryan wore when he pitched for them.

Basketball coaches say that you can't teach height; but baseball scouts know you can't teach speed either. Umpires liked to say that Ryan was the fastest pitcher they never saw. Players too. One time, after taking a third strike from Ryan, Mickey Stanley shook his head and decided, "Those were the best pitches I ever heard." Nobody liked to hit against him. But people would also say that the thing that made him so effective was his great curveball; once he proved that he could throw his curveball and changeup for strikes, hitters couldn't sit back and wait for his fastball. Maybe, but the fact that he struck out 5,714 batters means that there were a lot of people who could be waiting for that fastball for a couple of weeks and still couldn't hit it.

Randy Johnson was the scariest pitcher I ever saw. He's six-ten, and when he strides forward and brings his arm around he looks like he's reaching out to pick your pocket. From behind. A lot of people have asked me to describe Johnson's fastball, or Ryan's express. To hit it, you have to start your swing in the on-deck circle. Both Johnson and Ryan had the added advantage of being really wild when they were younger. They just reared back and threw it as fast as they could. Their pitches were all over the place. Hitters used to thank me for calling them out on strikes. *Hey, Kais, nice call, I'll be heading back to the safety of the dugout now. Nice seeing you.* Who could blame them? Johnson threw 500 miles an hour and had no idea where the pitch was going. It could just as easily bounce up to the plate as sail over the batter's head. Randy Johnson is the only pitcher I ever heard of who killed a bird with a pitched ball. That is absolutely true. In spring training he hit a dove with a pitch. Well, obviously he had that good, high fastball working.

Hitting that bird created an interesting rules problem for the umpires. What do you call it? There is a rule that states, "If a batted or thrown ball strikes a bird or other animal on the playing field, consider the ball alive and in play."

So, under that rule the bird was dead and ball was live. But the rule doesn't mention a pitched ball. The umpires called it no pitch. That meant that both the bird and the ball were dead.

Because Randy Johnson had the same last name as umpire Mark Johnson they used to call each other "Cuz." *How ya doing Cuz? What's up, Cuz?* But, one night in Seattle when Mark Johnson was behind the plate, Randy bounced one up there and the ball hit him right in groin. Mark Johnson went down hard. He was rolling around on the ground in pain, his face was turning blue, he was moaning. Randy Johnson stood over him, genuinely upset, "You all right, Cuz?" he asked.

"Ummphh," Mark Johnson replied. "Oooshhooot."

He was really in pain, but there wasn't much anybody could do for him on the field. I'll tell you one thing they weren't going to do for him, they weren't going to rub it. They carried him off on a stretcher. I found him in the training room after the game, a large ice pack sitting right where he got hit. "How you doing?"

"Ooggkkk," he explained. "Oooo."

No matter how fast the pitcher was, a pitched ball never caused me to blink. You blink once and the ball is in the catcher's glove. But I did blink on some swings—okay, on a lot of swings. I think pretty much every umpire does. It's an involuntary response, particularly after you've been hit in the mask by foul tips a few times.

As pitchers get older or hurt their arms they lose velocity. It may be just a little, but it makes a big difference. You can see it happening. After you've been behind the plate for enough games you can see the beginning of the end of a career. Everything starts and ends with the fastball. The fastball just isn't as crisp. Suddenly it's hittable. And that affects all the other pitches, the break of the curveball just isn't quite as sharp, the slider doesn't drop so suddenly. Roger Clemens threw hard for a lot of years. When he started losing velocity he worked to develop a new pitch, a splitter, that kept hitters off balance. I had the plate for Clemens' two hundredth win. What helped make Clemens so successful for so long was the fear factor. His control was just bad enough to keep hitters real loose at the plate.

The slowest-working pitcher I ever saw was Luis Tiant. Tiant's windup looked like a movie clip in which every third frame had been cut out and then put back in the wrong place. No one ever had a windup anything like it. I could have balked him on every pitch he threw. He would . . . raise his . . . arms and . . . kick up a . . . leg, then bring . . . his arm . . . his arm . . . his arm . . . back, and start to push . . . forward. . . . He was as hard to follow as that sentence. I think he was so successful because batters got bored waiting for the ball to reach home plate. Believe me, it's easier to get a plumber on Sunday than it was to time a Tiant pitch. He'd go into his windup, and into his windup, and continue his windup—hey, let's go Luis we're all getting older back here—and continue his windup and then, continue his windup, and finally throw the ball. By that point the batter's timing was destroyed. But umpires liked him. He never complained, he never said much of anything, and his pitches looked so hittable his games moved pretty quickly.

The slowest pitches were knuckleballs. Attempting to hit a knuckleball was like trying to punch a dandelion. The ball was never where it was. Trying to call it wasn't a picnic in the ballpark either. You had to wait, wait, wait, wait, and then wait, and wait until it crossed home plate. And then call it. It's hard to have ball-and-strike arguments with a knuckleball pitcher. Charlie Hough was pitching one day in Texas when Bobby Valentine was managing the Rangers. He threw a pitch, I called it a ball. Nobody complained, but when the inning was over Bobby came over to me and asked, nicely, "Kais, what was wrong with that pitch?"

I said, "Bobby, you know what? When he throws it he doesn't know where it's going. Your catcher can't catch it. The batter can't hit it. You can't see it, but you expect me to call it?"

Like most knuckleball pitchers, Charlie Hough started in professional baseball as a normal person. He was a light-hitting infielder in Single-A ball when Tommy Lasorda told him that unless he came up with some sort of miracle he was going to be released. Thrown out of baseball. So Charlie learned to throw the knuckler in about a week—and two years later he was making his major league debut. Lasorda brought him in to face the Pirates' Hall of Famer Willie Stargell late in a game with two out and the bases loaded. Hough threw five straight knuckleballs and went to a full count. Then he figured, "I know what I'll do, I throw him my fastball. He definitely won't be expecting a fastball in this situation."

Hough went into his windup and as he got ready to release the ball he suddenly remembered, *I don't have a fastball. That's why I learned how to throw a knuckleball.* But it was too late. He was committed to the fastball. Or in his case, the mediocreball. Stargell was so surprised that he took the pitch for a called third strike.

Hough had a good one, but Wilber Wood threw the best knuckler I ever saw. That thing moved around more than a butterfly in a hurricane. And that was the first knuckleball I ever saw. I was still in Double-A ball. I was assigned to work a spring training intrasquad game for the Pirates in Bradenton. For me, this was a big break, a chance to get noticed. I was doing great behind the plate with fastballs, curveballs, change-ups, sliders—and then Wilber Weed came in. He went into a nice easy windup and sort of pushed the ball towards the plate. Suddenly it started dipping, rising, curving, dropping, sliding, up and down and in and out. I had never seen anything like that in my life. At least when I was sober. *What the %$# was that?* I wondered.

Then he threw another one. That's just about all he threw. I had real problems calling it, and I figured there had to be something wrong with me. And I felt that way until Richie Zisk got up to bat. Wood threw his first pitch to Zisk. It looked like it was going to break down and away. Zisk leaned over the plate and took a hell of a cut at it.

It hit him in the forehead.

Knuckleballs aren't thrown hard enough to hurt anybody. Zisk was more embarrassed than hurt. To be able to throw that pitch for a strike was amazing. But Hough could do it, Wilber Wood could do it, Phil Niekro could do it. Mike Mussina throws a knuckle curve, which looks a lot like a curveball to me. I saw thousands of pitches during my career. Ryan and Johnson were the fastest. Wood threw the best knuckleball. Bert Blyleven had the best curveball I ever called—it broke a foot and a half in any direction he wanted it to. For a while at least, Ron Guidry threw the best hard slider I ever saw—the bottom would drop right out faster than a lead anvil in a wet carton. Relief pitcher Doug Jones had the best change-up—his pitches seemed to change speeds in mid-flight. Gaylord threw the best doctored ball, obviously, followed not too far behind by Ray Miller. The toughest motion to follow was Tiant's, and right behind his was the Royals reliever Dan Quisenberry's, who threw full sidearm, and sort of slung it towards the plate. He was tough to hit because the ball came at the batter from such an unusual angle, but that angle also made it easy to call balls and strikes when he was on the mound. Jack Morris had the best split-fingered fastball. Catfish and Frank Tanana had the best control. And Ed Figueroa was the most often out of control.

No one keeps any statistics about umpires—not even umpires—with the exception of how many ejections you get a season. So I don't have any idea how many times I worked the plate in my major league career. At an average of about forty times a year it would have to be close to a thousand plate jobs. I can't even guess how many batters or pitchers I saw, or pitches I called. Working the plate was a tough job. It required complete concentration. So when the game was over I was exhausted. It was like being on stage for three or four hours, and it takes a little time to come down after a game. I'd usually sit around the dressing room, maybe have something to eat, shower, and talk with my partners about the game. And when I left the ballpark there were often a few fans who would recognize me and ask for my autograph. If I paused to think about my next game, which I didn't do that often, there were two beautiful words I focused on: third base.

6

Strike zones are like personalities; everybody's got one, and no two are the same. The strike zone is probably the most important part of the playing field, even though it doesn't really exist. It's an imaginary box. Umpires don't even have a rigid strike zone—it changes from batter to batter. And, unlike those big mattress protectors, the strike zone is really easy to carry with you from city to city.

Everything in the game begins with the strike zone. In umpire school the strike zone was one of the first things they taught us. They showed us a diagram of a batter standing almost upright with a darkened box in front of him. There it is, that's the strike zone. If a pitched ball passes through any part of this imaginary box and the batter doesn't swing at it, it's a called strike. If a pitched ball is outside the box and the batter doesn't swing, it's a ball. That's it, that's all there is to it. *Whoa, this is easier than I thought it was going to be.*

That would have been great, as long as that diagram didn't move. But when they started putting real people up to bat who crouched down, and then they started throwing pitches that didn't go straight, it got a little more complicated. The problems are that every hitter is a different height and uses a different batting stance, and that pitches rise, drop, and curve inside and outside as they reach the strike zone, and that catchers stand up or move inside or outside and tend to block the umpire's view of the pitch.

The strike zone was defined in the rules for the first time in 1907. "A fairly delivered ball is a ball pitched or thrown to the bat by the pitcher . . . that passes over any portion of the home base before touching the ground, not lower than the batman's knee nor higher than his shoulder. For every such fairly delivered ball, the umpire shall call one strike." Since that time baseball has tried to change the strike zone every few years. If they wanted to speed up the game, for example, or increase scoring, they would tell umpires to make their strike zone wider, or start calling higher pitches strikes, which would force batters to swing at more pitches. And, if they wanted to decrease scoring they would . . . well, they never wanted to decrease scoring.

Every umpire has to determine his own strike zone. For Doug Harvey the ball had to be over the plate and between the imaginary parallel lines. Durwood Merrill's strike zone was wide in the first few innings, but would change during the game. Ed Runge, who retired in 1970, was known for supersizing his strike zone. They used to describe his strike zone as "toes to nose, dugout to dugout." When Runge worked the plate in the fifteen-inning-long 1967 All-Star game, twenty-nine batters struck out. That's twenty-nine All-Stars going down. They were going down in waves. Twenty-nine strikeouts. For Vic Voltaggio a strike basically had to be somewhere between first and third base. Home plate is seventeen inches wide, Voltaggio's strike zone was good enough for a first down. He was behind the plate on April 29, 1986. Roger Clemens was pitching for the Red Sox against Seattle. I watched this game on television. I suspected in the first inning that it might be a special night when Clemens threw a fastball maybe a foot outside and Voltaggio called it a strike. Well, I figured, he missed one early. No big deal. We all do. Every umpire knows that if you get them swinging the bat everybody goes home sooner. But then Clemens threw another pitch that was even further outside. And Vic called it strike two.

Clemens was overpowering that night. Then you add to that a strike zone about the size of, say, Sacramento and he was practically unhittable. I don't think Babe Ruth could have hit him that night. The Mariners definitely couldn't. That night Clemens set the major league record with twenty strikeouts, eight of them called third strikes. And, of course, he didn't walk anybody.

The fact that Voltaggio had a very big strike zone that night doesn't mean he had a bad game. Vic Voltaggio was a good umpire. The size of a man's strike zone doesn't really matter—there are some fine umpires known for their small strike zones—what does matter is that it's exactly the same for both teams and that it's consistent from the first pitch to the last out. Teams play with the same ball, they can play with the same strike zone.

The strike zone as defined in the rule book, "that area over home plate the upper limit of which is a horizontal line at the midpoint between the top of the shoulders and the top of the uniform pants, and the lower level is a line at the hollow beneath the knee cap," is a myth. It doesn't exist. It's a nonexistent imaginary box. It has always not existed, but the situation used to be much worse. When the American League was using the mattress we would crouch directly behind the catcher, while National Leaguers used the inside protector and had to get down much lower. As a result, American Leaguers called higher strikes and National Leaguers got a better look at lower pitches, while never getting a real good look at the outside corner.

No two umpires have the same strike zones. People see differently, they stand in slightly different positions behind the plate, they react differently to pitches, they have different philosophies of what a strike is. I was always considered a very good ball-and-strike umpire. I got a good look at pitches as they crossed the plate. I didn't really have a firm definition of my strike zone, except to say that I knew a strike when I saw it. It varied from batter to batter, pitcher to pitcher. The little guys who crouched over the plate were tough to call. Rickey Henderson, for example, was almost impossible. Generally, umpires call strikes that are on the plate between the top of the batter's belt and his knees. Rickey was small to begin with, and then he'd crouch over and hang his hands out over the plate and his belt was practically resting on his knees. According to the current interpretation, his strike zone was maybe a couple of inches high. For me, a pitch had to be close enough to the plate for the batter to hit it to be a strike. I missed a few, everybody did, but I tended to agree with Hall of Fame umpire Nestor Chylak, who advised umpires, "Never ever call a strike a ball. You can call a ball a strike once in awhile, but never the opposite, because it slows down the game."

Every few years major league baseball decides it's time to change the strike zone. They usually announce it to the media like they were tailoring a suit, *We're just going to add an inch to the top*. They pretend that the strike zone is uniform, and that by changing it they are going to make a significant change in the game. This will force pitchers to be make better pitches, causing batters to swing the bat, increasing scoring. Or this will restore the competitive balance between pitchers and batters. Or this will make the network executives think we know what we're doing.

So they would send a directive around during the winter announcing that the strike zone has been changed. Most umpires treated these notices as seriously as they did letters from Publisher's Clearinghouse telling them they'd won a million dollars. The reality is that there have been very few significant changes in baseball rules in the last half century. One was the addition of the designated hitter. The other prohibited players from leaving their gloves on the field when they were at bat. That's it. So nobody took these strike zone directives seriously. The fact is, you can't change the uniform strike zone, because it doesn't exist to begin with. Changing the strike zone is like buying new clothes for the invisible man.

A few years ago, the American League president Dr.

Bobby Brown announced that he wanted umpires to begin calling strikes as it is defined in the rule book, from the knees to the letters and over the plate. Everybody listened carefully. We all nodded in the right places. In spring training we called strikes that way, which was great, because it definitely speeded up the games, and then, as soon as the season started, we went back to doing what we had been doing for our entire careers and never heard another word about it from Dr. Bobby Brown.

Dr. Brown would have had a better chance to make square clouds. But again, before the 2001 season, baseball announced that the strike zone would be strictly enforced. During spring training they had training sessions. They taught umpires to call the high pitch a strike. To illustrate the new strike zone, they put masking tape on players uniforms at the top and bottom of the strike zone and had them bat against pitching machines set to throw high pitches. Umpires listened and learned and practiced and then had a one-word response: Ball!

Two things that are never going to change are the undefineable strike zone and players complaining about it. When a batter doesn't swing at a pitch he's convinced it was a ball—while the pitcher knows it was a strike. One night Steve Palermo, who was a great ball-and-strike umpire before he got shot risking his life trying to stop a mugging, called a strike on Wade Boggs. Boggs grimaced, then stepped out of the box and said, "Geeze, that pitch can't be a strike."

"Hey, don't get mad at me," Palermo said, then pointed out to the mound, "he threw it, get mad at him. All I did was report it."

One time Lou DiMuro called a close pitch a strike and

Willie Wilson complained, "Oh man, that pitch was definitely inside."

The legendary umpire Jocko Conlon used to tell young umpires, "Son, if you got the right answer you got 'em screwed," and DiMuro remembered that when he told Wilson, "You know what, Willie, you're right."

Wilson couldn't believe it. This was probably the first time in his career that an umpire had agreed with him. So he asked suspiciously, "What do you mean, I'm right?"

"You're right, that pitch was probably a quarter inch inside. See, my eyes aren't that good anymore, so when you see a pitch that close you better be swinging at it."

Somebody once asked Doug Harvey what was the main difference between those players who complain all the time and the players who rarely say a word—and he answered, "About a hundred points in their batting average." His point was that good hitters don't complain, or they're such good hitters that they don't need to complain. As far as I was concerned, that wasn't necessarily true. Nobody complained about pitches more than Doug DeCinces, for example, who was one of the greatest hitters in the history of baseball. A lot of people don't know that, but he must have been great because he played fifteen years in the big leagues and, according to him, he never took a strike. He was so good that he also was never fooled on a pitch and took a half swing. He always checked his swing, always. Truthfully it was sort of silly, DeCinces would take a cut strong enough to hit the ball out of the park—of course that assumes he could hit it—but claim that he had checked his swing. So he's got to be the greatest lifetime .259 hitter ever.

Paul O'Neill really was a very good hitter, but he never

stopped complaining. He was another one of those players who never took a strike in his entire career. He was always whining that umpires were sticking it to him. And if they did, once in awhile, it was because he was whining all the time. I was at third base one night in New York and O'Neill was on third with a triple. While the other team changed pitchers I was talking with the Yankees' third base coach, Willie Randolph. Willie is a really good guy. We've known each other for most of our careers. Suddenly O'Neill called my name. "Hey, Kaiser," he said, "remember last night, that second strike you called on me?"

I had made at least three hundred ball-strike calls the night before. Remember a second strike I'd called on Paul O'Neill? I barely remembered the score of the game. But I knew where O'Neill was going. "No," I admitted, "but let me tell you something, Paul. You're a great hitter. Can you just imagine how good you would be if I gave you all three strikes?"

He didn't understand. "What?"

I looked at Willie, who had a big smile on his face, then I told O'Neill, "Ask Willie to explain it to you."

Remember the second pitch to Paul O'Neill? When I was behind the plate I really had to concentrate on what I was doing. Most of the time I didn't even know who was at bat—and all of the time I didn't care. Even if I had wanted to help a player, or screw him, I couldn't have done it. I didn't have time to think before I called a pitch. If a pitch had been a ball for fifteen years, it didn't suddenly become a strike because Eddie Murray was the batter.

Most people don't believe that. I was behind the plate one day in Boston and Mike Greenwell was the batter. While the other team was making a pitching change we were standing by the plate as the new pitcher warmed up. Greenwell started talking about Wade Boggs, how much he admired him, what a great hitter he was. But then he told me how unfair it was that umpires always gave Boggs a break on close pitches, because we knew he was so good, while we never gave him the same breaks. I laughed at him. He may have believed that, but he was wrong. Umpires don't have time to remember who's batting before calling a pitch: *Boggs is up, and if he didn't swing it must be a ball. Ball!* Or in the field, on a close play on the bases, *Rickey Henderson's running, he must be safe.*

In September 1972, Bruce Froemming was behind the plate when the Cubs' pitcher Milt Pappas went into the ninth inning with a perfect game against the Padres. A lot of pitchers had thrown no-hitters, but at that point there had only been seven perfect games in the history of baseball. It was one of the rarest feats that could be accomplished. Babe Pinelli, for example, was behind the plate for Don Larsen's perfect game in the 1956 World Series, and is remembered mostly for calling pinch-hitter Dale Mitchell out on strikes, on what was probably a high pitch, for the final out of the game. The Padres' twenty-seventh batter was a pinch hitter, Larry Stahl. He was Pappas' ticket to immortality.

In fact, Froemming didn't even know Pappas was pitching a perfect game. He knew it was a no-hitter, he could look at the scoreboard and see that San Diego had no hits, but it didn't even occur to him that the Padres had not had a base runner. Pappas got two quick strikes on Stahl, then threw two consecutive pitches off the plate. He wanted the last strike desperately, and when Froemming called the second pitch a ball Pappas took a couple of steps towards the plate and shook his head in disbelief. Randy Hundley was catching, and Froemming warned him, "If he gets down here, he's gone. I'm not going to have a guy come off the mound at me." Just imagine what would have happened if Froemming had ejected a pitcher one strike away from a perfect game? But Bruce would have done it.

The count went to 3-2. Stahl may have fouled off a pitch, but Froemming called the next pitch he took ball four. That ended the perfect game. Pappas started to come in and just sort of bent down on the grass. Cubs manager Whitey Lockman grabbed him and put him back on the mound, where he finished his no-hitter.

After the game, Pappas admitted to reporters, "He called the pitches right, but I wanted them to be a strike."

The reporters descended on Froemming. One of them said, "You would have been famous. You would have been only the eighth umpire in baseball history to call a perfect game."

"Really?" Bruce replied, "Let me ask you, who was the plate umpire for the first perfect game?" None of the sportswriters knew the answer. "That's how famous I'd have been." Ironically, Froemming is probably better remembered for calling that pitch a ball than he ever would have been if Pappas had completed the perfect game.

Before the game the next day Pappas went up to Froemming and asked him how he could have called a pitch that close ball four. Froemming told him that he had no choice, if he'd called it the other way he wouldn't have been able to sleep at night. Pappas couldn't believe it, asking him, "Then how did you sleep at night after all the other lousy calls you made?"

There is no sentimentality on the field. They used to say that pitcher Early Wynn would knock down his mother if she crowded the plate. But if she swung at the pitch I would have called it a strike.

Only one time did I actually cheat for a batter. I was in Ft. Lauderdale during spring training. This was when Michael Jordan, the greatest basketball player in history, had retired and decided to try to make it in baseball. He was with the White Sox. He was a very good guy, friendly with everyone. But as great an athlete as he was, he was having trouble hitting the ball. That didn't surprise me, the skills required for baseball and basketball are completely different. Baskets don't curve. He hadn't gotten a hit the entire spring. So, when he came to bat I told him, "Look, Michael, I'm going to get you your first hit today. You're going to stay in there until you hit the son of a bitch."

The first pitch was right down the heart of the plate. "Ball one. Swing the bat Michael." It was an exhibition game, it didn't matter who won. The world was rooting for him. The next pitch was on the plate, "Ball two. Come on Michael, swing the bat or we're gonna be here all day."

Ball three. Ball who-knows-how-many?—*swing the bat, Michael.* Finally, he hit a rope down the left field line for a double. His first hit.

At the end of the inning he told me, "Hey, I owe you one." I agreed. If you see him, tell him he still does.

And, admittedly, on very rare occasions I've stuck it to a batter—but never in a situation where it would affect the outcome of the game. Absolutely never. One night in Detroit I got hit three times with foul tips. I got hit in the mask a lot because I stood up high behind the catcher. I pretty much had to replace my mask every season, sometimes twice a year. Getting hit by a foul ball at close range is like getting slugged in the mask by Mike Tyson. It shakes your resolve. That night, I got hit in the shoulder twice, and the mask once, and Kirk Gibson was sitting in the Tigers dugout breaking my hump. I was getting killed back there, and he was yelling and laughing. He thought it was really funny. He was injured, so he didn't start the game, but he came up to pinch-hit in a later inning. He looked at me and smiled. We both knew what was about to happen. The first pitch almost hit him. Good. "Strike one! How do you like that? Does it hurt as much as mine hurts? Want me to call another one?"

He struck out swinging. Before he went back to the dugout he glanced at me and, still laughing, told me, "Okay, you got me. We're even now."

"Not yet," I told him, "but we're getting there."

The legendary umpire Bill Klem always told people, "I never missed one in my heart." That's probably true, but on the field was an entirely different matter. I missed pitches. Every umpire misses pitches. One time I called a player out on strikes on a bad pitch. He swung and missed at the first pitch, fouled off the second pitch and took the third strike. I knew I'd missed it, the hitter knew it, the only person who didn't know it was the pitcher, who was standing out there on the mound thinking, *Yesssss, I got it going today.* The batter—it was a veteran infielder, but I can't remember who it was—started walking away from the plate, and as he did he kind of said over his shoulder to me, "You missed that last one."

I gave him the old reliable answer. "Well, that's possible.

But you missed the first two all by yourself, so you're doing twice as bad as I am."

Rod Carew had the best attitude about balls and strikes I've ever seen. Veteran American League umpire Ed Runge was behind the plate for one of Carew's first at bats in the major leagues. As Carew tells the story, the first pitch was about three or four inches outside, but Runge called it a strike. "I turned around to him and I said, 'Oh no!' " Carew said, "and he said, 'Oh *yes*, and you'd better be swinging the next time, too, kid.'

"I swung at the next two pitches because I wasn't taking any chances, and after that I never had real trouble with umpires. I developed the attitude that I'm going to make mistakes out there and that these guys are gonna make some, too. I haven't met anybody who's perfect yet. So, sometimes I rant and rave, but the nice thing about it is that I know they've been honest with me."

Almost as long as I've been in baseball they have been looking for a more reliable method of calling balls and strikes. The latest gimmick is the Questec Umpire Information System, the UIS, which they've installed in ten ballparks. This system was originally invented to be used by the military to track missiles; now it's being used by baseball to track pitches. So, if the situation was really desperate, it could probably shoot down a fly ball. It consists of six cameras, computers, and sophisticated tracking software. Four cameras take a series of pictures of the pitch as it travels to the plate, so that the path of the ball can be tracked by computers, and two cameras focus on the batter as he takes his stance. Supposedly this machine can determine the precise location and speed of every pitch and is accurate to within a half inch. Baseball insists that this is just a training tool to help umpires improve their weaknesses, that it is not intended to ever replace umpires. Yeah, and O. J. still insists he's innocent.

Baseball is always experimenting. More than three decades ago, for example, an inventor in San Francisco created a rearview mirror for pitchers. It hooked onto a cap and let the pitcher see what was going on behind him. In a practice game it worked really well—the inventor picked his brother-in-law off second three times. He claimed he had his mother-in-law picked off too, but his next door neighbor dropped the ball.

In the late 1960s, Joe Torre and his brother Frank invented the Iso-Swing Batting Coach in their basement during the off-season. Supposedly, it helped hitters develop muscles and work on their timing by making them swing a bat through two big rubber jaws. Frank Torre claimed that once the device got into general use, anyone with the desire to practice could become a .300 hitter.

A little more than two decades ago the equipment manufacturer Mizuno made gloves for the catcher and pitcher with a microwave communications system built into them that enabled the catcher to call for one of four pitches in any of four locations by pressing two buttons. And between innings maybe you cook a hot dog in it too.

You'll notice nobody's wearing electric baseball gloves. Baseball changes slowly. For example, the designated hitter was first proposed in 1928 by the president of the National League. And only fifty years later the American League jumped at the idea. So I don't think we're going to be seeing electronic umpires calling balls and strikes real soon.

Right now baseball is supposedly using the Questec UIS to enable umpires to see how well they're doing behind the plate. At the end of the game the home plate umpire is given a report that compares his ball-and-strike calls to the system's results. I understand why baseball eventually would love to utilize a device like this. It not only calls strikes, it can't *go* on strike. Computers don't join unions, they don't need vacations, they don't demand pay raises. There is no doubt that a computerized system would reduce the number of arguments and ejections over calls, although it would also be the first time in baseball history that a manager could scream at the umpire, "You're nuts! Bolts too!" and be absolutely correct.

Among many difficulties with the system is that somebody has to calibrate it, somebody has to program the machine—and that involves people. I was told that there has been quite a difference in strike zones from ballpark to ballpark because of the way the system has been set up. I have no idea if that's true or not. If it is, maybe they need to create a system to program the system.

Baseball doesn't want the umpires to know too much about this system. Makes sense to me—you can't expect baseball to reveal the secrets of its missile-tracking system. But the umpires didn't like it so much that during the 2002 season the union filed a grievance against management, pointing out that the commissioner hasn't allowed the union's experts to look at the system to determine if it really works as well as they claim it does. Considering the fact that baseball is making judgments of individual umpire's ability to call balls and strikes based on these reports, that seems like a pretty fair request. So, it probably isn't a big surprise that the owners responded by suing the union, which then brought unfair labor practice charges. For a system that is supposed to help cut down on arguments, this has created quite a big one.

Maybe baseball would like to expand the use of this system, but I guarantee you the players wouldn't like it and the fans definitely wouldn't like it. If a device like this could be perfected, which I doubt, it would take the human element out of the game. I don't know anybody who would like that to happen. They have been trying to develop a device like this one for a long time. In the mid-1980s an inventor got a patent for something called the Baseball Strike Indicator and Trajectory Analyzer, which was a machine that supposedly did the same thing as the Questec. Even then umpire Rick Reed knew it wouldn't work, saying, "It makes a player feel better to yell at someone he can relate to."

Even if the Questec UIS could accurately call strikes within half an inch, it couldn't possibly replace the home plate umpire. Maybe a computer can do calculations faster than a human being, or answer more questions, but it can't think, and it can't create, and it can't adapt to situations, and it can't speed up the game when necessary by making batters swing at close pitches, and it doesn't know when to stop a game because it's raining and order the ground crew to put the tarp on the field, or figure out if a pitcher is intentionally throwing at a batter or just has lousy control.

Maybe the only thing baseball has tried to do more often than change the strike zone is figure out how to speed up games. And the more they try, the longer games last. Practically every winter I would get a directive from the league office explaining what was going to be done to shorten games. One year it was making batters get into the batter's box faster, another year it was cutting down the time between innings. Baseball once gave stop watches to all the umpires and told us to enforce the rule that pitchers had twenty-eight seconds between the time they caught the ball and threw a pitch. Now, there was about as much chance of umpires pulling out a stop watch between pitches as there was of the players voting me Mr. Congeniality.

Believe me, no one would like to see games shortened more than umpires. Except maybe sportswriters. They're the people who are always writing about the games being too long. Truthfully, I'm not sure the fans want the games shortened. Tickets have gotten expensive—including food, bringing a family of four people to the ballpark could easily cost $200—and I never heard of anyone who spent a lot of money to buy tickets, came out to the ballpark with their family or friends, and then wanted to see the game end as quickly as possible. Actually, I'm not even sure the owners really want the game shortened. Remember, the longer a game lasts, the more food and souvenirs they can sell, the more time there is for TV and radio commercials.

I've never thought it was the length of time a game lasts that bothered people as much as how that time was filled—or emptied. A lot of time is wasted standing around waiting, and that gets tedious. When I was busy games went pretty fast. Or at least faster. The thing that bothered me was batters stepping out of the box after every pitch to adjust their uniform and swing the bat and move their wristbands and check their cap and swing the bat and then get back in the box. The worst used to be Mike Hargrove, who was known as The Human Rain Delay. Hargrove is a very good guy, but when he came to bat I knew I'd have time to watch rocks grow on the infield. Chuck Knoblauch was almost as bad—adjust, fix, move, swing, move, fix, dig in, swing. I could move in all my furniture and get settled in a new house faster than some players got settled in the batter's box. But, probably the all-time worst at wasting time in the batter's box is Jeff Cirillo. Umpires are now entitled to take a vacation during the season; the story is that someone left on his vacation when Cirillo came to bat and when they came back he was still up. Houdini could get comfortable on a bed of sharpened nails faster than Cirillo gets ready to hit.

But if every player was like Lee May games would be over in an hour. Lee May swung at everything. He never took a pitch. He didn't even need an umpire, if he could reach it he was swinging. I always wanted to thank him, but he was never up there long enough. *Uh, Lee, I just want to* . . . boom. Umpires just love players like Lee May and the Yankees' Alfonso Soriano, who averages about one base on balls every five games and strikes out just about one time a game. He doesn't take a lot of pitches. Anything near the plate, he's swinging. He's swinging the bat before he gets into the batter's box, he's swinging from the dugout, he's swinging when he gets up in the morning. You've got to really want to walk him to walk him.

Even when the batter finally gets ready to hit, the pitcher has to throw the ball. Tug McGraw used to have a theory about why pitchers hold on to the baseball. He called it his Frozen Iceball Theory. Early in Tug's career, Gil Hodges brought him in to face Johnny Bench with the bases loaded. As McGraw stood on the mound he realized that as long as he held onto the baseball nothing bad could happen. So he stood there. Then he started thinking, *In ten billion years the sun is going to burn out and the Earth is going to become a giant iceball flying through space. And when that happens nobody is going to care what Johnny Bench did with the bases loaded.* That gave him the confidence to finally make a pitch.

Satchel Paige got it right when he said, "Throw strikes. Home plate don't move."

One change in baseball strategy that has really slowed down the game is the use of so many relief pitchers. When I came up to the major leagues, teams had starting pitchers, middle-relievers, and their closer. Closers would pitch two innings, on occasion three. Managers almost never brought in a pitcher to pitch to one batter. By the end of my career it was common to see three, even four pitchers used in the same inning. And, on occasion, managers will take advantage of a pitching change to start an argument.

Managers and players are not allowed to argue about strike and balls. If they do it's an automatic ejection. So what some managers do is go out to make a pitching change and wait there on the mound until the umpire is forced to come out to tell him to make his decision—and then he gets into it about some calls; *I'll stand here as long as I want to, I wouldn't even be out here if you knew a strike when you saw it.* Or—*Don't go telling me my job until you figure out how to do yours.* One time, Tommy Lasorda waited patiently on the mound until Lee Wyer finally came out to break up the meeting. Then Lasorda started complaining about a strike call Wyer had made an inning earlier. "How can you make a call like that?" Tommy said, or at least that's the printable version.

Wyer threw him out of the game. "It's automatic," he said, "you can't argue balls and strikes."

"Wait a second," Lasorda said, "what do you mean it's automatic? I'm asking you about it an inning later."

"That doesn't matter," Wyer told him, "it's automatic. It's in the rule book."

"In the rule book?" Lasorda said. "You mean to tell me that if I came out here next week and complained about that call you'd have to throw me out?"

"That's right."

"How about next spring? Would you have to throw me out then?"

Wyer had the right answer for him, "Tommy, there's no statute of limitations in the rule book."

And Lasorda, who never forgets, had an answer for him, "Oh yeah? Well then let me ask you, if you can throw me out for arguing about a call six months later, how come you can't call Reggie Jackson out for interference in the fourth game of the 1978 World Series?"

Of course, there were a lot of umpires, as well as some players, who referred to Tommy Lasorda as Walking Eagle. They called him that because he was so full of it he couldn't fly.

Regulation games last long enough when you've got the plate, but most of the time a game that goes into extra innings is worse than an appointment with Dustin Hoffman's dentist in *Marathon Man*. The longest game I ever worked was seventeen innings—seventeen long innings—the Angels against the White Sox on a Sunday afternoon in Anaheim. If there was one thing I learned during my career, it's that on Sunday afternoons in California, when we were scheduled to fly back east right after the game, we were going to play extra innings. We were going to miss our flight and have to stay over and leave the following morning. There was never any doubt about it, that's what was going to happen.

In that seventeen-inning game I was on the field more than five hours. There were times when I thought that the game would never end. I was mad at everybody, but I was just too tired to get angry. By the thirteenth or fourteenth inning I was beyond exhausted. Now, I love the game of baseball, but I have to admit that by the fourth hour I was beginning to lose some of my passion for it. You can love ice cream, for example, but after eating the first gallon, it begins to lose its appeal. Try wearing a heavy steel mask and standing in pretty much the same place for four or five hours—it's okay to move around every ten minutes or so to get loose—and then bend over as if peering over a catcher's shoulder three hundred times—without stopping for anything to eat.

The players get to sit down half the game. And, unlike the umpires, they get relief from the heat or the cold. The old-time umpire Bill McKinley used to talk about the longest game of his nineteen-year big league career. The Yankees and the Tigers played twenty-two innings in only seven hours. Twenty-two innings—seven hours on the field. Now that should be a *Survivor* challenge. McKinley was working the plate, and towards the end of the game his back and legs were aching. About the twentieth inning Yogi Berra asked him to clean off home plate. Believe me, there was no chance of that happening in the twentieth inning. "Brush it off yourself, you dago," McKinley told him, "I know where it is." After twenty innings he sure did.

It used to be the unwritten rule that umpires would never eat, drink, or leave the field during a game. We demolished those rules pretty good. But as games got longer, and then longer, there was an additional problem. In the fifth game of the 1999 National League Championship, the Mets and Braves played fifteen innings in a quick five hours and twenty minutes, making it the longest playoff game in major league history. Jerry Layne worked the plate and considered it one of the best games he's worked in his career. He was really proud of the job he did. After the playoffs, he was home, and he was taking his youngest daughter to school. As he was walking into the school a classmate of hers told him that he had watched the game. He had seen every inning, every pitch. "I have one question for you, Mr. Layne."

Jerry was pretty modest about the fine job he did. But he had made some difficult calls during that game and sort of assumed the young man wanted to know something about one of them. He was ready to explain the details of the play, ready to talk baseball. "Yes?"

"Well, that was a really long game," the boy said, "so Mr. Layne, what happens if you have to go to the bathroom?"

Baseball's unspoken secret. What happens when somebody has to go to the bathroom during the game? The reality that baseball never talks about: Sometimes umpires have to go to the bathroom. I don't know how people like Bill "Old Iron Kidneys" Klem managed to avoid it, but I can verify that there are times when umpires have to respond to the call of nature. When that happens the last thing you want to do is make a public announcement. A lot of people are sort of shy about this subject, so imagine what it would feel like to be in the men's room knowing that 48,000 fans are waiting patiently for you to come out. Or Bob Costas has informed the millions of people watching the game, "We're going to pause for a commercial while Ken Kaiser goes to the bathroom."

Actually, when we were working in the field we had a little sign for it, you move your thumb and forefinger up and down, like you were opening or closing a zipper. Then at the end of the half inning, as quietly as possible, trying real hard to attract no attention, you kind of wander off the field into the rest room. The other three umpires cover for you, and most of the time the fans don't even realize you're missing. And at the end of the half inning, as the teams are running in and out of the dugouts, you wander back onto the field, newly refreshed and ready to go. Or, more accurately in this case, not go.

In Houston one night, Paul Pryor was working first base, and between innings he ran into the bathroom in the dugout. He was real quick and he turned around to get back to his position—and discovered that some Houston players had locked the door from the outside. He was trapped in the bathroom. Maybe the worst thing was that no one on the field even realized he was missing. After a few pitches the Astros let him out.

When you're behind the plate there are no options. You just do what you have to do. And you try to do it as fast as you can. The only difference is, in this situation all the people in the ballpark and the millions watching at home know that you're in the bathroom.

I've also had real bad headaches on the field. Imagine this, your head is throbbing, you've got a splitting headache—and you're surrounded by 35,000 screaming people, ready to scream even louder. That happened to me in Chicago one night. To make it worse, I had a bang-bang play at second and I called the White Sox runner out. Manager Tony LaRussa came sprinting out of the dugout, but I was waiting for him. "Did you get that play right?" he asked.

LaRussa and I had a good relationship, he knew I was going to be honest with him. If I had kicked it I would have admitted it. So, before he could open his mouth I told him, "Don't give me a hard time, Tony. It wasn't even that close and I got it right. I got this splitting headache, and I don't want to get into it with you."

LaRussa came right up to me and asked, "When did that start?"

"A couple innings ago. Do me a favor, between innings have Hermie bring me out a couple of aspirin and a glass of water." Hermie being trainer Herm Schneider, whom I'd known since we were in the minor leagues together. In fact one time in Syracuse I'd actually thrown him out of the game just to make him feel wanted.

In order for LaRussa and I to hear each other, he had to stand real close to me. To the fans it looked like he was arguing about my call, so they started cheering loudly for him, making my headache even worse. The louder they yelled, the closer Tony had to stand, the more they yelled encouragement. "Sure," Tony said really loudly. And at the end of the half inning Herm came out with several aspirin and a glass of water.

My seventeen-inning game was bad enough, but it really didn't compare to the long game umpired by National Leaguer Andy Olsen when he was in the minors. Olsen had the plate in an Eastern League game in May 1965, between the Elmira Pioneers and the Springfield Giants, that went twenty-seven innings. It lasted six hours and twenty-four minutes, at that time the longest game in professional baseball history. But it was even worse than that. The start of the game had to be delayed so the field could dry after a heavy rain storm. But that was not the worst thing either. The game was scoreless until the twenty-sixth inning, when Springfield scored a run—letting the umpires think they were finally going to finish the game—and then Elmira scored a run in the bottom of the inning to tie it. But even that was not the worst thing. The worst thing was that Elmira's manager was Earl Weaver. Olsen had to listen to Weaver for twenty-seven innings: *Pitch is high. Pitch is low.* Twenty-seven innings of Earl Weaver! I thought that kind of torture had been outlawed by the Geneva Convention.

In the bottom of the twenty-seventh—that's a triple-header, three complete games—Elmira's leadoff hitter tripled. After the next batter struck out, the Pioneers hitter bounced a routine grounder to the shortstop. The runner broke from third. There was a close play at the plate, but Olsen called the runner safe. Springfield's manager, Andy Gilbert, was very upset. After twenty-seven innings after six and a half hours of baseball, after the equivalent of three games, he actually complained to Olsen, "Andy, you shortened the game on us."

If major league baseball really wanted to make the games shorter, it could be done easily. All you got to do is take off an inning. Who decided a game had to be nine innings long? Play eight. The fact is that, other than doing that, there isn't too much that can be done. You can't force pitchers to throw more strikes. Here's the reality of the situation: The reason that baseball games last so long is that there is a two-minute and forty-five-second break every time the teams change sides. Figure it out, that, times however many breaks there are between half-innings is . . . is a lot of time. TV uses that time to show commercials. That two minutes and forty-five seconds is what helps keep a lot of teams in business. The same thing is true when a relief pitcher is brought in. Does TV show viewers the pitcher warming up, or do they show more commercials? When I first started, the break between half innings was a little more than a minute. Every few years it got a little longer. And longer. Two minutes and forty-five seconds is a long time to wait, but that was the directive.

Anything baseball does to shorten the game is going to cost baseball teams money. So you know that's not going to happen. If the game is shorter fans will leave the ballpark sooner, meaning they'll spend less money there. If the time between innings is cut down, TV will lose commercial time, making TV rights worth less money.

The reality is that there is almost nothing the plate umpire can do to speed up the game. If I could have, I would have. Making batters get into the box a little quicker, or getting pitchers to take less time between pitches won't solve the problem. A few seconds saved here, a few seconds saved there, and before you know it you've saved . . . a few seconds.

Maybe the only thing on the field that the home plate umpire has no control over is a fight—which is sort of how I began my baseball career. For a non-contact sport, there is definitely a lot of contact in baseball. There are people who will tell you that baseball players don't fight, that they just sort of push each other around. That's definitely not true. They fight. Big time. The biggest fight I saw in my career actually took place while I was still in the minors, in Pittsfield, Massachusetts. Pittsfield was a Washington Senators farm club, playing the Pirates' Waterbury, Connecticut, club. Bill "Mad Dog" Madlock was with Waterbury and Toby Harrah was with Pittsfield. A Waterbury player named Dick Sharon was trying to break up a double play and slid hard into Harrah. That started it. Both dugouts emptied onto the field. I mean, this was a real brawl. A lot of young, aggressive players with a lot of enthusiasm just went at each other. There was nothing I could do to stop it. This wasn't baseball, this was hockey on grass. What was I going to do? I didn't have to get hit in the head to know enough to stay out of it. The fight lasted about a half hour. It didn't slow down until we heard the sirens. When the police arrived, they drove their cars right onto the field.

I didn't know how to handle the situation when the fight ended. I knew I couldn't throw out both teams—I had to keep enough players in the game to finish it. So I started picking off the players who were obviously in the middle of the brawl. One kid from Waterbury, an Italian kid, an ex-major leaguer named Lou Maroni, had taken a beating. His shirt was ripped half off, there was blood all over his face and his uniform. His cap was long gone. "You're done," I told him.

That got him really angry. "What are you throwing *me* out for?" he screamed, "I wasn't in no fight."

There was blood all over his uniform. His jersey literally had been at least partially ripped right off his body. "Well if you weren't," I said, pointing at the remains of his uniform, "you better get yourself a new tailor."

I never saw a better fight than that one. Never. But I did witness a lot of brawling during my career. Baseball fights don't make a lot of sense to me. Most fights on the field begin when a pitcher throws inside or intentionally tries to hit a player. With even the minimum big league salaries at $300,000 a year, the batters are afraid that they might get hurt, which would affect their career and their ability to earn. So what do they do? They start a fight—which is where they really might get hurt.

But they never think about that. I know that's absolutely true because George Brett told me it was. Let me tell you, everybody in the big leagues knew which players would be in the middle of a brawl if one broke out and who would be standing over on the sidelines holding back somebody from the other team who also wanted to be standing on the sidelines. Guaranteed, when Kansas City got in a fight George Brett was going to be right in the middle of it. Brett wasn't afraid to fight anybody. For example, the toughest ball club I ever saw was the late 1970s Texas Rangers. They had players like Dock Ellis and Johnny Ellis, Gaylord Perry, who was as tough as anybody, Willie Horton, Toby Harrah—that team had some strong people. George Brett's Royals and the Rangers didn't like each other. They would fight all the time. One night Brett got brushed back and went after the pitcher. I don't remember who it was and it doesn't matter. Brett didn't hesitate. He dropped his bat and went racing towards the mound.

Now, in retrospect, I think even George would have had to admit that it turned out to be a mistake. I liked George a lot, everybody did, but I didn't like him enough to get in the middle of that fight. The catcher, Johnny Ellis, was as tough as any player in the league. It wasn't so much what he hit for the club as who he hit for the club. This time it was George.

When I saw George the next night he was really banged up. "Man," I asked him, "what were you thinking to go charging out there?"

"See, Kais," he admitted, "that was the problem. If I had been thinking I wouldn't have gone out there."

I don't know who I would have picked in a fight between Ellis and Willie Horton. Willie could fight. One night the Oakland A's pitcher Mike Norris kind of whizzed one by his head and Horton started going out to the mound after him. The A's catcher, Mike Heath, stepped in front of him and said, "Willie, you don't want to do this."

"I don't huh?" he said.

"Well, if you're going out there I'm gonna have to stop you."

Willie looked him up and down, then told him, "Then you just better jump on my back and I'll take you out there with me."

While Heath and Horton were arguing with each other, the dugouts emptied as players ran onto the field. The fighters and the holders started pairing off. When it became obvious that Horton wasn't going to be able to get at Norris, Willie really got angry. His own teammates were holding him back. Finally, finally, we got things quieted down. Nobody got tossed. Everybody went back into the dugouts. I got back behind the plate, I put on my mask and bent over. Heath squatted down. Horton got in the box and just as we were ready to go, Heath said quietly, "I would have stopped him."

I got to know who had the worst tempers, and generally I could tell when a fight was brewing. When two teams playing each other had a history of fighting the league would send a memorandum to umpires working their games telling them to be alert for problems. Currently baseball has what's called a "Heads Up" program where they e-mail information and warnings to umpires. For example, if the Indians and Red Sox had a brawl last time they played, umpires will get an e-mail telling them exactly what happened and who was involved. It makes sense.

But you can't stop everything. Rod Carew, for example, was generally even tempered. He rarely complained or argued. One time though, when he was with the Angels he fooled me. Oil Can Boyd was pitching for the Red Sox and a couple of his pitches came close to hitting Carew. Finally, Carew hit a routine ground ball to second. The second baseman made the play, but after being thrown out at first Carew, instead of turning around and going back to his dugout, made a hard left and went after Boyd. He took a swing at him, then tackled him. Eventually we pulled Carew off him; I'd never seen him so angry. "Who do you think you are?" I asked him, "Rocky Balboa?" He was not amused.

I guess I knew what Carew was feeling. Even I got into a fight on the field. Once. It was in Chicago. I was working the plate and I'd had a close play in the bottom of the sixth. I called the White Sox runner out when he'd tried to score on a sacrifice fly, and Tony LaRussa and I got into a real good one. So, the fans were already incensed at the end of the inning when the White Sox mascot came out onto the field. Here's how I feel about mascots: you don't want to get me started about mascots. That's how I feel about mascots. They're ridiculous. The White Sox had a mascot. Ribbie. There is no way to accurately describe it. It was fat and had a big head and an elephant's nose. So Ribbie came out onto the field and thought he would be clever. He came to home plate as if he was arguing with me about the play. He started swinging that nose at me. And the fans, who had quieted down, got started again. I looked at him and said, "Who do you think you are, the Phillie Fanatic?"

Then I picked him up and held him over my head—and body-slammed him onto home plate. Return of the Hatchet! Okay, I beat up a mascot. But he deserved it. The truth is that, after I hit him I got a little nervous. I thought I really hurt him. But he was fine. He walked off the field dejectedly swinging his nose.

Every single day of the thirty-three years I spent on a baseball field was different, but somehow all of it was the same. It's a long season, times thirty-three. I came up to the big leagues before memorabilia had any real value. In the 1970s nobody was interested in buying used gum chewed by major league players. So, like every other umpire, I used to send items into the clubhouses to be signed and then give them to friends or charities or people who had been nice to us. At one time I had a nice collection of souvenirs, but I gave almost everything away. Today the only real souvenirs I have of a lifetime spent in professional baseball are pretty much the same thing every umpire gets at the end of his career: a gold pass that gets me into any baseball park in America, bad knees, and a very bad back. But I do have my memories, I've got a lot of wonderful memories. I can close my eyes and see a Nolan Ryan fastball—and I can hear him grunt as he releases it. I can see Bo Jackson catching a fly ball against the fence in Seattle and throwing out Harold Reynolds trying to score. It was the most amazing throw I ever saw—the ball came in on a line 350 feet and was never more than five feet off the ground. I can close my eyes and see Cal

Ripkin Jr. at shortstop going to his left—maybe his range wasn't as good as Derek or Nomar or A-Rod—but if he could get to the ball he would make the play. I can hear the sound of Weaver's whining voice. I've seen so many different players, so many games. Along the way I made a lot of friends as well as a few not-so-friends. I've worked playoff and World Series games and I've marched on picket lines. I've seen the best and worst of baseball, both on and—unfortunately—off the field.

But I don't think anything that I'd done, anything that I'd seen, anything that had happened to me, prepared me for the abrupt end of my career.

7

The easiest part of the job was the job itself. Ball-strike, safe-out, fair-foul, balk, it was no more complicated than that. It was life off the field that made the job as tough as it was. Basically, the job consists of one long road trip. Umpires are never the home team. When I first came up we got no time off at all during the season. From April to October we lived on the road. We only saw our families on an occasional off day, if we were lucky enough to be in a city close by, or if they came to games we were working. When I was working in Toronto, for example, my dad would drive the family up there for the games. But we couldn't get home for weddings, graduations, anniversaries—any of the celebrations of normal family life. One time, Durwood Merrill's daughter was having an operation and he wanted to go home to be with her. When he asked for permission, Dick Butler, the supervisor of umpires, turned him down, saying, "What are you, a doctor? You aren't gonna do any good there." It was a hard way to live, and it caused a lot of marriages to fall apart.

During the season your family consisted of your crew, the umpires you worked with. You got to know those people real well. In the old days the crew traveled together, stayed together in the same hotel, and ate most of their meals together. The crew chief gave the orders and expected them to be obeyed. He was the captain. When they drove anywhere he always sat in the front passenger seat. When the phone rang in the locker room after a game he was the only one allowed to answer it. After a game the crew chief was the first person into the shower. If he wanted coffee or a soda the new man would get it for him.

That had started changing by the time I got to the big leagues. Haller was my first crew chief and he ran a pretty independent crew. With Luciano and me he didn't really have much choice. In our crew we all carried our own bags. Haller knew how much I loved pro basketball, and if the NBA finals went down to a seventh game—this was our secret—he would give me the night off to watch the game. It was the old my-grandmother-died-and-I-have-to-go-to-her-funeral excuse. Everybody knew about it. People used to say, if it goes to a seventh game it's bad news for Kaiser's grandmother. A lot of fans call in sick to go to a baseball game, I was the only umpire I knew who got sick to miss a game.

When I joined the crew Luciano was responsible for making the hotel reservations. That lasted about two cities. After

I saw the second-rate places they stayed in I volunteered to make the reservations. I always believed in going first class. The job was tough enough without staying in hotels where rooms were priced by the hour. I'd served my time with sausage dogs in the lobby.

I just never believed that a crew had to travel together and stay together and eat together to do a good job on the field. I didn't believe that my life off the field had to be ruled by the crew chief. I already had a wife. One was plenty, I didn't need three more. There were some umpires who didn't like my attitude. As far as I was concerned, that made us even.

Life with Haller and Luciano was always an adventure. One day after a game they went ahead of me to get the car. As they came out of the locker room a parking lot attendent stopped them and asked Ronnie if he knew a man named Charlie Arnott. Apparently, a man named Charlie Arnott claimed he knew Ronnie and wanted to say hello to him. Ronnie made friends wherever he went, although he never remembered anybody's name. So he figured he must have met this guy somewhere. "Sure," he said, "it's okay."

As Bill and Ronnie continued walking towards the car this man approached them. "Hey," he said, extending his hand, "it's good to see you again!"

"You bet," Ronnie said, "good to see you too." Ronnie had no memory of ever meeting this person, but he didn't want to hurt his feelings. As Haller got in the car Ronnie stood by the door and continued the conversation.

"You still bowling?" the man asked.

Ronnie had never bowled a game in his life. "Aw, you know, once in awhile."

The fan nodded, "I know what you mean. But hey, we sure did have some good times bowling, didn't we?"

My guess is that this was probably about the time Ronnie began to get a little nervous. There were often people hanging around umpires trying to get anything from an autograph to information. The best thing to do with people like that was humor them and keep walking. "You bet," Ronnie told him, as he opened the car door. "Well, it's been nice seeing you. . . ."

The man leaned on the car, "My brother was a really good bowler. You remember?"

He began easing into the car. "Oh yeah, he sure was. How is your brother?"

The man looked stunned. "He's dead," he said. "Don't you remember, you were a pallbearer at his funeral?"

Uh-oh. Ronnie kind of eased into the car, not wanting to make any fast moves. "Oh yeah, oh my goodness, I totally forgot. Well, um . . . how's . . . how's his wife doing?" Ronnie just took a shot that the man had been married.

"Oh, she's dead too. Don't you remember the accident?"

Haller started the car. Ronnie opened the car window a few inches, "Well then, how about you? How's your wife? She's okay, right?"

The man shook his head. "No," he said, "she left me after I got fired. She took the kids and moved away. And then I got sick. . . ."

They started backing up. "Well, Charlie, it's been nice seeing you. We've gotta go . . ."

The man grasped the top of the window and started walking along with the car. "Hey listen, while you're in town why don't you come over for dinner one night?"

Ronnie wasn't much of an actor, but he did his best, "I'd really love to, but we're really busy while we're here. We got the three games, you know. Hey, I'll call you!"

"No," the man said, "I'll call you. What hotel you staying at?"

"The Hyatt," Ronnie said. We were staying at the Sheraton. "Give me a call there," Ronnie continued, "maybe we'll have dinner."

Haller began speeding up. "Good," the man said, "but it can't be anything fancy. You know, I pretty much lost everything in the fire. . . ."

Finally they pulled away. They drove around to the gate and picked me up. As Haller started driving us back to the hotel he asked, "Hey Ronnie, did you ever meet that guy Charlie Arnott before?"

Ronnie shook his head. "Never saw him before in my life."

I couldn't believe it. "Charlie Arnott?" I said. "Hey, I used to bowl with him!"

Eventually I was assigned to Larry Barnett's crew. Barnett was one of the hardest-working umpires I'd ever seen. He made himself a very good umpire. I respected him, but that still didn't mean I was going to carry his bags. I had the least seniority on the crew. On our first road trip they just sort of assumed that I would be responsible for the luggage. Believe me, there was no chance of that happening. I just left the bags at the airport. So, when we were registering at the hotel Larry asked me, "Where's my suitcase?"

I told him the truth. "Damned if I know," I said. "Last time I saw it, it was spinning around that thing at the airport."

Well, joining this crew was good for my grandmother's

health. She never got sick again. Over time and through various union contracts the rigid structure of crew responsibilities disappeared. By the time I retired, for the most part everybody was making his own flight and hotel reservations. The responsibilities had changed. The new man on the crew, for example, is the computer man. He carries a laptop computer supplied by the league and has to check in with the office through e-mail every day to get updates and messages. The computer is also used to file reports when someone is ejected from the game. We've finally made it to the electronic age.

I spent thirteen years in the minor leagues because there were very few job openings in the big leagues. At most, one or two jobs a year opened up. At most. So there was always strong competition to be hired by one of the two major leagues. A lot of very capable umpires never got to the big leagues. That changed in 1999. After two thirds of all the major league umpires submitted letters of resignation in 1999 as a strategy to force baseball to negotiate a new contract—although some people almost immediately took back their letters—the commissioner accepted these resignations and promoted twenty-five minor leaguers. Think about that, twenty-five young umpires, several of them with limited minor league experience, became major league umpires. When they get more experience some of these people will turn out to be very good, but it's going to take time. Managers and players don't talk about it publicly because they understand the problem, but everybody knows that the quality of umpiring in the big leagues has gone way down. Too many of the experienced people are gone.

What these new people didn't get was the chance to break

in slowly under the supervision and protection of experienced umpires. I don't mean just on the field, but surviving off the field. People who a few years ago would have been the junior member of a crew are now running crews. Like Haller and Luciano made me a major league umpire, I broke in Mark Johnson. He was a kid out of the hills of Kentucky. The first time I met him was in Bradenton, at the Pirates' spring training facility. In those days the umpires would eat meals with the club. I met him on the way to dinner; he was dressed in a pair of jeans with holes in them, a T-shirt, and he wasn't wearing shoes. "Where you going?" I asked him.

"Down to eat."

"Not dressed like that. Go put on your nice clothes." So he did. He came back wearing a different pair of jeans with smaller holes in them, the same T-shirt, and sandals. The next day I took him downtown and loaned him money to buy slacks and a sports jacket. That's the way it worked, we protected each other.

On the field too. In 1995, Teddy Barrett was called up from the minors to fill in for major league umpires who were on vacation or injured. Baseball does that a lot now—they use umpires being paid minor league salaries to substitute for major leaguers. They pay them on a per-game basis, just like high school umpires. So, an umpire who is not officially on the major league staff, not being paid a major league salary, and not earning seniority might work 120 or more major leagues games a season. Teddy Barrett was one of these guys. He joined our crew in Cleveland. He had flown all day to get there and hadn't slept in almost a full day. He was exhausted. Just to make the situation a little more difficult, we were forced to work a three-man system because someone got hurt.

I had the plate, Teddy had second base. There was a bang-bang play at third. Ted came racing across the field, but never got a good angle on it. He kicked it—the base runner was safe and he called him out. Mike Hargrove, the Indians manager, realized what was going on. He made his objection known and left. It was a pretty calm discussion. But third base coach Jeff Neumann wouldn't let up, he wouldn't stop yelling at Barrett.

Eventually things got quieted down. It was over. History. Almost forgotten. Now, in that situation there really is only one thing you don't want to happen. And that is precisely what happened. The next batter, Albert Belle, hit a long home run.

Neumann stared at Barrett. He just glared at him. If anybody ever wanted the definition of a dirty look, it was the way Neumann was looking at Barrett. His meaning was obvious, you cost us a run with that bleeping call. Neumann just wouldn't take his eyes off him. Even when we resumed play, Neumann continued to glare at Barrett. Teddy didn't know what to do about it. I showed him what to do about it. I charged down the third base line and screamed, "Don't you stare at the kid."

"I'm not saying nothing," Neumann protested.

"Yeah, but it's the way you're not saying it," I said. "I know what you're doing. You keep your eyes to yourself, you're being unfair to him." I don't know if I could have ejected Neumann for staring but, fortunately Hargrove came out and made peace.

I took the heat for Teddy just like Haller and Luciano had

taken it for me. That's the way it was done, and that's the way it isn't done when you've got too many inexperienced umpires working in the same crew.

My job on most of the crews I worked with was driving the car. I like to drive. Guess I like to be in control. Now, there are people who will say I may not be the safest driver with whom they have ever had the pleasure of driving. It is not for me to disagree with them, rather simply to state, I got us there on time. Whatever I had to do, I got us there on time. I was never late for a game, though I did get real close to being late for a playoff game in New York. And okay, admittedly, sometimes getting there on time did take some doing. My basic philosophy of driving was to just keep going until I heard glass break.

I drove in every city. New York to Seattle. There were some times when maybe I played it a little too close. Mark Johnson and I were in Seattle, for example, and had about twenty minutes to get from our hotel over the bridge and to the ballpark. Traffic in Seattle is always awful—that evening it was worse than that. For a time even I wondered if I was going to be able to pull this one off. We got one big break, there was some sort of construction on the bridge, so the police had blocked off one lane with those orange barrels with flashing lights on top, forcing three lanes to merge into two. "Good news, partner," I told Mark, "we can use the umpire's lane." And I took off in that third lane.

I'd say we made it at least half a mile before a trooper stopped us. That big trooper stuck his head in the window and asked politely, "Sir, just what the hell do you think you're doing?"

I was almost always able to talk my way out of traffic

tickets, but this one looked tough even for me. The trooper took my driver's license and walked back to his car. "Well, Bud," I told Mark, "I don't think I'm going to be able to talk us out of this one."

Us? I was right, it was a tough one. It ended up costing me two Ken Griffey Jr. autographed baseballs—but, in return, that officer put on his siren and escorted us in that third lane all the way to the ballpark.

There were times when I had to be creative. In Toronto I had to take a real shortcut. The road I needed was on the far side of a parking lot. I pulled up to the lot attendant and he asked for the $5 parking fee. "That's okay," I told him, "we're not going to be here that long." I drove right through the lot and up a one-way street the wrong way, until I got where I needed to be. The man I was with, it probably was Johnson, couldn't believe it. "Kenny," he yelled at me, "this is a one-way street."

"That's okay," I told him, "we're only going one way."

In Detroit one afternoon an accident had the road completely blocked, so I had to drive along the shoulder. I was doing just fine until the shoulder ended. Then I had to cut through a residential area. I have to be honest, I don't remember why I had to cut across that guy's front yard, but I do remember looking in the rear-view mirror and seeing two parallel tire tracks across his lawn.

I loved driving in New York because the people there drive just the way I do. For a time though, I always had use of a limousine. That started with my very first trip into New York. My plane landed at LaGuardia Airport. I didn't know where I was or what to do. A man came up to me and said, "You going into the city?"

I said I was. "How much?"

He replied, "How much do you want to pay?"

Right then and there I knew we were going to get along just fine. I said, "Nothing."

He said, "Nothing?"

Gene Parada was his name, and we became good friends. Like family. Umpires are entitled to six tickets to every game they work. For the next twenty years two of those tickets went to Gene and his wife, Elizabeth.

Eventually though, I did start driving a rental car when we were in New York. I got to know my way around the city. One Saturday I had Larry Barnett and Rocky Roe in the car, and for some reason the road I wanted to take up to Yankee Stadium, the FDR, the East River Drive, was closed. "It's not a problem," I said optimistically. "We'll cut through the park." I knew I could go through Central Park all the way up to Harlem, then get the Madison Avenue Bridge and cut across the Harlem River to the stadium.

Admittedly, there might have been a few signs saying something about the park being closed to cars, but they weren't really that clear. "Uh, Kenny," Rocky said, "I don't think we should go this way."

"It's okay," I told him. "We're going this way." I was making great time through the park, there wasn't another car on the road—until I went around a corner—and saw hundreds of bicycles coming towards me. "Oh geeze . . ." Turned out I had driven right into the middle of a bicycle race. It was like being caught in a blizzard of bicyclists. They just whizzed by us. It was like being in Dorothy's house as it flew through the tornado. The three of us just sat there watching them, nobody saying one word.

Which made it a lot easier to hear the names they were calling us.

In all the years I drove I had only one accident—and it wasn't my fault. No, it really wasn't. We were in Boston on our way to Fenway Park. I stopped at a red light and somebody rear-ended us. He was driving a pickup truck with a solid oak bumper. It was an old, beat-up truck, but, instead of having a metal fender in front he had the redwood forest. Man, he slammed right into us. We ended up in the hospital. Mark Johnson hurt his lower back and I really hurt my neck, injuries that we both still suffer from.

The real race usually took place after a game, when I was trying to get to the airport in time to make a flight. I made my flights. I made all my flights. I made flights that other people thought were impossible to make. I traveled light. One bag and the clothes on my back. My most memorable trip was from Milwaukee to the west coast. The flight left from Chicago. The game started at 1 P.M. and our flight out wasn't until 6 P.M., which should have given us plenty of time after the game to drive to Chicago from Milwaukee. The problem was that the game went twelve innings. It was quarter of five when I got off the field. One hour and fifteen minutes. The other three people on my crew gave up, they decided to stay over until the next morning. Not me. I was going to make it. I got stopped by the first cop not too far from the stadium. I explained that I was one of the umpires and I was trying to catch a six o'clock flight. He looked at his watch. "It's only five," he said, "you'll make it."

"Leaving from Chicago," I added.

"Oh no, no way. You can't make it," he said.

"I bet I can if you let me go," I told him.

The second cop stopped me about three miles later. Same story. Go!

The third cop stopped me maybe six miles later. He was riding a motorcycle. He asked me why I was doing eighty in a fifty-five-mile-per-hour zone. Truthfully, I was surprised when he said that. Only eighty? There must have been something wrong with his radar gun. I thought I was going a lot faster than that. When I told him my story he asked, "You the guy who just got stopped twice?"

If it wasn't me, then there were two people having a real run of bad luck. He let me go too. I got to the front of the terminal five minutes before my flight departed. I left the car right there and gave an attendant $20 to take it back to the rental agency. But I made my flight. I always made my flight.

For six months every year for more than twenty-three years I was on an airplane every three or four days. I flew in good weather and bad. If the plane got off the ground, I was on it. In all that time I only had one close call. I was still in Triple-A, flying from Washington, D.C., to Toledo, Ohio. Usually I'm the last person to get on the plane. For me, getting on the plane in time to sit there watching other people get on the plane has never been a major source of entertainment. But this time I got on first and settled into a window seat. It was a small plane, about forty seats. While I was sitting there waiting I smelled smoke. I glanced out my window—the entire wing was on fire.

Anybody who thinks I can't hustle when I need to should have seen me that day. I thought the whole plane was going to burst into flames. That was the last time in my life I got on a plane first.

Most flights are routine. By contract we always travel first-class, so I've had the opportunity to sit next to some interesting people. A. J. Foyt gave me his business card and invited me to visit him at his ranch in Houston. Christie Brinkley didn't give me her card and definitely didn't invite me to visit. I sat next to Herb Alpert and Dan Aykroyd, and I became friends with a wonderful character actor named Bob Ginty. Bob Ginty is one of those actors people know as *Oh look, there's what's-his-name again. I like him.*

Not everybody was nice. When you fly as much as I did you do meet some less-than-nice people. One time I was with another American League umpire on a very early morning flight from Kansas City to Los Angeles. This was some time ago. The plane was still on the ground, we hadn't even pulled away from the gate. We were exhausted, we had our heads back and were trying to sleep. A man sitting behind that umpire was reading a newspaper, and every time he turned the page he'd hit him in the back of his head. The umpire asked him once, twice, three times very nicely, "Please quit banging me with that newspaper." Each time the man said fine, and then proceeded to bang him on the head with the newspaper. Finally through gritted teeth, my partner said, "This is the last time I'm going to ask you. Please stop hitting me with your newspaper!"

The man agreed—and then hit him in the head with his newspaper. With that, this umpire reached in his pocket—and the next thing I saw was the newspaper in flames! He'd lit the newspaper on fire! "Geeze," I said, "don't you think maybe that was a little extreme?"

"Yeah, maybe," he agreed, "but one thing I guarantee you, he ain't going to be hitting me with that newspaper again."

Life on the road was pretty simple. Meals, movies, reading, more meals, work out in the hotel health club, relax, maybe see friends in that city for a quick bite to eat, walking around malls, take a nap. It may not be a lifestyle that appeals to everyone, but it was comfortable for me.

In most cities the restaurants are closed after a game, so you try to find a reasonable place to eat. In Texas, for example, I had a good friend, a wrestler known as The Angel of Death, and after the game Death and I would go to one of the only places opened that late that served a good meal—a big strip club named The Fantasy Ranch. I'd often run into ballplayers there, although, admittedly, it was a little strange when I introduced my friend to them. "I'd like you to meet my good friend, The Angel of Death."

Other people would resort to all kinds of activities to kill time. Bill Kunkel had fish calling him. The hotel we stayed at in Seattle was right on the Puget Sound. You could stick a fishing pole out your window. Literally. Bill Kunkel liked to fish when we were there. I was eating lunch in the restaurant there one day when he walked in. "Hey, I thought you were fishing," I said.

"I am." He had rigged up an ingenious system, which I admit I never quite understood. He had the telephone in his room all set to call his cell phone. Then he attached a fishing line to the receiver of that phone. When a fish hit the line it would pull the receiver off the hook causing it to dial his phone. And when his phone rang he knew there was a fish on the line, and he'd go up to his room and reel it in.

Luciano was another umpire who loved to fish from his hotel room. One time I got up in the middle of the night to go to the bathroom. I was in a complete daze. I turned on the light and looked down—and looking right back at me was this big fish! That fish was swimming around in the bowl. I don't know who was more scared, me or that fish. But I know I got out of there before it did.

This is the kind of thing that happens when people have too much time and too little to do. Luciano, in particular, liked to play practical jokes. He would put the plate umpire's shoes in the freezer until about five minutes before game time. One time he and Haller soldered closed the straps on Jim Honochik's shin guards. It was Luciano who sewed closed all George Maloney's shirts.

George did get even with him though. He bought a battery-operated metronome, that ticking device that musicians use to keep time, set it to tick very slowly, then hid it in an air-conditioning duct in Luciano's room. For three days Ronnie was listening to a faint tick . . . tick . . . tick. . . . It was like water torture. It was driving him crazy. He wanted to change rooms but—again, thanks to Maloney conspiring with the front desk—there were no other rooms available. At one point he asked me and Maloney to come into his room to hear it. And so we did: *Gee, Ronnie, I don't hear anything. You hear something, George? Nah, I don't hear anything either. What did you say it sounded like again, Ronnie?*

It went on . . . and on . . . and on for three days, until the battery wore down. Maybe on the field we were mature authority figures, but off the field it sometimes was like summer camp. Other people, not me, definitely not me, would do things like put Saran Wrap over the toilet bowl. Or put itching powder in a jock. Food was always a good prop. Mustard in underwear. Pickles in pockets. Believe me, after a week in an equipment bag, a hamburger begins to smell really awful. Rocky Roe once put half a pound of chewed tobacco in Durwood Merrill's ball bag just before Durwood went out to work the plate. In the first inning he reached into his bag to pull out a new ball—and stopped. It was clear from the expression on his face that he'd found the chewed tobacco. One time I got Bill Kunkel. He had an important appointment and put on a nice black suit. I took about four pounds of baby powder and put it under a towel. When he sat down on the towel to put on his shoes he looked as if he was sitting in the middle of a white fog.

The late Lee Wyer stopped at . . . well, he didn't stop. When a female passenger fainted on a flight from New York to Chicago, for example, the plane made an emergency landing in Detroit. Paramedics came on board and revived her and said she was fine. When the plane took off again, Lee reached into his bag, pulled out his headphones, and went to the back of the plane. *I'm a doctor,* he told her, *and I just want to check you out.* He put his hand under her sweater right on her breast and asked her to breath in and out. Which she did. He started moving the headphones around, leaning down as if listening through them. Occasionally he'd nod and say *uh-huh, uh, interesting.* Finally he told her she seemed to be fine, but then said he would like to examine her again at the baggage claim in Chicago.

Lee Wyer was very tall, maybe six-five, and in Chicago this woman was met by a man just as big as Lee. Lee watched as she told this man what happened and pointed at Lee. The man immediately walked really fast directly towards Lee. And when he got right in front of him he said, "Aren't you going to check her out again, doctor?"

You bet, Lee agreed enthusiastically. And he went through the whole routine again.

Lee and his partner Eddie Montague both did magic tricks. But the trick Lee was best known for in baseball was known as the Baffling bra. Montague bought it for him at a magic shop. It was pretty simple: He would take two scarves and tie them together. Then he would ask a woman to work with him. He'd knot the scarves together, then push them right down the front of her dress or blouse or whatever she was wearing. And at the count of three, he would pull them out—with the woman's bra attached to it.

Don't ask. But it worked. One season he set a goal of performing this feat two thousand times. He did it everywhere, he did it on planes, in restaurants, hotel lobbies. Occasionally, women would lift up their blouses just to show Lee that they weren't even wearing a bra. He and Montague kept count. By the last day of the season he had successfully done the trick 1,998 times. They had one more game, one more shot. The pressure was enormous. They were working in San Francisco. The game went thirteen innings and didn't end till after eleven. Lee had less than an hour to reach his goal. He raced to a club and did it six more times before midnight, ending the year with an official total of 2,004. That's a major league record that probably will never be broken.

In the off-season several years later, Montague was playing golf with Bruce Froemming. Montague told him he had been hired to go to Japan for three weeks to conduct clinics for Japanese umpires. The sponsor wanted him to bring another umpire with him. They would each be paid $50,000. Montague asked Froemming if he wanted to go. Three weeks, all-expenses-paid in Japan? $50,000? "I'm your buddy, right?" Froemming responded.

Montague set up a luncheon meeting between Froemming and the Japanese representatives in the Hilton Hotel in Philadelphia. Unfortunately, he himself was on vacation and couldn't attend this meeting. There were seven or eight Japanese there. They put a kimono on Froemming, and a small hat, and everybody started bowing to each other, and Froemming bowed right along with them. It was quite an elaborate lunch, during which they toasted each other with an unusual drink. Bird sweat, they told Froemming when he asked—bird sweat. It came from bird droppings. A very special drink. Because the Japanese spoke with heavy accents he couldn't quite understand them. They were all drinking it, so he took a sip—and liked it. "This doesn't offend me," he said, and drank some more.

Eventually, the door opened and former major leaguer Jay Johnstone, the host of a sports show in which they play practical jokes on unsuspecting people, walked in. The whole thing had been a setup. There was no trip to Japan, although Froemming did admit that, for $50,000, he'd drink bird shit.

Recently, Montague and Jerry Layne had a new, young partner, an umpire just up from the minor leagues who had never been to several of the big major league cities. The first time this crew got to Philadelphia this young umpire said that he wanted to see the Liberty Bell. Montague and Layne volunteered to take him. Actually, they didn't exactly take him to see *the* Liberty Bell—they took him to see *a* Liberty Bell. In Philadelphia, several companies have small replicas of the Liberty Bell out in front for promotional purposes. They took him to see one of these bells. This young umpire was surprised. "Wow," he admitted, "I always thought it was bigger than that."

"Most people do," Montague agreed. The umpire was also surprised by the fact that it was just sitting out there in the open, and there were no other tourists looking at it.

Layne explained, "I guess we're just lucky. Normally there'd be big crowds around it." Then Jerry suggested that the young umpire have his picture taken with the Liberty Bell? How could he resist? "Go ahead, put your arm around it," he suggested. And when that photograph was developed they happily showed it to the embarrassed umpire's wife.

While there are people who refuse to accept it, umpires are human beings too. And they do things any normal man living on the road would do. In that same Seattle hotel from which the umpires fished, another umpire sitting in the hotel bar probably had a little too much to drink. He began talking to an attractive woman who told him she was waiting for her husband. Now, admittedly, it's possible that this umpire said some things better left unsaid. What he didn't know was that her husband was an offensive tackle for the Seattle Seahawks. When the husband finally arrived this umpire didn't back down. That was when the tackle picked him up and hung him out the window, holding onto him by his ankles, three stories above the Puget Sound.

Another umpire had close friends that he stayed with in Los Angeles, rather than staying in a hotel. In our locker room one day I noticed he was just covered with mosquito bites. I noticed because he was in agony, he couldn't stop scratching. What happened, he explained, was that he met a woman and couldn't bring her back to his friend's house, so they had made love out in a field—and that's where the mosquitoes got him.

He swore that would never happen to him again. So, at his next opportunity he was a lot smarter—he did it in a public fountain in Chicago. He was right. That time the mosquitoes didn't get him—the police did.

I've had my own share of interesting evenings. During spring training one year I was in a bar in Ft. Lauderdale with my girlfriend, Cheryl Bogner. I'm a lucky man, Cheryl is a very attractive woman. The place was crowded, and a college kid started hitting on my girl. Very politely, I suggested, "Why don't you just leave her alone?"

About eight guys stood up with him. "What are you," he asked, "her bodyguard?"

And there I was without my pool table. Fortunately, Orioles pitcher Arthur Rhodes was there with several other players. Never in my life did I think there would come a time when I would be happy to see Orioles. Baseball is like a brotherhood, we may fight on the field but . . . well, we may fight off the field too, but, most often, people protect each other. "We got your back, Kais," Rhodes said. That ended the confrontation.

As my son from my first marriage, John, got a little older I would take him with me on the road. The Ken Kaiser World Tour he called it. On one of our first trips I took J. K. and two of his friends to Baltimore. They sat in the stands. Only once in my entire life have I watched a major league baseball game from the stands. That was a World Series game in Toronto that Mark Johnson was working. I saw enough to know the view from the field was a lot better. But I knew what fans were like, I knew how rough they could be. So I told John very carefully, don't identify yourself, don't get into trouble. I definitely told him that. But he happened to be sitting behind a particularly loud and obnoxious fan, a man who spent half the game screaming at me. Finally, J. K. couldn't take it anymore, he said to the guy, "Why don't you shut your mouth. No one wants to hear you."

Apparently, the man was surprised. "What are you," he asked, "a fan of the umpires?"

J. K. followed my instructions. He didn't admit that one of those umpires was his father. No, *he* didn't, his friend did. He said something like, "That's his dad at third base. You gonna do something about it?"

Uh, yes he was. But, before he threw the first punch, he said loudly enough for everybody in the section to hear, "Oh, great. So, you're the umpire's kid!" That's when the fight broke out.

From the field I could see there was a fight going on in the stands. That's not unusual. I knew my son was sitting somewhere in that area, but it didn't occur to me that he. . . . So I wasn't that surprised, but I was disappointed. After the game I told him very specifically, "J. K., these are baseball fans. Don't get down to their level."

On the field I treated all players equally. Well, maybe Eddie Murray got a little special treatment, but off the field umpires and players do develop relationships. Like people who work in different divisions of the same company, I think each of us knew how hard the other one's job was. For example, on the field Paul O'Neill did nothing but complain. But, one day I was walking through the Yankee clubhouse with my son, I had been growing a goatee, it was kind of gray and black, and I thought it made me look quite distinguished. "Geeze Kais, what happened?" O'Neill said when he saw me. "It looks like a skunk sat on your face."

There were certain people you just couldn't help liking. Reggie Jackson and I got along really well. Reggie respected people who stood up to him. One time, I remember, I was walking past the Yankee locker room and I saw Reggie arm wrestling with Graig Nettles for $100. "Boy," I said to him, "you must think you're pretty strong." Well, Reggie was strong. He had massive forearms, that's where he got his great power. "Tell you what," I challenged him, "why don't you put another hundred down there and we'll see how strong you really are."

Reggie loved a challenge. His face just lit up. "Come on, big guy," he said. Now, I know Reggie Jackson is left-handed, I'd seen him bat and throw, but he didn't know I was left-handed. So I put up my right hand. "No, no," he told me, "I'm left-handed."

I hesitated. "Okay," I said, "I guess I could probably beat you left-handed too." Hands up. Boom. I put him down in about a second. Reggie was strong, but he wasn't tall. "You might be big for a small man," I told him, "but you aren't big for a big man." I took the $100 and left.

Only one time did I see Reggie back down to a challenge. The Yankees were playing Milwaukee, and a left-handed pitcher for the Brewers struck out Reggie on all off-speed stuff. Junk. Reggie was furious. He wanted that pitcher to challenge him. He wanted him to try to throw the fastball past him. "You got no balls, you gutless bastard," he screamed. "Throw that ball. I'll kick your ass."

Suddenly, from out of the Brewers dugout stepped Frank Howard, big Frank Howard. Frank Howard was about six-ten and as strong as anybody who ever played baseball. Looking at Reggie, he shouted, "Why don't you start with me?" Reggie turned around and went quietly back into the dugout. He didn't want any part of Frank Howard.

One of my favorite players was Fred Stanley. "Chicken" Stanley. He used to do an imitation of me. He'd take about six towels and stuff them down his shirt and walk up and down the dugout left-handed the way I do. He kind of ambled side to side. And then he would mimic my out call. It was pretty funny. Not *very* funny, just pretty funny. But funny enough that I knew I had to get even with him. I enlisted Catfish Hunter in my plan. After a game one day I got the keys to Hunter's van and kind of hid behind it in the parking lot. When Stanley walked by I kidnapped him. I mean, I literally leaped out and grabbed him from behind, picked him up over my head and body-slammed him into the back of the van. I shut the door and locked it. I'm sure he had absolutely no idea it was me. Catfish knew. And when he started driving I'm sure Chicken thought he was kidding. I'm sure he thought so all the way to Catfish Hunter's house in New Jersey where he had to spend the night.

Here's an admission. I took advantage of the relationships I made on the field off the field. St. Joseph's Villa in Rochester is a home for kids who get into trouble. With a little less luck, that could have been me. I wanted to help out, so I decided to host an annual sports dinner to raise money for their charity. Eventually it became a very big event. Don Mattingly came about six times, George Brett was always there, Kirby Puckett, Nolan Ryan, Roger Clemens, Rickey Henderson, Reggie, Paul Molitor, Billy Martin, Dave Righetti—it was an impressive list. I also invited my friends from pro wrestling, including The Road Warriors, Big John Studd, Hulk Hogan, Mr. Perfect, and The Angel of Death. The day before the dinner these people would go over to the villa to spend time with the kids.

It was a very successful event. In the ten years we held the dinner I had only one problem. After the dinner one year we all went to a club in Rochester. I was downstairs when a security guard found me. Three wrestlers, it turned out to be The Road Warriors, Hawk and Animal, and Big John Studd, were throwing plastic chairs off the balcony. They were competing to see who could hit the most cars. Throwing chairs? Didn't they know they were supposed to be hitting each other with them?

I went upstairs with four security guards. As it turned out, The Road Warriors were keeping score. The good news was that the only thing they were throwing was chairs—and that their aim was really bad. The bad news also was that they were throwing chairs. By the time I got there the score was still zip. One of the security people told me, "I'm sorry, Mr. Kaiser, you're going to have to get them to stop throwing chairs, or we're going to have to throw them out."

I looked at him. Then I looked at Big John Studd, who was about six-nine and three hundred pounds, and I said, "You're going to throw them out?"

Maybe that's when the guard was hit by reality—which was much safer than being hit by a chair. "You know what, Mr. Kaiser?" he said. "Try to keep those people under control." And walked away.

My career on the field made a lot of things possible for me off the field. Once I reached the major leagues I sort of stopped working in the winter. While The Incredible Umpire might have made a great wrestling character, I suspected baseball would frown upon seeing me get tossed around the ring. Throwing people out of a game was one thing, throwing them out of a ring was a whole different world.

Years ago umpires had to work in the winter to pay their bills. They took any kind of seasonal jobs available—working in a bar, driving trucks, several umpires worked in sporting-goods stores or officiated basketball games. Luciano was a substitute teacher, Larry Napp worked as a boxing referee. But, with the raises negotiated by the union, I earned a very good salary, more than I ever imagined possible, so I really didn't have to work like the old-timers. Several umpires, Richie Garcia, Jerry Crawford, and Jim McKean, for example, run clinics for college and high school umpires. I did a lot of different things during the winter. For a time I did a lot of speaking at dinners and charity events. I told them all the old stories, and some of them were even true! People would always ask me what really went on during an argument. And I would tell them what happened to me one day in New York. Lou Piniella was at bat and I called a strike on him. It was a good pitch, but he didn't like it. He stepped out of the box and looked back at me. "Hey, where was that pitch at?" he asked.

"Time," I yelled, and said, "Lou, you're a college graduate aren't you?"

He nodded his head. "Yeah. So?"

"So? So didn't they teach you in college that you're never supposed to end a sentence with a preposition?"

Lou thought about that for a minute, then said, "You know what, you're absolutely right. So where was that pitch at, asshole?"

And I loved to tell people about the game, during my first season in the big leagues, when Gene Mauch came out to discuss a call I made at second base. After a brief argument, Mauch asked me in a nice way, "Kaiser, huh? How do you spell that?"

I spelled it for him. "K-a-i-s-e-r, like it sounds."

He nodded, "Yeah, just like I thought. One eye."

At one point I was also invited to speak to a class at MIT. MIT? I could barely spell it. Naturally, I was pleased at the invitation. Truthfully, I didn't know what I was going to tell these kids. A college education doesn't help you call the low strike. The room was really crowded, and all these young people were looking at me with this kind of expectation. The professor running the class introduced me and I asked him, "So, how you doing?"

"Relative to what?" he replied. I figured I was in serious trouble right there—and the class hadn't even begun.

But I do remember that one kid asked me, "Mr. Kaiser, it says here in your bio that you've been an umpire since you were eighteen. Don't you feel you cheated yourself out of college?"

At that point in my life I was doing very well financially. "You know, that same thing occurred to me last year," I explained, "so I've been thinking about buying a college."

In my career I did have the opportunity to do two television commercials. Being a major league umpire makes you an expert on . . . on practically nothing. If Nolan Ryan was selling fastballs I could be a good pitchman. But I don't qualify for anything else. The first commercial I did was for a local company, the Charlotte Appliance Corporation. This is one of the best companies in Rochester; it has a long-standing reputation for excellence, and they were looking for a person who represented the image they wanted to convey, which was that they sold quality products and offered good service at low prices. Who better than an umpire? I was the perfect spokesperson for them, mainly because the owner of the store was a good buddy of mine, "TV Tony" Agostinelli, and I worked cheap. The commercial was written especially for me. "Shop here to buy good stuff," or something like that.

My second commercial was a national spot for Diet Pepsi. That was the closest I ever got to a diet. Actually, it was for Pepsi One, the soft drink with only one calorie. In the commercial an umpire made a call at home plate. I really was perfect for this part. I mean, what were they going to do, use an appliance salesman?

I got the commercial because I looked a lot like an umpire and I happened to bump into a guy I had known several years earlier who worked for Stolichnaya Vodka. Stoli is owned by Pepsi. Years earlier I had done some public relations for Stoli—I would take some of their salesmen or customers to lunch at the ballpark before a game. We filmed the commercial in Seattle. I also appeared on a twenty-second CD suggesting that people take the advice of someone who knows the rules of the game and try Pepsi One.

Hey, it really can be fun doing something you know nothing about. That's why I always figured Weaver would have enjoyed being an umpire. It took a full day to shoot a thirty-second segment. The runner slid across the plate and I called him safe. That was it. Then he slid across the plate again. He was still safe. And again. They didn't use professional ballplayers, but it didn't make any difference, the runner was safe every time. Time after time after time. They shot it from more angles than the Questec Umpire Information System. It was amazing, I'd finally found the perfect use for instant replay—and they wouldn't use it.

In 1990 I was invited to join a team consisting of Eric Gregg, Dan Morrison, and Mark and John Hirschbeck on the TV game show *Family Feud.* We played against five players: Joe Carter, Rick Sutcliffe, Ozzie Smith, Wally Joyner, and Ellis Burks in a week-long "Natural Enemies" special. The game is simple: before the show they asked a series of questions to one hundred people; when we were asked the same questions we were supposed to guess how those people answered. It actually sounds a little easier than it is to play. For example, there were four answers to the question, "Name a phrase women love to hear?" The first two were easy, *You're beautiful,* and *Will you marry me?* Then it was my turn. Those were the two answers I had, but then I had five seconds to come up with something else. So I said the first thing that came to my mind, "Your place or mine?"

That was not one of the answers.

I really did get a little nervous. I probably wasn't the best representative of the great game of baseball. To the question, "Name a really boring sport," I replied, "Baseball." Now, I don't really think that, I didn't believe it. But it was the first answer that came out of my mouth.

Of course, that wasn't as bad as Mark Hirschbeck's response to the question, "Name a sport that is run by a clock." Mark is a major league umpire. To become a major league umpire he had to have a thorough understanding of the rules. Therefore his answer, "Baseball," could only be the result of nervousness. Either that, or there was something I was missing for thirty-three years.

Probably my most accurate answer during the week was also not on the survey. The question was, "Name one thing athletes do for good luck." The answer was pretty obvious to me, I said firmly, "Count their money."

And maybe the funniest answer was Dan Morrison's response to the question, "Name something you played as a child you still play today?" Dan thought about it for a second, then said, "Doctor?"

I answered next. *What am I supposed to say after that,* I wondered, *nurse?*

While the players won more money for their charities than we did, we actually won more games, three to two. Not that I was keeping count, of course.

For a short time I was in the food business. What better business for me, right? I produced and marketed Ken Kaiser's Major League Salsa. A friend of mine in Rochester, Tommy Tescano, made the best Mexican salsa that I had ever tasted. Still does. I used to give it to the players that I liked. Cecil Fielder fell in love with it. He told me it was the best salsa he'd ever tasted. Couldn't get enough of it. He'd be up at bat, pitch would be two feet outside. Close enough! Strike three! *Okay, Kais, but can you get me some more of that salsa?*

I was well known in upstate New York. I was a local celebrity, so I knew a lot of people in the city. Among them was a top executive at Wagman's Grocers, one of the biggest and most prestigious food chains in the country. They tested this salsa and decided to market it. I was going to be the salsa king! What the colonel was to fried chicken I was going to be to salsa. The label was a picture of me in uniform. Okay, maybe there wasn't that obvious a connection between umpires and good salsa, but people liked the product. When we gave it away in the stores they ate it up. There was only one problem: It was a fresh salsa, so it could only stay on the shelves for a couple of days at most. It had the shelf life of a mayfly. It had to be used almost immediately. The expiration date pretty much read, "today." So, if you bought it in the afternoon you had to go home and use it.

It survived about two years. Instead of becoming the salsa king, I was more like the salsa peasant.

The last winter job I ever had was umpiring. Something I was really qualified to do. After the 1998 season, Durwood Merrill and I worked at Cal Ripkin Jr.'s fantasy baseball camp. I had known the whole Ripkin family—Senior, Junior, and Cal's brother Billy—just about their whole careers. The first day of camp Billy told the campers, "This is one umpire you do not want to mess with, because he does not take it." I liked that. I was proud of my reputation. And I proved it to them. I only knew one way to umpire. So, the first day of camp I threw a doctor out of the game.

What I guess I didn't know at that time was that the next person who was going to get thrown out of the game was me.

This is an example of how much major league baseball changed during my career: I knew Rickey Henderson for more than two decades. I probably worked more than two hundred games in which he played. I liked him but, as with George Scott, I don't think I ever understood three words that he said. *How's it going, Rickey?* "Mumble, mumble, mumble, Kais, mumble, mumble." They were far from the only players I couldn't understand—there were a lot of players who didn't speak Rochester.

In 2001, Ted Barrett's parents went to watch him working a game in Seattle. At one point between innings he was standing in the outfield talking to the Mariners' Japanese outfielder, Ichiro Suzuki. After the game his parents asked him what he was doing. "I was talking to Suzuki," he told them.

"Uh, Ted," they reminded him, "you don't speak Japanese."

"That's right," Teddy explained to them, "but we were talking to each other in Spanish."

When I came up, umpires were usually older than the players, and few of them had gone to college. The games were played outdoors in old stadiums and we still used the mattress protectors behind the plate. The American and National Leagues maintained their own umpire staffs and we each had our own system for working. Our association—the union—had very little power. Our maximum salary was $21,000, and the only time we got off during the season was the three-day break for the All-Star game.

That had all changed by the time I finished my career. By then, major league umpires were earning hundreds of thousands of dollars a year and working interleague games, we got a three-week vacation during the season, had job security—and were speaking Spanish to Japanese players. What had been a job had become a profession.

It would have been nice to have been able to enjoy all that I had worked for. That didn't happen. I'm not bitter towards baseball. I'm not angry about the way I was treated after spending thirty-six years in professional baseball. I'm not upset that baseball has refused to pay me and other umpires the money we've earned. It doesn't bother me that baseball won't even give me my health insurance benefits.

Okay, I'm lying. I'm definitely lying. I am bitter and angry. Upset? I'm furious. But like all the other umpires who have lost just about everything we worked for, there isn't very much I can do about it. When I first came up to the big leagues it wasn't unusual for retired umpires to drop by the locker room before the game. We'd sit around and they would tell their stories about the good old days. From their stories, it became pretty obvious that those good old days weren't all that good. Salaries were terrible, there were basically no benefits—after twenty-four years in the big leagues, Beans Reardon got a $200 monthly pension—and umpires were treated very badly. For example, until 1959, when American League umpires got to Chicago they had to report to the office of American League president Will Harridge every morning. They just had to sit there—and this was every day—waiting to see if Harridge wanted to speak to them. There were days he didn't even open the door to say hello. Even worse, baseball could hire and fire umpires without giving any reason at all. All they had to do was send the umpire a letter informing him that he'd lost his job. And only the umpires picked by league officials to work the World Series got any extra money, so there was always a lot of competition, jealousy, and anger among umpires. There were definitely a lot of major league umpires who didn't get along with each other.

Baseball had very little respect for umpires. One year when the umpires went on strike, for example, the great baseball executive Bill Veeck, who then owned the Chicago White Sox, told people that baseball didn't really need us, that they could get umpires just as good from any bar in town. You know how much we appreciated his support. Just as we went back to work it started raining in Chicago—so, for three straight days we had to postpone games. Veeck started screaming that these rainouts were costing him a fortune—and we explained that the guys in the bar said we couldn't play.

I remember one of the old-time umpires being asked what he remembered most about the New York fans. After thinking about it for a minute he said, "They had terrible aim."

The last thing most baseball people wanted was for the umpires to form any kind of association or union. Union? They didn't even want two umpires talking to each other. They wanted to be able to deal with each of us independently. Every umpire had to negotiate his own deal with baseball. And if an umpire dared complain publicly he got fired.

As far back as 1945, the commissioner of baseball, Happy Chandler, wanted to improve working conditions for umpires. Chandler was the commissioner—but he was actually a politician, a former senator, not a baseball man. He asked an umpire named Ernie Stewart to write to the other umpires and ask their opinion about what was fair. American League president Harridge got a copy of that letter and forced Stewart to resign.

The National League umpires formed the first umpires' association in 1964. Among the leaders were Al Barlick and Augie Donatelli, two of the toughest and most respected umpires in history. Because the National Leaguers stuck together, there wasn't much the league could do to stop them. But, when the American League umpires tried to do the same thing a year later, the league made the optional retirement age of fifty-five mandatory, and Bill McKinley, a twenty-year veteran who had helped organize a meeting, was through.

A few years later, two American League umpires, Bill Valentine and Al Salerno, again tried to form a union. As soon as the league found out about it both men were fired. I guess there's a reason it's called hardball.

In 1969, the major leagues began the playoff system and the umpires wanted to be paid fairly to work the extra games. When an agreement couldn't be reached, the umpires decided not to work the 1970 playoffs. For the first time umpires called their own strike. Baseball hired replacements. Among the minor leaguers they tried to recruit was Terry Tata, who was stuck in Triple-A. Barney Deary, the head of the Umpires Development Program, called him and said, "I want to put you on notice that I'm going to offer you a position to go up and umpire the National League playoffs between Cincinnati and Pittsburgh." In other words—well actually, it only takes one word—scab.

Tata had been in the minors for twelve years. This was his opportunity to get to the major leagues, at least for a few games. He really thought about it. But the next morning he called Augie Donatelli to tell him about the phone call and his decision. "I just want to tell you where I stand." And he turned down Deary's offer.

"We won't forget you," Donatelli told him, and two years later Terry was up in the big leagues to stay.

Baseball was forced to settle that strike when the Teamsters Union, the people who delivered hot dogs, popcorn, and soda to the ballpark, refused to cross our picket lines. Umpires could be replaced, but not hot dogs.

In all honesty, I've felt the same way at times myself.

I was buried in the minor leagues in 1970, so I didn't pay much attention to any of this. I just didn't think it affected me. At that time I was making less than $1,000 a month, and the only things I was interested in were getting gas money and what was for dinner. But, when the association went out on strike in 1979, I was in the big leagues. I was a member of the Major League Umpires Association. I had never been in a labor dispute before, but I was ready to do whatever I was told to do. They told me to picket. Picket? I'll do more than that, I'll put it in bales and throw it up on the wagon. Our leader was a Philadelphia lawyer named Richie Phillips. Richie had a way of motivating us. He knew how to use the language. The particular words he used were *more* and *money.*

Richie Phillips was a tough lawyer, agent, and union leader. How tough was he? When he was thirteen years old he was the head of the Altar Boys Society at his church—and he led them out on strike when a priest tried to take away their tips. He was thirteen years old and he was leading a strike against God. I mean, what chance did the American League have? He grew up to become a criminal lawyer, then he went to work in the Philadelphia District Attorney's office prosecuting murderers. He was the perfect guy to deal with baseball's owners.

We really didn't know quite how tough he was, but it was obvious he was a strong leader. It was a rough time for the umpires. We didn't have a real union yet, so every umpire still had to sign an annual contract. Richie Phillips convinced everybody not to sign a contract for the 1979 season. Without signed contracts baseball wouldn't let us go to spring training. During the spring, baseball sent us all letters warning that if we didn't return our signed contracts before the season opened we would be replaced. We had to choose between the union and our jobs. It was really a scary decision to make. I thought my career was going to end just when it was beginning. For me, though, it wasn't much of a choice. I didn't have that much to lose. If things didn't go right, I figured I could always get my old job back at the bank—where I would probably be in the strange position of having to repossess my own furniture. But veteran umpires were risking twenty years of benefits, including their pensions and health insurance. They put their future on the line. Richie Phillips held us together.

When the season began I walked the picket line in Boston and New York. It was sort of strange—the fans were very supportive of us not working. They were much nicer to us when we weren't doing our jobs than when we were at work. We elected Ron Luciano as our first president, because we figured no one knew more about getting his picture in the paper than Ronnie. Major league baseball tried to prove that Veeck was right, they hired replacement umpires from the minor leagues. The scabs. The strike lasted more than seven weeks. A lot of mortgages and car loans didn't get paid, there were some tears, but nobody even suggested giving in to the owners.

Richie Phillips traveled with a group of umpires to several cities to try to get other major unions to publicly support our strike. In Boston, the AFL-CIO announced its support. Detroit was next. As the center of the auto industry, Detroit is one of the most pro-union cities in America. A meeting was scheduled at our hotel headquarters with representatives of several important unions. Richie had invited the press to cover the meeting, and camera crews from three TV stations, and reporters from about five radio stations and every local newspaper showed up. They were waiting patiently outside the room for a statement from the union officials.

In fact, just about the only people who didn't show up were the union officials. One person showed up, a member of the service union that represented the people who worked inside ballparks. But he had no power, he was just supposed to observe the meeting and make a report. While Richie got on the phone and tried to find officials from the other unions, just about everybody relaxed with a drink or two. Richie didn't want the media to know what was really going on, so he encouraged everybody to pretend a raucous meeting was in progress. Every few minutes somebody would stand up and scream, "They can't treat us like that anymore!" and the rest of us would cheer, *That's right!* And pour another drink.

I don't think I had realized that being a member of an organized union was such tough work.

After almost two hours, it was obvious that no other union representatives were coming to the meeting. The one actual union member who was there didn't say a word. Just every once in awhile someone would pour him another drink. This was potentially a very embarrassing situation. Finally, Richie Phillips came up with a plan: because Detroit was an American League city the reporters didn't know the National League umpires. So, one of the National Leaguers would pretend to be a union representative. Luciano would walk out of the room with him and, as they walked by the reporters, the National Leaguer would say loudly, "Don't worry, we're going to be behind you all the way on this one." He wouldn't stop to answer any questions, and Ronnie would promise the reporters that the union would be issuing a statement soon.

It was finally decided that Dutch Rennart would play the union official. Dutch looked the part; he was short and very compact, and he smoked a cigar. The problem was that, while waiting, just about everybody in the room had been drinking. Richie explained the plan to Dutch. "The only thing we want you to say is that you're behind us all the way."

"You bet," Dutch said firmly, "I'm behind you all the way."

"Yeah, we know that," Richie said, "but you have to say it to Ronnie."

"Okay, you got it." He looked at Ronnie and told him, "Hey, Ronnie, I'm behind you all the way."

Richie tried to make it a little simpler, "No, see Dutch, all you have to do is go with Ronnie and say loudly that you support the association."

"That's right," Dutch said really loudly, "I support our association."

Everybody cheered.

"All right, here we go, Dutch. You and Ronnie are going to go out there. If anybody asks you any questions, you just tell them that you're a good union man. Got it?"

"I'm a good union man."

Ronnie walked over to the door and opened it. Then he looked at Dutch and said—so that all the reporters could hear him—"Thanks a lot for coming. I want you to know we appreciate your support."

Dutch turned around to see who Ronnie was talking to; when he realized Ronnie was looking at him he said, "Don't worry, Ronnie, I'm not going anywhere. I'm with you all the way."

Everybody cheered. Richie Phillips shut the door.

Eventually an official of the AFL-CIO did show up. And, when he heard from Richie that a representative of the

Teamsters Union had been there earlier and before leaving had pledged that union's support, he agreed to make a statement of support. By then, I think, people were looking under the table for that Teamsters Union representative. And, before the meeting was done, that representative of the service union had pledged the support of his union too.

The next day we walked a picket line outside Tiger Stadium. There were probably about twenty of us. I read in the paper the next day that Phillips had estimated that 200 people had walked the picket line. I must have missed that 180 people, because I never saw them.

I hated being on a picket line. If working third base was dull, just imagine walking around in a circle carrying a sign. It's dull and tiresome. Hey, I wasn't walking that fast—if people couldn't read my sign the first time, they weren't going to get it the twenty-fifth time.

Richie Phillips did a tremendous job of holding the union together. That wasn't easy. This was new to all of us. We didn't know what to expect, but we knew our jobs were in jeopardy. There were some people who suggested going back to work. It's amazing how good a bad salary can look when you're not getting it.

Baseball pretended the replacement umpires were doing an acceptable job. I was told that they sent a memo to the clubs explaining the situation and asking managers and players to take it easy on the replacements. But it was a joke. Those people could call balls and strikes, safe and out, but they had no control over the games. The real problem was that they were inconsistent. I think it was Yankee manager Bob Lemon who told me when the strike ended, "The problem with those guys was that we never knew what to expect. At least you guys are bad consistently."

The strike lasted seven weeks. Seven weeks of wondering if we were ever going to work again. Finally, the league presidents, Chub Feeney of the National League and Lee MacPhail of the American League, met with the association's board and reached a settlement. In addition to a substantial salary increase, we just about doubled the starting salary to $22,000, we got a two-week vacation during the season, which meant we could spend at least a little time during the season with our families, and annual contracts offering some job security. But probably the most important thing was that we had established an association, a union. By sticking together we'd proven that we had real strength, we had a union.

I was thrilled to be back to work. Thrilled to still have a job. I loved being a major league umpire. The players were obviously thrilled we were back too. When we came onto the field to work our first game, they actually stood on the top step of the dugout and started clapping. There was a lot of kidding too; for a while, every time we had a disputed call someone would shout from the dugout, "Bring back the real umpires!" or, "The scabs could've missed that one just as good as you!" but it was in fun. Mostly. I think. I hope.

That strike marked the beginning of more than two decades of bitter fights between our association and major league baseball. As a labor leader, Richie Phillips was tenacious, he never let up on baseball. He made a lot of enemies. Supposedly, at one point during negotiations he got so upset he literally threw a chair through a wall. Richie produced for us, but the fact is that very few members of our association really knew what was going on in negotiations. We'd usually have one meeting a year, just before the start of spring training. Generally, our negotiating position could be defined as, "whatever Richie says it is." Most of the time I didn't even know what we were asking for in negotiations.

Richie Phillips was completely in control of the Major League Umpires Association. Pretty much nobody questioned him. We said anything we wanted to say; first Richie told us what we wanted to say, then we said it. In 1984 we went on strike during the playoffs. Only a few umpires were assigned to work the playoff games. So, for most of us the playoffs was the perfect time to strike—we were refusing to work when we weren't scheduled to work anyway. But it was embarrassing to baseball to have scabs working what were supposedly the most important games of the season. We settled that strike for an agreement that the bonus money paid for working post-season games would go into a pool and be distributed equally among all umpires. That was really important, because it eliminated all the jealousy and backbiting. Working the post-season games became a matter of prestige, rather than a financial bonus for getting along with baseball's executives.

Richie demanded respect for umpires. When baseball added games to the playoffs in 1985 without our permission, we threatened another strike. Nobody could complain that umpires weren't calling enough strikes. But that strike was averted when we agreed to binding arbitration. The arbitrator was Richard Nixon. Richard Nixon, the former president of the United States. It wasn't like former president Jimmy Carter, who was busy negotiating peace treaties between nations, but it was still pretty impressive to have a former president negotiating peace between baseball and its umpires. Nixon gave us a forty percent pay increase for the playoffs.

This was the first time in baseball history that umpires had any real power off the field, and a lot of people didn't like that. There was a lot of resentment, a lot of people who thought umpires had become too arrogant, that we had come to believe that we were as important to the game as the players. These people didn't like umpires showing any personality on the field. The fans knew who Ron Luciano was and there was no question that he added some fun to the game. A lot of people just loved Eric Gregg. There were a lot of people who recognized me—I was the guy whose arms were on backwards—and every National League fan was familiar with Dutch Rennart's exaggerated strike call. Baseball officials didn't like any of that. None of it. Umpires weren't supposed to be noticed. So, baseball did everything possible to tone us down.

At times it felt like we were in a constant battle with baseball. When Terry Cooney threw Roger Clemens out of a playoff game in 1990 the complaints about umpires having too much power got much worse. Just who did we think we were, getting angry just because players cursed at us? We were umpires, we were supposed to take abuse. What were we getting so upset about? Screaming at the umpire is an American tradition. Like pushing cake in the bride's face at a wedding, or the car mechanic charging for repairs he never did.

Basically, our feeling was that we were the best in the world at what we did, that our presence guaranteed that the game would be fair, and that it was the players and managers who wouldn't leave us alone to do our job and who were the people who were hurting the game. Here's the reality of the job: One time, just before I came up, the old National Leaguer Tom Gorman was working first base during a Pirates-Cubs game. Danny Murtaugh was managing the Pirates and Leo Durocher was managing the Cubs. Gorman and Durocher really didn't like each other very much. On an infield ground ball, the runner, the Cubs' Paul Popovich, and Pirates first baseman Al Oliver collided, and Oliver went flying into Gorman. Gorman went down hard. He was knocked unconscious and, as it turned out, his leg was broken. When Gorman regained consciousness Murtaugh and Durocher were standing right over him. The first thing Durocher said to him, long before *Are you okay* or *are you breathing,* was "What is he, Tom, safe or out?"

Gorman whispered, "Who's that talking?"

Durocher said, "It's me, it's Leo."

"Well then," Gorman decided, "if it's your runner Leo, then he's out!"

And Durocher started arguing with him! The umpire was lying there on the ground in pain, half conscious, and the manager was arguing with him about his call!

No wonder baseball thought the umpires had too much power.

We also felt strongly about the fact that the league office would not back us up in a dispute with players or managers. In 1996, for example, the Indians and the Brewers had a real brawl. Umpire Joe Brinkman tried to break it up, grabbing Cleveland's Julian Tavarez from behind and trying to hold onto him. Tavarez flipped Brinkman, then body slammed him to the ground. Tavarez was suspended five games—for fighting the Brewers. The league did not penalize him for flipping Brinkman. So we pretty much knew that, except for all the protective equipment we wear and Richie Phillips, we were out there naked.

Believe me, naked is not the way you want to see me. Or Eric Gregg, either. If anyone doubted that baseball would not protect its umpires, we got more proof in October 1996. Just a few days before the end of the season, Roberto Alomar got into an argument with John Hirschbeck and spit in his face. Point blank, he spit at him. Having known Alomar since he was a baby, I knew he was a decent man who just lost control. Of course, while something like that has never happened to me—you calling me a liar?—I kind of understood what happened. What I didn't understand is the response of the league. Alomar was suspended for five games—at the beginning of the following season. The league allowed him to participate in the playoffs.

In the locker room after the argument, Alomar said some personal things about Hirschbeck that he never should have said. He was wrong. When Hirschbeck heard these comments he tried to get into the Orioles locker room to confront him. But the bottom line was that baseball failed to back the umpires. By letting Alomar participate in the playoffs they were basically declaring open season on the umpires. Let me make this suggestion: spit on an IRS agent and see what happens to you. Spit on a police officer and try to figure out how you're going to raise bail. Or, just imagine what would have happened if an umpire had spit on the commissioner of baseball. Think that umpire would have been working the playoff games?

I believe what happened after that confrontation was that

baseball decided it had to try to take back some of the power that had been gained by our association through our several contracts. Several steps were taken. By the end of 1999, the league presidents, who had always controlled their umpires, were eliminated, and the commissioner's office became our direct boss. The traditional American and National League structure was ended for umpires. Our schedules were no longer controlled by the leagues, and we began working in all the major league cities. Instead of going to a city ten times during the season, at most an umpire now goes there four times. The theory was that, by working in every big league city, umpires wouldn't get to any single city too often or work too many games featuring the same teams. That would make it much tougher for players, managers, and umpires to form the kind of relationships we used to be able to make. Both good and bad—it would also help prevent feuds from developing. Eliminating the league identification would also promote uniformity of umpiring styles throughout baseball. But it also meant that the fans wouldn't get as familiar with the individual umpires.

In theory, this new system would cut down on travel during the season—but not in reality. Umpires make just as many trips, it's just that the distances traveled are shorter. Maybe if I was younger I would have enjoyed going to some different cities. It definitely could have been fun. But, having been in the American League for twenty-three years, I knew all the good restaurants and hotels. I knew the places to shop and I knew the maitre d's and the limo drivers, and I had friends just about everywhere.

In addition, Commissioner Bud Selig hired Sandy Alderson to be the executive vice president in charge of operations. Alderson was a lawyer who had served as president and general manager of the Oakland A's. One of the first things Alderson did was make it clear he was going after the umpires. Put them in their place. Show them who was boss. In July 1999, umpire Tom Hallion got into an argument with the Colorado Rockies pitching coach Milt May and catcher Jeff Reed. During the argument Hallion bumped into Reed. As a result, National League president Len Coleman, in one of the last actions he took before resigning, suspended Hallion for three days without pay. A lot of baseball people believed the decision to suspend Hallion was forced by Alderson. Supposedly, the commissioner's office had drafted other directives to the umpires in Coleman's name that Coleman refused to issue. Who knows? The only thing for certain was that Hallion was suspended. No one could remember an umpire ever being suspended for a run-in with a player. This was a big deal. It was like a declaration of war against the umpires.

There was also a very strong rumor that, when our contract expired at the end of the 1999 season, Alderson intended to get rid of twenty of the sixty-eight permanent major league umpires. When I first heard that I really wasn't too concerned. Richie'll take care of it, I figured. It was obvious they were trying to break the union, but they had tried that before and failed. There were also a lot of people who believed that the commissioner's office wanted to force a confrontation with our union as a means of sending a message to the Player's Association—whose contract with baseball expired in 2002—that it was no longer baseball-business-as-usual, that, unlike every other time, this time the owners were going to take a really hard position and stick firmly to it. Compared to the impact on the game of those negotiations, our new contract had about as much importance as garnish at a banquet.

During the All-Star break in July we had a big meeting to discuss our strategy. I came to the meeting on crutches. My knee had been injured and I'd had an operation.

We discussed the situation in the usual way—Richie told us what our strategy would be. He came up with an interesting concept: under the terms of our existing contract we were prohibited from striking. But, if we waited until the end of the season to act, our contract would expire and Alderson legally could fire people. We wouldn't have any leverage. In the winter, an umpire is about as necessary as a snowplow driver in Florida. But if we all submitted our resignations effective in September, baseball would either have to bring in sixty-eight minor league umpires to work the pennant races or negotiate with us. I mean, what else could they do?

What else could they do? What else could they do? Hmmm. Maybe that's what the guy who decided Volkswagen didn't need to keep making the same old Beetle said. Or the guy who told Coke that there would be no problem if they changed the formula.

In retrospect, this has to rank as one of the worst decisions made in the whole history of labor negotiations. Baseball was threatening to fire twenty umpires? We'd show them—we'd all file letters of resignation! That would certainly scare them. You can't fire just twenty of us, you have to fire all of us. I can just imagine the response when Sandy Alderson heard about this.

They were telling me that the best way to keep my job

was to resign. Hey, made sense to me. I'd like to say that I knew it was a bad idea and fought against it. Oh, would I like to say that. I can't. I had always gone along with Richie Phillips and, as a result, I was making almost $200,000 a year. Since he had become head of our association, our salaries had been raised 600 percent, we got five weeks vacation, traveled first-class, received a fair per diem on the road, and had good health insurance and retirement benefits. In the past Richie had done things I didn't quite understand, but as long as everybody stuck together it had always turned out well. As long as everybody stuck together. But this time there were some people who weren't happy with Richie Phillips' leadership. A dissident group led by Joe Brinkman and John Hirschbeck felt he had become too confrontational, that he was too tough on baseball. There had been some conversations about dumping him and hiring new leadership. At a meeting on February 14, an attempt had been made to get rid of Richie Phillips, but it was defeated by a large margin.

The major league umpires had always been one big happy family. Right, like the Addams family. In fact, there had always been some tension between the American League and National League umpires.

While I definitely was among Richie's supporters, I was a little uncomfortable signing my letter of resignation. Resign? I wanted a new contract. I had a conversation with a union representative in which I said, "Davey Phillips and I are both out on medicals. I don't think we should sign these papers, because we're still getting paid." As long as I was on a disability leave I didn't think I could resign my job. I was the last person to hand in a letter of resignation.

"Don't worry about it," I was told, "we're not really going to send yours and Davey's in." I think they told me that while they were on the way to the post office to send them in. There were fifty-seven umpires at the meeting. Two people who were there, Jim McKean and one other person, wanted to take home the letters and read them before signing. They never signed. Of the eleven umpires who didn't attend the meeting, initially six agreed to sign. Of the five umpires who did not want to sign the letters, two of them were scabs—umpires who had gotten their jobs by working during the 1979 strike—and were not members of the association. So, while there wasn't unanimous agreement, it was still an overwhelming majority.

I still believe that if the union had stuck together we could have forced baseball to negotiate with us, and we probably would have saved those twenty jobs that Alderson supposedly had threatened to eliminate. There just was no way sixty-eight umpires could be replaced right in the middle of the pennant race and through the playoffs and World Series if baseball was to maintain its credibility. No way—unless you really believe the quality of umpiring isn't essential to the conduct of the game. And this strategy wasn't so different from the threats Richie Phillips had made in the past. There had always been a lot of posturing—a lot of the *Oh, Yeah?* kind of threats, and then everybody calmed down and negotiated a deal. I admit that I assumed this was just more of the same.

Alderson responded to this strategy by calling it "either a threat to be ignored, or an offer to be accepted." Some people started panicking. Most of the American League umpires who had resigned called the league office and rescinded their letters of resignation. I wasn't too nervous. One of the vice presidents of the league told me that the league had not set a deadline for taking back these resignations. Then things began to get a little complicated. Baseball accepted the resignations.

That's when I began to get nervous. They knew we had resigned because we wanted to keep our jobs. Eventually, twenty-seven umpires either didn't sign or rescinded their resignations. That meant that about forty-two umpires had lost their jobs. I figured forty-two was still too many for baseball to replace at one time. As Richie Garcia said later, "[Resigning] didn't turn out to be the right move, because we had defectors." But then Jerry Crawford, the union president, made a deal in which baseball agreed to take back another twenty umpires and pay $1.36 million in post-season bonuses in return for the union dropping its lawsuit. I couldn't believe that the union would do that. I can still hear Crawford saying, "I've got to put these twenty guys back to work. These people [baseball executives] are different. They will fire everybody."

I can just imagine how tough that decision must have been for him to make. It was either get the jobs back for about half the members and take the risk that the others would be left hanging, or gamble that everyone would get back his job. I fought against his decision. I knew that once the union was split we couldn't win. Our power was in our unity. It was a game of chicken, and the union squawked. I will always believe that if those twenty umpires had refused to return to work, baseball would have had to negotiate. But adding them to the original defectors gave baseball enough umpires to do the job.

That left twenty-two umpires without jobs. Baseball hired twenty-five new umpires to replace them. The twenty umpires who went back to work made certain promises to those of us left behind. We're still waiting.

Still, the union told us not to worry. That we had a clear case and would win our jobs back in arbitration. That didn't happen. Eventually an arbitrator gave nine more guys their jobs back, for technical reasons, but four of those people retired and accepted buyouts. Some of them got a payout of more than $1 million. That left thirteen people without jobs. Richie Garcia eventually accepted a job inside baseball as an umpire supervisor. That left twelve people. Three more guys got their jobs back when a judge ruled that baseball had to offer them arbitration. That left nine guys out. Nine. Ironic, isn't it.

The defectors won. Richie Phillips was fired, and Brinkman, Hirschbeck, and Tim Welke formed a new union. Baseball negotiated a contract with this union.

While the money is good, a lot of job security has been lost. A lot of umpires now are scared to death about losing their jobs. They've seen what baseball does to its own. They should be nervous, they should be looking over their shoulder. About twenty-five years of gains in job security has been lost.

If I seem bitter, it's only because I am. I'm mad at everybody. The commissioner, Richie Phillips, Abner Doubleday, everybody. I'm mad at the people who broke the union. I've lost everything, everything that I've earned during my life spent in baseball. I haven't gotten any money from baseball since I lost my job. By comparison, these people make the Enron executives look generous. Baseball has refused to give me the severance pay and pension that I earned by working for thirty-six years. Baseball won't settle with the remaining nine umpires until all the lawsuits are dropped or settled. And there are a lot of lawsuits. People are suing and being sued. Richie Phillips has a lawsuit against baseball. Several umpires, including me, have a lawsuit against Richie. Baseball wants us to pressure Richie to drop his lawsuit and, in return, they'll pay us the money they owe us and we can happily go on with our lives—but we can't do that because we're suing him.

I haven't spoken with Richie Phillips since this happened. He won't talk to any of us. But it's been very tough for everybody. People have lost their homes. Our kids have had to drop out of school because we can't pay the tuition. We lost our health insurance; I have diabetes and I haven't been able to pay for the medicine I need. My friend, Dr. Stephen Whittlin, has pretty much saved my life. Three days after our resignations were accepted, Drew Coble's wife died. Drew Coble wasn't even at the meeting—he was with his wife while she had chemotherapy—and never signed a letter of resignation—but they accepted it anyway.

A lot of long-time friendships ended because of that strike. For example, Bruce Froemming and Mark Hirschbeck, John's brother, had worked together for five years and had become best friends. Their families had become close. Froemming considered him like a son. But they haven't spoken in years.

In addition to everything else, the reaction of fans and sports reporters has also been really disappointing to me. There are a lot of people who seem to feel that we umpires got what we deserved. Those are people who have never been umpires. A lot of sportswriters and broadcasters have written or said that this was our own fault, that somehow we deserved it because the umpires had become too powerful. We abused our position. What we were trying to do was protect our jobs, and for that we've received the economic death penalty.

Obviously, baseball has survived without us a lot better than we have done without baseball. But I'm told that the umpires—particularly the new umpires—are running scared. They're afraid to make a call that could end up costing them their job. The commissioner's office now has the power to fire them, and apparently it is utilizing a computerized system that may or may not be accurate, nobody really knows, to evaluate umpires and determine their ability. *That's* pressure.

As part of the settlement of the 1979 strike, several replacement umpires—scabs—were given major league contracts. There was tremendous resentment against these people. While umpires worked with them, some of them never spoke to the scabs off the field. Probably the biggest difference between the umpires hired to replace those of us who lost our jobs in 1999 and those scabs who were hired in 1979 was simply the number of them. Just about a third of all the current major league umpires got their jobs as a result of the labor dispute. Some of them are talented and eventually would have made it to the major leagues; others have less ability and never would have made it, but benefited by being in the right place when warm bodies were needed. Getting to the big leagues doesn't make someone a big league umpire. That takes time and experience.

I guess what surprised me was how some of the people

who benefited most from the earlier strikes so casually and permanently abandoned the rest of us. Well, they got what they bargained for, literally.

I think a lot of people will describe what I have to say as sour grapes. That's not really accurate. It's probably more like sour vineyard. How could anyone feel differently? Until I could no longer pay for the medicine I needed, or the tuition or the mortgage, I probably felt worse for the young umpires at the beginning of their major league careers who lost their jobs than I did for myself. Those people had no real choice but to go along with the union. They were without any power, and yet baseball showed absolutely no sympathy for them. Truthfully, I don't know how much longer my career would have lasted. Twenty-three years in the big leagues is a long, long time. It has been a real physical grind. But I wanted to make the decision when to end my professional career. It was a matter of pride and pension.

I'm very proud of my career. At times I was rated one of the best umpires in the league—and I was also rated one of the worst. There are people who claim I was too flamboyant, and others who said that I didn't run enough on the field. I never paid attention to any of that. To those people who criticized me I always had the same answer: show me. Show me one play in which I was out of position to make the call.

Accepting criticism is part of the basic umpire job description. And from my first days in the minor leagues I got a lot of practice at it. Like every umpire who has ever put on a mask I made mistakes, I kicked plays, I blew calls. It's probable that I never called a game perfectly behind the plate—I don't know any umpire who has—but one thing I know for sure is that I never lost control of a game. If I didn't have the respect of the players and managers, I definitely had their attention. When I was on the field, they knew that if one of us was going to be intimidated it wasn't going to be me. Which is why the last five years of my career were so peaceful.

I don't spend a lot of time looking back on my career. Not too many people would describe me as sentimental. I live right in the present; my all-time favorite meal is my next one. But, when I do think back over my three decades in baseball, it really does surprise me how much the game has changed. Naturally, to me the biggest change in the game over the last few years has been the fact that I'm not there anymore. But, that aside, it's a whole new baseball game. Only the rules are the same. In the past, baseball history was divided into two eras, the dead ball era and the lively ball era. It seems to me that baseball has now entered a third era. Maybe you can call it the supersized ball era.

At some point, the people running baseball must have thought the expression "run for the money" meant that if more runs were scored they would make more money—because everything possible has been done to make it easier to score runs. In fact, maybe the game should be called McRuns. Just about everything in baseball has gotten bigger—the players, their salaries, the number of home runs hit, the distance the ball travels, batting averages, pitchers' earned-run averages, the cost of a ticket, even the price of ballpark hot dogs. I guess the only thing that has gotten smaller is the distance to the fences.

The game changed a lot during my career. I remember day games during the week, double-headers, ladies' day, pitchers throwing complete games, and shutouts. I remember Tiger Stadium, Comiskey Park in Chicago, Cleveland's Municipal Stadium, Baltimore's Memorial Stadium, Milwaukee's County Stadium, Minnesota's Metropolitan Stadium, Seattle's Kingdome, and the heat in Texas' Arlington Stadium. I remember the managers Billy Martin, Earl Weaver, Sparky Anderson, Tom Kelly, Whitey Herzog, Chuck Tanner, Dick Howser, and Gene Mauch. I definitely remember Weaver, I just wish I could forget him. I remember when you couldn't buy pizza at the ballpark, but you could buy a fifty-cent scorecard instead of a $5 program. I remember all the old team logos and uniforms and mascots.

I even remember the one year the Yankees had a mascot. After Lou Piniella got in a fight with another team's mascot, George Steinbrenner banished the Yankee mascot—which looked a little like Sparky Lyle on steroids—to the upper deck at Yankee Stadium. He had to have two bodyguards with him at all times—and his mother made him quit after one season. I remember Reggie Bars and inflatable chest protectors and the American and National League presidents. All of them. I remember when the players actually cared which league won the All-Star Game, when there were no division playoffs and no Wild Card, when World Series games ended before midnight on the east coast, and baseball wasn't afraid to compete against football for the weekend TV audience. I remember when players considered a million dollars a decent salary, and when the starting salary of major league umpires was raised to $22,000.

I remember the insults and the arguments and the friendships. I remember the taunts and teases and the threats. I remember Chicken, Rooster, and the Goose, I remember The Bull and The Bulldog, Mad Dog and The Mad Hungarian, two Pudges and two Counts, Disco Dan, Junior, Inky, The Boomer, Bam-Bam and Bye-Bye, Pags and Rags, Kong, Big Mac, Moose and Buck, Rock, The Big Hurt and The Big Unit, Sweet Lou and Sweet Music, The Rocket, Spaceman, Bird and Gator, I remember The Terminator, Knucksie, and The Road Runner. I can see them in my mind, I can hear their voices in my head.

Do I miss it? Absolutely. I loved baseball. I loved the job, even with all of its difficulties, most of the time I loved the job. I don't miss all the travel, I don't miss running for planes or looking for a place to eat after a game, I don't miss the screaming—but I miss that feeling of being part of something special. I miss being on the field on a gorgeous June night. Occasionally I'll get to yell at one of my two kids, but it's not the same thing. My kids have gone off on their own, so I can't even eject them from the house. And most of all I miss the camaraderie.

I had a great run, or some people might argue I had a great fast walk. It was the shortest thirty-six years in history. It seems like just yesterday that I was a kid without a plan hitting a minor league catcher over the head with a pool table.

I wonder what ever happened to that table?

ACKNOWLEDGMENTS

I have been so fortunate to have had the friendship and assistance of many people. In particular I would like to acknowledge Red Fedele and suggest that anybody visiting Rochester should visit his Brookhouse Restaurant. I probably wouldn't be alive without Dr. Stephen Whittlin. I made many friends in baseball and would like to acknowledge Bobby Valentine, Don Zimmer, and George Steinbrenner, all people who cared to help me when I needed help.

This book would not have been written without the assistance of David Fisher, and both of us will forever lovingly remember our friend Ron Luciano. Our publisher, Tom Dunne, and editor, Sean Desmond, of Thomas Dunne Books at St. Martin's Press, made it easy to tell all the stories and were unfailingly supportive—they went a lot further than required by a contract.

And finally, I want to thank the woman in my life, Cheryl Bogner, and my children J. K. and Lauren, for their unconditional love. I'm so lucky to have them all in my life.